A Cosmopolitanism of Nations

A Cosmopolitanism of Nations

GIUSEPPE MAZZINI'S WRITINGS ON
DEMOCRACY, NATION BUILDING,
AND INTERNATIONAL RELATIONS

Edited and with an introduction by
Stefano Recchia and Nadia Urbinati

Translations by Stefano Recchia

PRINCETON UNIVERSITY PRESS

PRINCETON AND OXFORD

Copyright © 2009 by Princeton University Press

Published by Princeton University Press, 41 William Street, Princeton,
New Jersey 08540
In the United Kingdom: Princeton University Press,
6 Oxford Street, Woodstock, Oxfordshire OX20 1TW

Library of Congress Cataloging-in-Publication Data

Mazzini, Giuseppe, 1805–1872.
    A cosmopolitanism of nations: Giuseppe Mazzini's writings on democracy, nation
building, and international relations / edited and with an introduction by Stefano
Recchia and Nadia Urbinati; translations by Stefano Recchia.
        p.   cm.
    Includes bibliographical references and index.
    ISBN 978-0-691-13611-0 (hardcover : alk. paper)   1. International relations.
2. Democracy.   3. Nation-building.   4. Cosmopolitanism.   I. Recchia, Stefano, 1978–
II. Urbinati, Nadia, 1955–   III. Title.
JZ1308.M397 2009
    320.01—dc22
    2009011028

British Library Cataloging-in-Publication Data is available

This book has been composed in Palatino

Printed on acid-free paper. ∞

press.princeton.edu

Printed in the United States of America

10 9 8 7 6 5 4 3 2 1

Contents

Preface

THIS VOLUME is the result of a fruitful cooperation between a political theorist and an international relations scholar. Having both independently done some research on Giuseppe Mazzini in recent years, we were impressed by the originality and timely character of several of his writings on democracy and international relations. Mazzini set forth some pioneering reflections on, among other things, the ethics and strategy of guerrilla warfare, the normative dilemmas of military intervention and democratic regime change, and the possibility of a more just and peaceful international order. Although he quite obviously discussed these issues within, and in relation to, the specific political context of nineteenth-century Europe, he first conceptualized and tried to disentangle several of the dilemmas that political theorists, international policymakers, and ordinary citizens are still often grappling with today.

Mazzini ranked among the most influential European public figures of the mid nineteenth century. He crucially anticipated and theorized about the democratic role of the nation and thought of inclusive, participatory democracy as a necessary condition for international peace. Today Mazzini is largely remembered as the spiritual father of the Italian political nation. Yet as a public intellectual and political agitator, he inspired several patriotic and anticolonial revolutionary movements in different parts of the world well into the twentieth century. In recent decades his writings and ideas had fallen into virtual oblivion, especially in the Anglo-American world. Some of his seminal political essays had never been published in English to begin with, and existing translations were often of rather poor quality. Hence, with this anthology we would like to contribute to a fresh reexamination—but in many regards this will be a genuine *rediscovery*—of Mazzini's political thought.

For the present edition, Stefano Recchia newly translated some foundational writings by Mazzini on democracy, revolution, and international relations. Rebecca Bauman provided helpful assistance during the initial stage of the translation. About half the essays in this volume are first-time translations. The other essays reproduced here had been written in English by Mazzini himself or were originally translated under his supervision; in these latter cases we have sought to retain the original text as much as possible, while partially updating language and sentence structure and correcting some obvious misspellings.

The following essays have been newly translated from their Italian or French originals: (1) "Manifesto of Young Italy"; (2) "On the Superiority of Representative Government"; (3) "Humanity and Country" and "Nationalism and Nationality"; (7) "Toward a Holy Alliance of Peoples"; (8) "From a Revolutionary Alliance to the United States of Europe"; (9) "Against the Foreign Imposition of Domestic Institutions"; (10) "To the Patriots of Serbia and Hungary"; (11) "Letter to a Polish Patriot"; (12) "For a Truly National War"; (13) "Neither Pacifism nor Terror"; (14) "On Publicity in Foreign Affairs"; (21) "To Our Friends in the United States"; and (22) "Principles of International Politics." We are grateful to Annie Stilz and two anonymous reviewers for their helpful comments on a draft of the introduction. Nathan Carr and Jack Rummel at Princeton University Press and Nick Serpe at Columbia University provided valuable editorial assistance. This project received financial support from the Comitato Nazionale per le Celebrazioni Mazziniane (Italian National Committee for the Celebrations of Mazzini's Bicentennial). We would like to thank in particular its executive director, Mario di Napoli, who has strongly supported this project since its early stage.

A Cosmopolitanism of Nations

Giuseppe Mazzini's International Political Thought

GIUSEPPE MAZZINI (1805–72) is today largely remembered as the chief inspirer and leading political agitator of the Italian Risorgimento. Yet Mazzini was not merely an Italian patriot, and his influence reached far beyond his native country and his century. In his time, he ranked among the leading European intellectual figures, competing for public attention with Mikhail Bakunin and Karl Marx, John Stuart Mill and Alexis de Tocqueville. According to his friend Alexander Herzen, the Russian political activist and writer, Mazzini was the "shining star" of the democratic revolutions of 1848. In those days Mazzini's reputation soared so high that even the revolution's ensuing defeat left most of his European followers with a virtually unshakeable belief in the eventual triumph of their cause.[1]

Mazzini was an original, if not very systematic, political thinker. He put forward principled arguments in support of various progressive causes, from universal suffrage and social justice to women's enfranchisement. Perhaps most fundamentally, he argued for a reshaping of the European political order on the basis of two seminal principles: *democracy* and *national self-determination*. These claims were extremely radical in his time, when most of continental Europe was still under the rule of hereditary kingships and multinational empires such as the Habsburgs and the Ottomans. Mazzini worked primarily on people's minds and opinions, in the belief that radical political change first requires cultural and ideological transformations on which to take root. He was one of the first political agitators and public intellectuals in the contemporary sense of the term: not a solitary thinker or soldier but rather a political leader who sought popular support and participation. Mazzini's ideas had an extraordinary appeal for generations of progressive nationalists and revolutionary leaders from his day until well into the twentieth century: his life and writings inspired several patriotic and anticolonial movements in Europe, Latin America, and

---

[1] Alexander Herzen, *My Past and Thoughts*, trans. C. Garnett, intro. Isaiah Berlin (New York: Knopf, 1968), 687, 694.

the Middle East, as well as the early Zionists, Gandhi, Nehru, and Sun Yat-Sen.[2]

It was Mazzini's conviction that under the historical circumstances of his time, only the nation-state could allow for genuine democratic participation and the civic education of individuals. To him, the nation was a necessary intermediary step in the progressive association of mankind, the *means* toward a future international "brotherhood" among all peoples. But the nation could never be an end in itself. Mazzini sincerely believed that cosmopolitan ideals and national sentiment would be complementary, so long as the rise of an aggressive nationalism could be prevented through an adequate "sentimental education." As we will argue in more detail below, he was thus a republican *patriot* much more than a nationalist. The nation itself had for him a primarily political character as a democratic association of equals under a written constitution. Like a few other visionaries of his time, Mazzini even thought that Europe's nations might one day be able to join together and establish a "United States of Europe." His more immediate hope was that by his activism, his writings, and his example, he would be able to promote what today we might call a genuine *cosmopolitanism of nations*—that is, the belief that universal principles of human freedom, equality, and emancipation would best be realized in the context of independent and democratically governed nation-states.

Mazzini clearly believed that the spread of democracy and national self-determination would be a powerful force for peace in the long run, although the transition might often be violent. Where oppressive regimes and foreign occupation made any peaceful political contestation virtually impossible, violent insurrection would be legitimate and indeed desirable. Democratic revolutions would be justified under extreme political circumstances. However, he expected that once established, democratic nations would be likely to adopt a peace-seeking attitude in their foreign relations. Democracies would become each others' natural allies; they would cooperate for their mutual benefit and, if needed, jointly defend their freedom and independence against the remaining, hostile despotic regimes. Over time, democracies would also set up various international agreements and formal associations among themselves, so that their cooperation would come to rest on solid insti-

[2] Gita Srivastava, *Mazzini and His Impact on the Indian National Movement* (Allahabad, India: Chugh, 1982); Jorge Myers, "Giuseppe Mazzini and the Emergence of Liberal Nationalism in the River Plate and Chile," in C. A. Bayly and E. F. Biagini, *Giuseppe Mazzini and the Globalization of Democratic Nationalism, 1830–1920* (Oxford: Oxford University Press, 2008); Denis Mack Smith, *Mazzini* (New Haven, CT: Yale University Press, 1994), 219; Michael Howard, *War and the Liberal Conscience* (New Brunswick, NJ: Rutgers University Press, 1978), 49.

tutional foundations. In this sense, Mazzini clearly anticipated that constitutional republics would establish and gradually consolidate a separate emocratic peace" among each other. He did so much more explicitly than Immanuel Kant, as we will argue below.

For these reasons, Mazzini deserves to be seen as the leading pioneer of the more activist and progressive "Wilsonian" branch of liberal internationalism. There is indeed some evidence that President Woodrow Wilson, who later elevated liberal internationalism into an explicit foreign policy doctrine, was quite influenced by Mazzini's political writings. On his way to attend the 1919 peace conference in Paris, Wilson visited Genoa and paid tribute in front of Mazzini's monument. The American president explicitly claimed on that occasion that he had closely studied Mazzini's writings and "derived guidance from the principles which Mazzini so eloquently expressed." Wilson further added that with the end of the First World War he hoped to contribute to "the realization of the ideals to which his [Mazzini's] life and thought were devoted."[3]

His Life and Times

Mazzini was born on June 22, 1805, in Genoa, a city with a glorious republican past that was quite arbitrarily handed over to the Kingdom of Piedmont-Sardinia at the Congress of Vienna in 1815. The Kingdom of Piedmont-Sardinia itself was one of eight Italian states that had been reinstated after the defeat of Napoleon in 1815. All those states were ruled by nonconstitutional, autocratic governments. They were nominally independent, although most of them depended on Austrian protection and were de facto satellites of the Austrian Empire (with the exception of sizeable territories around Venice and Milan, which were directly ruled by Austria). Patriotic sentiments had begun to spread among Italian elites during Napoleon's rule (1805–14), when large parts of the Italian territory had been politically unified. The ensuing Restoration and renewed political dismemberment of Italy led to growing demands for the granting of constitutional charters and independence from foreign rule.

Italian patriots were inspired by the example of constitutionalist insurrections in Spain in 1820, which also rekindled older memories of the Neapolitan revolution of 1799 that had resulted in a brief republican interlude. A first wave of uprisings took place in the kingdoms of Naples and Piedmont between 1820 and 1821, yet all those movements

[3] Woodrow Wilson, "Remarks about Giuseppe Mazzini" and "Further Remarks in Genoa," *The Papers of Woodrow Wilson*, ed. Arthur S. Lind (Princeton, NJ: Princeton University Press), 53:614–15. See also Mack Smith, *Mazzini*, 221.

were brutally and quite easily crushed. In 1821 an Austrian expeditionary corps was sent to Naples for "peacekeeping" purposes under the auspices of the Holy Alliance (the alliance of Europe's counterrevolutionary great powers, led by Russia, Austria, and Prussia); this emboldened the local Bourbon king to repeal even the modest constitutional reforms he had previously granted. The repression was extremely harsh, with the execution or imprisonment of many revolutionary leaders and patriotic conspirators throughout Italy. It was in this tumultuous political environment that the young Mazzini was coming of age.

Mazzini's middle-class background (his father was a medical doctor) allowed him to pursue advanced studies in law as well as literature. Very soon he became attracted to and familiar with romantic poetry and idealist philosophy: he read and admired the works of Vico, Herder, Goethe, Fichte, the Schlegel brothers, and Schelling, and he wrote some innovative essays on the character of Italian literature from Dante Alighieri to Ugo Foscolo (a poet of great patriotic appeal in Mazzini's times). Later in his twenties, he turned his attention more explicitly toward social and political thought: his main points of reference during this period were the French priest and democratic philosopher Félicité de Lamennais and the Saint-Simonians. But Mazzini's temperament did not fit him for a life of tranquil intellectual pursuits. He soon became involved in the Italian struggle for national independence and quickly emerged as its leading theoretician and most charismatic political agitator. Already as a young lawyer and promising literary critic, Mazzini had joined the secret Carbonari society, an offshoot of Freemasonry that organized the Italian patriotic resistance throughout the early decades after the Restoration. However, he soon broke with the Carbonari over disagreements concerning their excessive secrecy and detachment from the people. Mazzini believed that what Italy needed was not an elitist constitutionalist conspiracy but instead a truly popular movement, based on a clear and well-defined republican revolutionary program.[4] In this sense he held a consistently democratic outlook, not only concerning his ultimate goal—government by the people and for the people—but also with regard to political action as a means to get there.

In 1830, after a short time in prison on charges of subversive activism against Austria's imperial rule, Mazzini left Italy. He spent most of his remaining life in exile, and from 1837 onward London became his home of choice. In London he continued to publish assiduously, while also attempting to coordinate what he saw as an emergent pan-European struggle against the imperial domination of the Habsburgs, Romanovs, and Ottomans over Italy, Central Europe, and the Balkans. As early as 1831, as an exile in France he had founded the revolutionary organiza-

---

[4] See Indro Montanelli, *Storia d'Italia 1831–1861* (Milan: RCS Libri, 1998), 40.

tion "Giovine Italia" (Young Italy), which promoted the patriotic ideal among Italy's educated middle classes and coordinated insurrectionary activities throughout the Italian Peninsula. Mazzini's organization became Italy's first political party, with its own newspaper and propaganda apparatus, although given the lack of constitutional freedoms it operated largely underground or from abroad (about one hundred years later, his method would inspire Italian anti-Fascist organizations in their fight against a new kind of tyranny).[5] Alongside Young Italy, Mazzini tried to set up similar patriotic organizations for Germany, Greece, Spain, Russia, and Poland. In 1834, while in Switzerland, he founded a new revolutionary association ambitiously called "Young Europe," with a dozen refugees from Italy, Poland, and Germany. This was one of the first transnational political associations, and it fostered a lively exchange of ideas among its members. Most of the ensuing insurrections and guerrilla operations inspired by Mazzini in Italy and elsewhere were utter failures from a strictly military point of view. Nevertheless, at least as far as Italy is concerned, Mazzini's revolutionary activism probably contributed more than anything else to the spread of patriotic sentiments among the politically alert population.[6]

Mazzini's influence and his actual political career reached their zenith in the spring of 1849. For a short period of about three months, he was able to return to Italy and stood at the center of European events. Following a popular revolt against the pope's despotic and theocratic regime in central Italy, in March 1849 a constituent assembly abolished the temporal power of the papacy and proclaimed the Roman Republic. Mazzini's popularity in revolutionary circles virtually preordained him to become the republic's de facto political leader. This was the only time during his entire life that he held any kind of political office. Several independent observers and foreign diplomats stationed in Rome admitted that during his short tenure, Mazzini displayed surprising administrative capacity and diplomatic skills. (Lord Palmerston, then British foreign secretary, reportedly described Mazzini's diplomatic dispatches from Rome as "models of reasoning and argument."[7]) The republic's citizens universally enjoyed personal and political freedoms, including press freedom, religious freedom, due process, and equality among the

---

[5] This was certainly the case for the clandestine movement "Giustizia e Libertà" (Justice and Freedom) founded and led by Carlo Rosselli (himself a Mazzinian) during his exile in Paris, until he was assassinated by the Fascists in 1937. See Nadia Urbinati, introduction to Carlo Rosselli, *Liberal Socialism* (Princeton NJ: Princeton University Press, 1994).

[6] Mack Smith, *Mazzini*, 5–8. For a detailed history of Young Italy and Young Europe, see Franco Della Peruta, *Mazzini e i rivoluzionari italiani: Il partito d'azione, 1830–1845* (Milan: Feltrinelli, 1974), chaps. 2–3.

[7] Quoted in Martin Wight, *Four Seminal Thinkers in International Theory: Machiavelli, Grotius, Kant, and Mazzini* (Oxford: Oxford University Press, 2005), 113; see also Mack Smith, *Mazzini*, 67.

sexes, as well as some basic social rights, to an extent unequalled anywhere else in Europe at the time. But faced with such a radical political challenge, Europe's conservative powers did not simply look on. Under France's leadership (France, led by Louis Napoleon, was itself a crumbling republic at the time), they quickly organized a military intervention to crush Mazzini's political experiment in Rome and reinstate the pope. The Roman Republic eventually succumbed in June 1849, after a fierce and in many regards honorable resistance (hundreds of French war prisoners were regularly set free under Mazzini's orders as a sign of republican friendship). A merciless papal restoration ensued, and Mazzini soon returned to his exile in London. But the passionate defense of Rome by an army of volunteers under Giuseppe Garibaldi's command had been a considerable moral success. Mazzini's personal reputation among republicans and progressives in Italy and all over Europe came out greatly enhanced, and the siege of Rome probably won him more widespread support than he enjoyed at any other time in his life.[8]

After the failed uprisings and republican experiments of 1848–49, Mazzini slowly became detached from the Italian popular masses, who were increasingly drawn toward communist and socialist doctrines. As a republican, Mazzini had always been first and foremost the representative of middle-class aspirations; he was scarcely familiar with the popular "multitudes," and in turn the illiterate masses of nineteenth-century Italy knew little of his revolutionary project. But his explicit opposition to any form of organized class conflict in later years of his life, and his related insistence that the "social question" ought to be resolved in a consensual, nonconflictual manner, undoubtedly contributed to diverting large sectors of the nascent urban working class into the socialist camp. Revolutionary socialists, that is, followers of Karl Marx's International, regarded Mazzini as their opponent. Their antagonism was not unfounded, as suggested by Mazzini's harsh condemnation of the Paris Commune in 1871.[9] With Mazzini, Italian republicanism became divorced from socialism and in particular Marxist socialism.

From the late 1850s onward, Mazzini also grew increasingly disenchanted with the advancement of Italian national unification under Piedmont's monarchical leadership, which he saw as utterly incompatible with his republican ideals. Throughout his life, he feared that if patriotic movements lost their sense of humanitarian *duty* and ended up exploited by a short-sighted monarchical leadership or by self-serving oligarchies, they might quickly degenerate into a chauvinistic and bel-

---

[8] Mack Smith, *Mazzini*, 75.
[9] See Mazzini, "Neither Pacifism nor Terror: Considerations on the Paris Commune and the French National Assembly," [1871] chapter 13 of this book.

licose nationalism.[10] Nevertheless, Mazzini remained a highly influential moral voice in Italian and European republican circles until his death in 1872. He actually produced some of his most original essays, especially on international relations, in this latter period.

DUTIES BEFORE RIGHTS: MAZZINI'S MORAL AND POLITICAL PHILOSOPHY

With the French Revolution, and as a reaction against Napoleon's subsequent expansionism, the *individual* and the *nation* emerged as the two modern agents of political legitimacy. They became the symbols of political and moral resistance against all kinds of imperial projects, as brilliantly illustrated by Kant's 1795 warning against a "despotism without soul" or Benjamin Constant's 1814 dissection of Europe's illiberal and belligerent imperialism.[11] Undoubtedly Mazzini is part of this legacy, which he actually advanced further by emphasizing the importance of national independence and self-determination as *means* to human progress and emancipation.

Mazzini clearly believed in cosmopolitanism as a *moral* ideal, although he was somewhat ambivalent toward the actual term *cosmopolitanism*, which he associated with Benthamite utilitarian philosophy. Speaking for his republican movement, he claimed in 1847: "We are all Cosmopolitans, if by Cosmopolitanism we understand the love and brotherhood of all, and the destruction of all barriers which separate the Peoples."[12] Yet in his view, those who merely asserted their belief in

[10] Mazzini opposed in particular Prime Minister Cavour's political realism, which manifested itself in an international alliance policy devoid of moral scruples. For its part, the conservative Piedmontese government eventually understood that it could not defeat the Mazzinian revolutionaries; hence after 1850 it increasingly began to exploit them for its own purposes. In particular, the Piedmontese government was able to gain French support for its own expansionist policy, which it justified as necessary to "contain revolution." By late 1860, the Piedmontese had successfully annexed most of the Italian territories. Italy's national unification was thus completed in a top-down fashion, and it largely succeeded thanks to Prime Minister Cavour's astute international alliance diplomacy. All this stood in open contrast to almost anything that Mazzini had ever taught about the need to unify Italy *with* the popular masses, not against them or without them, and above all by painstakingly avoiding tactical alliances with foreign despots. See Montanelli, *Storia d'Italia*, 77, 413–15, 444.

[11] Immanuel Kant, "Perpetual Peace: A Philosophical Sketch" [1795], in *Kant: Political Writings*, ed. Hans Reiss (Cambridge: Cambridge University Press, 1991); Benjamin Constant, *De l'esprit de conquête et de l'usurpation dans leurs rapports avec la civilisation européenne* (Paris: Flammarion, 1993 [1814]). The following two sections of the introduction partially build on Nadia Urbinati, "In the Legacy of Immanuel Kant: Giuseppe Mazzini's Cosmopolitanism of Nations," in *Giuseppe Mazzini and the Globalization of Democratic Nationalism*.

[12] Mazzini, "Nationality and Cosmopolitanism" [1847], chapter 3 of this book, 58.

humanity and fought for individual freedoms without also struggling for national self-determination were bound to fail, for disjoined individuals would at best only "be able to worship Humanity in idle contemplation."[13] The specific stage of development reached by humanity in nineteenth-century Europe required that people become associated with each other in democratically governed nation-states, in order to further advance along the ladder of human progress.

Mazzini's entire political thought pivots around the notion of duties: toward oneself, the family, the nation, and humanity as a whole. Indeed, it would not be too far-fetched to identify Mazzini as the prophet of a "religion of duty." He became increasingly obsessed with the idea of duties—and patriotic duties in particular—after the defeat of the democratic revolutions of 1848–49, when many Italian patriots increasingly came to rely on the leadership of the king of Piedmont-Sardinia. Mazzini felt that the goal of *popular* self-determination was being abandoned for the sake of mere national unification, without regard to the form of government that would be established. He sought to counter this trend, which he perceived as potentially dangerous, by insisting on the need to believe in and fight for the nation conceived as a patriotic association of equals.

Yet while stressing the importance of patriotic duties, or national solidarity, Mazzini never meant to dismiss the value of *individual rights*. He actually thought that individual rights were an unquestionable achievement of the modern age. This is a characteristic of his political thought that has often been overlooked, if not outright misunderstood. Both the constitution of the Roman Republic of 1849 and his rough constitutional proposal for a future Italian republic were based on civil and political individual rights, and their equal distribution.[14] Mazzini believed so much in rights as to give them moral and political primacy over collective self-determination. Thus in principle, he placed individual rights above popular sovereignty: "But there are certain things that are constitutive of your very individuality and are essential elements of human life. Over these, not even the People have any right. No majority may establish a tyrannical regime."[15]

[13] Mazzini, "Nationalism and Nationality" [1871], chapter 3 of this book, 63. See also Bolton King, *The Life of Mazzini* (London: Dent and Sons, 1911), 306.

[14] See "On the Superiority of Representative Government," chapter 2 of this book.

[15] Mazzini then goes on to enumerate those rights: "You have a right to liberty in everything that is necessary to the moral and material sustenance of life: personal liberty; liberty of movement; liberty of religious faith; liberty of opinion; liberty of expressing that opinion through the press, or by any other peaceful means; liberty of association, in order to render that opinion fruitful through contacts and exchanges with others; liberty of labor; liberty of trade." Cf. Mazzini, "On the Duties of Man" [1841–60], chapter 5 of this book, 97. See also Alessandro Levi, *La filosofia politica di Giuseppe Mazzini*, ed. Salvo Mastellone (Naples: Morano Levi, 1967 [1916]), 202.

What Mazzini questioned was that one could rely on the language of rights to justify and advance the politics of nationality. He correctly perceived rights in their liberal formulation as antagonistic to political power and as protective shields against power. Yet liberal rights in and of themselves would be unable to *mobilize* the people, to *sustain* associations among individuals, and finally to *morally justify* national self-determination. Living in London, the capital city of utilitarianism, during the golden age of laissez-faire liberalism, Mazzini came to believe that the "theory of rights" was essentially a theory of selfishness, or self-centeredness. The Enlightenment theory of rights taught that society had been instituted to secure material interests. In his view, this philosophy encouraged everyone to look only "after his own rights and the improvement of his own position, without seeking to provide for others."[16]

In other words, Mazzini regarded liberal rights discourse as conservative in relation to a good (the individual) it essentially took as a given. Mere belief in liberal rights would be unsuited to galvanize the people into a life of sacrifice and struggle, which would be necessary to overthrow Europe's despotic regimes and bring about genuine popular self-determination. He therefore insisted that the "struggle against injustice and error for the benefit of one's brothers is not only a *right* but a Duty."[17] Like the Saint-Simonians, Mazzini thought that the new age would be one of collective purposes, marked by the primacy of duty and various forms of association. He saw national self-determination as a *constitutive* politics, and thus as the necessary condition for the implementation of liberal rights, rather than a liberal right itself.[18]

In contemporary language we might say that Mazzini gave the name of rights to what we call negative liberty (freedom as noninterference), while he linked his notion of duty to what we call positive liberty (freedom as autonomy and self-development.) The former lies at the origin of any bill of rights and aims at power limitation; the latter is an expression of self-determination that is essential to any democratic political founding. But Mazzini did not articulate this distinction in clear language

[16] Mazzini, "On the Duties of Man," chapter 5 of this book, 82.

[17] Ibid., 83. See also E. Vaughan, *Studies in the History of Political Philosophy before and after Rousseau* (New York: Russell and Russell, 1960), 266. As Carlo Cantimori perspicaciously argued, Mazzini's intuition was that the criterion to judge a philosophy ought to be practical—we should look at it from the point of view of the actions it inspires. Theoretical truth lies in practical reason. Cf. Cantimori, *Saggio sull'idealismo di Mazzini* (Faenza: Montanari, 1904), 285.

[18] In Mazzini's own words, the cause of nationality should not be "one of simple reaction, or of material well-being, or of mere rights to be recognized." Cf. Mazzini, *Letters*, trans. A. De Roses Jervis, introduction and notes by Bolton King (Westport, CT: Hyperion Press, 1979), 76.

and with an adequate political terminology. Furthermore, like other theorists of positive liberty from which he drew inspiration (most notably Rousseau), he did not translate his religion of duty into a fully developed theory of constitution making and institution building. He believed it was not the task of revolutionary agitators and political thinkers like himself to enter into the specifics of democratic constitutional design, which should rather be dealt with by future constituent assemblies according to the specific circumstances of time and place. In Mazzini's own words:

> We have always been careful to lay out the moral principles from which we derive our right and our duty to act. . . . But beyond this, we believe that it is for the people themselves, with their collective wisdom and the force of their intuition that have been sharpened by the experience of great insurrections, to resolve the problem at hand. To put it differently: the people themselves ought to erect the specific institutional structure that will allow future generations to benefit from peace and development for many centuries to come.[19]

Mazzini had a wholly modern view of democracy as a popular form of government based on the sovereignty of the nation, where the nation is a political association of citizens represented by elected representatives. The terms *democracy* and *republic* are virtually synonymous to him; they symbolize a political project against oppression and despotic rule, and their ultimate goal is the emancipation of individual human beings. Yet Mazzini appears to have fundamentally underestimated the importance of constitutional safeguards to actually protect those individual liberties whose primacy he proclaimed in the abstract. His ambivalence in this regard emerges most clearly from one of his early writings, where he straightforwardly claims that "the nation's power is unlimited" and then goes on to insist that "any restrictions brought to . . . the deputies' ultimate choice would contradict the principle of national sovereignty."[20] This complete reliance on citizens' republican virtue and their sense of duty, combined with an apparent lack of awareness that individual rights need to be constitutionally protected, have led some critics to portray Mazzini as a quasi-Jacobin.[21]

---

[19] Mazzini, "Toward a Holy Alliance of Peoples" [1849], chapter 7 of this book, 124.

[20] Mazzini, "On the Superiority of Representative Government" [1832], chapter 2 in this book, 51.

[21] See, e.g., Gaetano Savemini, *Mazzini*, trans. I. M. Rawson (Stanford: Stanford University Press, 1957), 56–61; Luigi Salvatorelli, *The Risorgimento: Thought and Action*, trans. M. Domandi (New York: Harper and Row, 1970), 97; and Bruce Haddock, "State and Nation in Mazzini's Political Thought," *History of Political Thought* 20 (1999): 324–27.

A Democratic Conception of the Nation

One of the most puzzling questions for theorists of nationalism has always been to explain why some forms of nationalism are a threat to peace and democracy while others are not, or how to recognize, in Michael Walzer's words, "exactly when nationalism turns into chauvinism and under what conditions."[22] Scholars in the twentieth century developed the distinction between, on the one hand, a "naturalistic" or organicistic conception of the nation, and on the other hand, a "voluntaristic" or associational one.[23] The former assumes the existence of some prepolitical factors without which a nation cannot exist; the latter pays attention only to the political factor—it insists on the popular *will* to become a nation and draws on Ernest Renan's famous statement that "the nations' existence is . . . a daily plebiscite."[24]

This scholarship claimed that "bad" chauvinistic nationalism had evolved out of the naturalistic conception of the nation first put forward by German romantic philosophers, while the "good" democratic cause of national self-determination was seen as an offspring of the voluntaristic conception developed by French republicanism.[25] The distinction is perspicacious but not quite satisfactory. Putatively "voluntaristic" nations such as France have not necessarily been less prone than others to develop chauvinistic and imperialist policies, as attested by two French empires and their attendant expansionism. Furthermore, the dualism between naturalistic and voluntaristic conceptions of the nation does

[22] Michael Walzer, "Only Connect," *The New Republic*, August 13, 1990, 34.

[23] A cornerstone in this research is Friedrich Meinecke's *Cosmopolitanism and the National State* [1907], a political treatise in the anti-Enlightenment tradition that laid out an organicist conception of the nation as "a natural core based on blood relationships." Cf. Friedrich Meinecke, *Cosmopolitanism and the National State*, trans. R. B. Kimer, ed. Felix Gilbert (Princeton, NJ: Princeton University Press, 1970, 9. Meinecke's analysis and definition of the nation would later encourage Hans Kohn and Federico Chabod, two influential historians, to distinguish between "naturalistic" and "voluntaristic" conceptions of the nation. See Hans Kohn, *The Idea of Nationalism: A Study of Its Origins and Background* (New York: Macmillan, 1944); Federico Chabod, *L'idea di nazione* (Bari: Laterza, 1962); see also Anthony D. Smith, *Theories of Nationalism*, 2nd ed. (New York: Holmes and Meier, 1983).

[24] Ernest Renan, "What Is a Nation?" [1882], in *The Poetry of the Celtic Races and Other Studies*, trans. W. G. Hutchison (New York: Kennikat, 1970), 80–81. Renan was rephrasing Michelet who had written forty years earlier that "la volonté de s'unir, c'était déjà l'unité des coeurs, la meilleure unité peut-être." Cf. Jules Michelet, *Histoire de la révolution française*, ed. Gérard Walter, 2 vols. (Paris: Gallimard, 1952), 1:423.

[25] Kohn, *The Idea of Nationalism*; Chabod, *L'idea di nazione*; see also Johan Huizinga, "Patriotism and Nationalism in European History," in *Men and Ideas: History, the Middle Ages, the Renaissance*, trans. J. S. Holmes and H. van Marle (Princeton, NJ: Princeton University Press,1984), 108.

not allow us to properly situate and understand Mazzini's own peculiar idea of *democratic nationality*.

Mazzini's conception of the nation does not imply, and certainly does not require, indifference toward the so-called prepolitical factors. He considered language, territory, and ethnicity to be *indications* of the nation—probably necessary but not sufficient for the emergence of self-determining political units, and certainly unable in and of themselves to legitimate national independence. Hence Mazzini looked beyond the prepolitical factors. Political equality and popular consent play a decisive normative role in his democratic conception of the nation, because without them, no political autonomy is possible, and the prepolitical factors remain without a legitimating voice. The nation, he wrote in 1835, has to stand "for equality and democracy"—only under this condition does it represent a genuine "commonality of thought and destiny." In a Rousseauian vein, he was convinced that without "a general and uniform law" there could be neither peoples nor nations, but only castes and privileges—at most a "multitude" of interest-bearers bound together by convenience alone.[26] Mazzini's conception of the nation is therefore inherently democratic, and it stands in outright opposition to the aristocratic principle.[27] However, according to his demanding standard of political legitimacy, political factors such as consent and the popular will are ultimately not sufficient either. In particular, they cannot by themselves make national self-determination democratic.

The originality of Mazzini's democratic conception of the nation springs from his intuition that although national politics must be legitimized by the popular will, *the popular will itself should actually be restrained*. This restraining force can only result from people's acknowledgement of a superior "law of Humanity"—that is, of a universalistic criterion that ought to guide them domestically, as well as in their interaction with other nation-states. Relying on the will and consent alone, and without certain fundamental moral constraints, the nation-state can become whatever it wants and even pursue a politics of hegemony and expansion. Hence for Mazzini, any legitimate patriotic pursuit always needs to be limited by reference to a universal maxim that bears some striking resemblance to Kant's categorical imperative: "Always ask yourselves . . . : *If what I am now doing were done by all men, would it be beneficial or harmful to Humanity? And if your conscience tells you it*

---

[26] Giuseppe Mazzini, "Nationalité. Quelques idées sur une constitution nationale" [1835], in *Scritti editi ed inediti*, 100 vols. (Imola: Tipografia Galeati, 1906–43), 6:125, 134. See also Mazzini, "Nationality and Cosmopolitanism," chapter 3 of this book.

[27] Mazzini, "Nationalism and Nationality," chapter 3 of this book, 65.

would be harmful, desist from acting; desist even though it might seem that an immediate advantage to your country ... would be the result."[28] Ultimately, Mazzini's fundamental distinction between a benevolent, republican *patriotism* and a belligerent, chauvinistic *nationalism* hinges precisely on the awareness of such universal moral restraints.

In early-twentieth-century Italy, Mazzini's democratic political thought and his related conception of the nation were deliberately perverted by the Fascist regime. Fascism aimed at imposing its cultural hegemony over the Italian nation by depicting itself as the heir of the Risorgimento. Thus Giovanni Gentile, the leading philosopher of Fascism, set out to fabricate an image of Mazzini that was meant to exalt an expansionist ideal of the nation. Gentile went about his task by intentionally underplaying and misrepresenting Mazzini's democratic republicanism. He also quite skillfully exploited several ambiguities inherent in Mazzini's philosophy and flowery political rhetoric. In short, Fascism ended up constructing an influential image of Mazzini as the father of an idea of "national mission" that could be used to support an aggressive foreign policy and the sacrifice of individual freedom to the supreme good of the state.[29]

Mazzini certainly believed that each nation, like each individual human being, ought to pursue a specific "mission." But the Fascist reading stretches Mazzini's political thought beyond recognition. Indeed, his idea of national mission cannot be adequately understood outside of his democratic and universalist political philosophy. For Mazzini, each nation can accomplish its own mission only insofar as it acts according to the universal "law of Humanity"; this requires that it grant civil and political rights to all its citizens, while also educating them according to an ethos of republican duties and international brotherhood.[30] Thus Mazzini spoke of "mission" in a peculiarly idealistic manner, to suggest the specificity and unique character of different individual and national vocations. Like the American transcendentalists and German romantics who were his contemporaries, he used the concept of mission as a counterpoise to Enlightenment philosophies built on

---

[28] Mazzini, "On the Duties of Man," chapter 5 of this book, 92; emphasis in original.

[29] See Giovanni Gentile, "Mazzini," in *I Profeti del Risorgimento Italiano* (Florence: Sansoni, 1944 [1923]), 26ss.

[30] Mazzini, "On the Superiority of Representative Government," and "Humanity and Country" [1836], in chapters 2 and 3 of this book. Italy's own specific mission, Mazzini argued toward the end of his life, "consists in promoting the principle of Nationality as the supreme foundation of international order and as a guarantee of future peace." Cf. Mazzini, "Principles of International Politics" [1871], chapter 22 of this book, 232.

abstract views of reason and the individual. Mazzini's frequent and admittedly somewhat vague references to distinct national missions are best understood as an effort to emphasize each people's unique contribution to the progress of humanity as a whole. The nation should embody the universal language of humanity, spoken in the tongue of each specific people.[31]

For Mazzini, only if the nation respects humanity (and thus not merely its own citizens, but also foreigners in its midst and abroad) does it properly deserve international recognition and respect. He identified two principal kinds of duties that ought to guide human behavior: duties toward humanity and duties toward one's own polity, respectively; hence *moral* and *political* duties. Duties toward humanity come first, and they confer moral legitimacy to a people's will to become a nation.[32] Hence in his view, the "nation" was not merely a political concept or a descriptive term but above all a *principle*—a normative ideal whose goal was to elevate and dignify the political practice of nation-building and self-determination.[33]

In Mazzini's view, all nations have an equivalent moral value; there is no hierarchy among them. Like the romantic philosopher Johann G. Herder, he saw each nation as contributing to the life of humanity in its own peculiar and irreplaceable way.[34] Yet Mazzini restated Herder's idea with an important variation: while Herder had emphasized prepolitical factors, such as race or ancestral traditions, as constitutive of the nation, Mazzini gave the nation an essentially political meaning as "commonwealth" or government by the people, based on a written constitution.[35]

---

[31] Mazzini's idea of a "Universal Mind" frequently evoked in this context echoes one of the themes most recurrent in the writings of American transcendentalists, like those of Margaret Fuller Ossoli and Ralph Waldo Emerson, who knew and admired Mazzini's work and political project, and, in Fuller's case, actually devoted their lives to his cause. Cf. Margaret Fuller Ossoli, *Memoirs*, 2 vols., ed. Ralph Waldo Emerson, William Henry Channing, and James Freeman Clarke (New York: Burt Franklin, 1972 [1884]), 2:266–67.

[32] For a more detailed discussion, see Nadia Urbinati, "'A Common Law of Nations': Giuseppe Mazzini's Democratic Nationality," *Journal of Modern Italian Studies* 1 (1996): 207–8.

[33] See Levi, *La filosofia politica di Giuseppe Mazzini*, 202.

[34] An important contribution to the diffusion of Herder's ideas in Mazzini's time, and particularly in the 1830s, was the French edition of Herder's *Ideen zur Philosophie der Geschichte der Menschheit* [*Idées sur la philosophie de l'histoire de l'humanité*] by Edgar Quinet in 1837.

[35] Mack Smith, *Mazzini*, 6. For this reason, Mazzini has been recently included among the theorists of a liberal, as opposed to communitarian, nationalism. See especially Yael Tamir, *Liberal Nationalism* (Princeton, NJ: Princeton University Press, 1993), 96–97; Margaret Canovan, *Nationhood and Political Theory* (Cheltenham, UK: Edward Elgar, 1996), 6–9; and Michael Freeden, *Liberal Languages* (Princeton, NJ: Princeton University Press, 2005), 212.

For the German romantic philosophers, the nation was a defensive project—an organic body with some pristine and unique characteristics to be protected from the infiltration of any foreign culture, at the political and ethical level. According to this view, the nation had *constitutive* qualities that communication with the outside could weaken but never alter significantly, and the organization of the state ought to follow and respect the national character. The nation's temporal dimension was the past. What for Mazzini were "indications" of the nation (language, territory, literature, ethnicity), were here its ultimate foundations and legitimate justification. In short, for the German romantics the nation was morally and politically prior to its own members—a communitarian ethical unity that gave meaning to the life and identity of individual human beings.[36]

For Mazzini, on the other hand, the politics of nationality was primarily a process aimed at redefining the legitimacy of sovereign power. Hence the achievement of national self-determination and independence would be an accomplishment of, rather than an alternative to, the message of the Enlightenment and the legacy of the French Revolution.[37] Equality, popular participation, and an awareness of universal moral duties were the principles that made Mazzini's nation the agent of a new cosmopolitan order. He understood quite well that by celebrating the "purity" of a supposedly prepolitical entity, nationalism could easily deteriorate into an aggressive chauvinism.[38] This led him to insist that the nation was actually not the last word of history, but only a necessary intermediate step toward further stages of human progress:

We do not believe in the timelessness of races. We do not believe in the timelessness of languages. . . . We believe in a sole and constant general law.

[36] The philosopher Johann G. Fichte, for instance, had no doubt that the German nation was essentially timeless: it was a unity "already achieved, completed, and existing," waiting to be liberated from the influence of "its fusion with foreign people" by means of a "new education," which would "mold the Germans into a corporate body." Cf. Johann G. Fichte, *Addresses to the German Nation*, trans. and ed. G. A. Kelly (New York: Harper and Row, 1968 [1807–8]), 45, 3, 12, 49. The philosophical perspective of Herder was not markedly different, even though he never translated his cultural nationalism into a political one. Herder's polemic was with imported culture (primarily French culture) and abstract universalism. Cf. Johann G. Herder, *On Social and Political Culture*, trans. and ed. F. M. Barnard (London, UK: Cambridge University Press, 1969), 186–87.

[37] Not surprisingly, among those who best understood the revolutionary implications of Mazzini's political conception of the nation was an antidemocratic liberal, Lord Acton, who listed Mazzini's idea of nationality, together with democracy and socialism, as ideologies "impugning the present distribution of power" in the name of political equality. Cf. Lord Acton, "Nationality" [1862], in *Essays on Freedom and Power*, ed. Gertrude Himmelfarb (Glencoe, IL: The Free Press, 1948), 169–84.

[38] Nationalism, he wrote, would drive each people "to break the intimate bond among human beings" and undermine "the perception of mutual needs that unites the nations with one another." Cf. Mazzini, "Nationalité," 127, 132–33.

Therefore we also believe in a sole and constant general objective; and we believe in progressive development toward this given objective, which can only be achieved by means of coming closer together—that is, through *association*.[39]

Mazzini rejected nationalism as both politically dangerous and morally wrong. Nationalism—that is, an ideology of national self-assertion untempered by the awareness of universal moral duties—interrupts what Mazzini took to be a natural process of *communication* and even empathy among peoples. It turns nationality into a zero-sum game—a contest between supposedly different degrees of human perfection. Mazzini's harsh criticism of the post-1849 politics of national unification and independence in Italy and elsewhere under the banners of monarchical regimes was a lucid diagnosis of the abandonment of democratic patriotism in favor of a crude and chauvinistic nationalism. National unification had become a largely top-down enterprise—the achievement of diplomatic and military elites rather than of popular movements. With the democratic movements sidelined and oppressed, he pointed out, "the question of *territory*" had wholly overshadowed "the question of *liberty*." Nation-building had thus become a question of force and self-assertion, leading "to a narrow and mean *Nationalism*" that was inherently "jealous of everything that surrounded it."[40] In sum, whereas communitarians and romantic nationalists theorized the idea of mutual impermeability and untranslatability among cultures and languages, Mazzini proposed instead the idea of a subterranean unity of the human race. The active participation of individuals in free democratic nations, he believed, would teach them to sympathize with foreign peoples and look beyond the narrowness of their own national culture and prejudices.

Democracy and Self-Determination as Means to Global Peace

The modern ideal of a peaceful international order based on liberty was first put forward by cosmopolitan philosophers in the eighteenth century. Beginning with the Abbé de Saint-Pierre, Immanuel Kant, and the Saint-Simonians, European democrats and republicans had outlined the idea of a voluntary "federation," or association, of autonomous nations in a covenant of mutual assistance and cooperation. In the nineteenth century, Mazzini reinterpreted this tradition and developed it further in his own original way.

[39] Mazzini, "Humanity and Country," chapter 3 of this book, 55; emphasis in original.
[40] Mazzini, "Nationality and Cosmopolitanism," chapter 3 of this book, 60; and "Letter to a German," in *Letters*, 19, 21.

According to Mazzini, the main problem of Europe in the past had been the lack of a common belief in democracy as the universal form of political organization. "Humanity was still ignored. . . . Each nation . . . had foreigners or barbarians in its own midst; millions of men not admitted to the religious rites of citizenship and believed to be of an inferior nature—slaves among the free."[41] Yet he observed that in the mid nineteenth century, across Europe increasingly large segments of society were demanding to participate in politics, while subject peoples claimed the right to shape their own destiny by means of national self-determination. Based on this observation and his own deepest convictions, Mazzini identified an "indisputable tendency" in his epoch toward a reconstitution of the European political order in accordance with the principles of nationality and democracy.

Mazzini also crucially believed that the moral progress achieved through the establishment of independent, democratic governments at the domestic level would greatly facilitate the emergence of a more peaceful international order. Once established, free democratic nations based on political transparency and popular consent would gradually establish a new type of international relations among themselves:

> These states, which have remained divided, hostile, and jealous of one another so long as their national banner merely represented the narrow interests of a dynasty or caste, will gradually become more and more intimately associated *through the medium of democracy*. The nations will be sisters. Free and independent . . . in the organization of their domestic affairs, they will *gradually unite around a common faith*, and they will enter a common pact to regulate all matters related to their international life.[42]

The English political realist E. H. Carr once suggested that according to Mazzini, the spread of popular government and national self-determination would result in a natural "harmony of interests" among democracies.[43] Mazzini was certainly an idealist, but he was less politically naïve than several of his critics, including Carr, have tended to assume. For Mazzini there was little doubt that democratically governed nation-states would continue to have many different and often outright conflicting interests. However, he anticipated that established constitutional democracies would be able to resolve those differences in a nonviolent, cooperative manner. Mazzini's intuition was highly original,

---

[41] Mazzini, "On the Duties of Man," chapter 5 of this book, 90.

[42] Mazzini, "From a Revolutionary Alliance to the United States of Europe," [1850] chapter 8 of this book, 126; emphasis added.

[43] E. H. Carr, *The Twenty Years' Crisis* (London: Palgrave, 2001), 45.

and it went beyond Kant's previous theory on the peaceful inclinations of republican governments in some important regards.

Mazzini's argument about a separate peace among democracies relies on both popular education and what he expected would be the international incentives facing democratic regimes. First, Mazzini identified a crucial pedagogical element in universal suffrage and other forms of popular participation. He believed that genuine democracy *within* states, combined with a generalized humanitarian education, would put in motion a moral culture that would challenge existing practices of exclusion and discrimination in the name of a common humanity. In other words, democratic citizens would learn to recognize all human beings as equals and to respect the freedom and independence of other nations.[44] Mazzini thus considered democratic government at the domestic level and the ensuing moral progress to be necessary conditions for a more peaceful international order. Yet they would hardly be sufficient. At best, the citizens of democratic nation-states would come to recognize their duties toward humanity and therefore broadly support a peaceful foreign policy.

But Mazzini was also acutely aware of international systemic constraints resulting from the condition of anarchy among nations and the related, permanent insecurity. He understood that democratic nations, although peacefully inclined, would not be able to fully renounce war so long as powerful and potentially aggressive despotic states continued to exist in their neighborhood. Mazzini expected, not without reason, that the old European despots would "for a long time look down with instincts of envy and suspicion" on any newly arising democracy.[45] He was convinced that even the survival of democracy itself would be constantly threatened under similar circumstances: "No conquest of liberty in a nation can function for long unless an analogous process is achieved in the nations that surround it."[46]

Young and still fragile democracies would therefore have strong incentives to enter into a mutual defensive "pact," or alliance, with other democracies, aimed at defending their shared values (what Mazzini calls their "common faith") and domestic political achievements. Ideally, one of them would take the lead to overcome what in contemporary language we might call collective action problems and constitute a focal point for their federal association. Not surprisingly,

---

[44] Mazzini insists that for this purpose, "there shall be a universally applied plan" of popular education, "various encouragements shall be offered to the arts and sciences," and "the founding of public libraries, newspapers, prizes, and universities should be actively promoted." Cf. Mazzini, "On the Superiority of Representative Government," chapter 2 of this book, 52.

[45] Mazzini, "Principles of International Politics" [1871], chapter 22 of this book, 236.

[46] Mazzini, "From a Revolutionary Alliance to the United States of Europe," chapter 8 of this book, 132.

Mazzini insisted toward the end of his life that a newly united Italy, having the potential to become a liberal great power, should accomplish this leadership function: "If Italy wants to be able to influence future international developments, its first priority in foreign policy should be to make itself the soul and center of a League of Europe's smaller States, closely united in a *collective defence pact* against the possible usurpations of one or the other great Power."[47] But on several occasions he speculated that perhaps Great Britain, or even the United States, might be better equipped to fulfill this function of democratic leadership.[48]

Europe's new democracies would have to pursue a principled foreign policy and make their peaceful intentions as explicit as possible, to increase their mutual trust and reduce the likelihood of accidental conflicts: "What applies to all nations is especially true of rising nations. The morality . . . of the standards that guide their political conduct is not just a matter of duty; it also affects their future to a significant degree."[49] Mazzini generally saw publicity in all matters related to foreign affairs as an absolute practical and moral requirement for democratic nations, particularly in their relations with other democracies: "Disclose everything to the people. Not even a single negotiation should be kept secret; not a single demand should remain hidden from the public eye."[50]

The argument that transparent behavior in accordance with certain basic moral standards can foster the buildup of mutual trust among nations has since become a central tenet of liberal thinking on international relations. John Rawls, for instance, argues that when basic standards of international morality (enshrined in what he calls the "Law of Peoples") are "honored by peoples over a certain period of time . . . peoples tend to develop mutual trust and confidence in one another"; this makes it possible to approach genuine "democratic peace" and thus achieve international "stability for the right reasons."[51] It may be interesting to note that Mazzini himself sometimes referred to the settled norms of international morality as the "Law of Peoples," drawing on the ancient Latin notion of *jus gentium*.[52]

Mazzini was no political economist; yet he shared with political thinkers and philosophers of the eighteenth and early nineteenth century, such as Adam Smith, Montesquieu, Kant, and J. S. Mill, the belief that

---

[47] Ibid., 236, emphasis added.

[48] See, e.g., Mazzini, "On Public Opinion and England's International Leadership" [1847] and "America as a Leading Nation in the Cause of Liberty" [1865], chapters 17 and 20 of this book.

[49] Mazzini, "Principles of International Politics," chapter 22 of this book, 224.

[50] Mazzini, "On Publicity in Foreign Affairs" [1835], chapter 14 of this book, 172.

[51] John Rawls, *The Law of Peoples* (Cambridge, MA: Harvard University Press, 1999), 44–45.

[52] Mazzini, "On Publicity in Foreign Affairs," chapter 14 of this book, 169.

growing *economic interdependence* could be a powerful stimulus for peace in its own right. He thought that liberal Europe in the mid nineteenth century was "so closely united . . . at the level of commercial interests" that no rise or fall of exchange rates could take place in London or Paris without the shock being felt elsewhere.[53] Any hypothetical war among liberal states would now inevitably undermine the transnational financial foundations of their prosperity. The anticipated enormous costs of war among liberal democracies would result in powerful additional incentives to resolve disputes peacefully and preserve the peace.

Finally, Mazzini expected that democratic nations would increasingly establish various covenants and federative arrangements among themselves to put their alliance on more solid institutional foundations. Yet he remained short on details concerning the specific institutional structure of these future international federations. He thought that the specific configuration of international federative arrangements, like the domestic constitutional structure of democracies, would best be determined by future generations according to their particular preferences and their needs.[54] At the European level, the growing trust among democracies and their common interests would probably lead to the establishment of a "large international democratic association" with its own parliamentary committee. Each nation would be represented on the parliamentary committee by an individual plenipotentiary with an equally weighted vote, according to the principle of one-nation, one-vote. Presumably one day there would also be a European Court of Arbitration to adjudicate international disputes, which would further reduce the state of lawlessness among nations.[55] Ideally, the European federation of democracies would culminate in the constitution of a fully integrated United States of Europe. Although Mazzini's immediate concern was the revolutionary transition from despotism to democracy, he insisted on several occasions that "our [long-term] goal is to create the United States of Europe."[56]

[53] Mazzini, "On Public Opinion and England's International Leadership," chapter 17 of this book, 201. Liberals since Montesquieu have pointed out that growing international interdependence and the related, greatly increased costs of any violent disruption would produce powerful incentives for peace. For an influential recent reformulation of the classical liberal argument, see Robert O. Keohane and Joseph S. Nye, *Power and Interdependence: World Politics in Transition* (Boston: Little, Brown, 1977).

[54] To Mazzini this was quite obvious: "We cannot at this time fully erect the Temple of our faith; the peoples will erect it when the time is ripe." Cf. "Toward a Holy Alliance of the Peoples," chapter 7 of this book, 128.

[55] Mazzini, "On Nonintervention" [1851], chapter 19 of this book, 218; and "Toward a Holy Alliance of the Peoples," chapter 7 of this book; see also Mack Smith, *Mazzini*, 154.

[56] Mazzini, "From a Revolutionary Alliance to the United States of Europe," chapter 8 of this book, 135. For an early, enthusiastic assessment of Mazzini's pan-European vision, see Gwilym O. Griffith, *Mazzini: Prophet of Modern Europe* (London: Hodder and Stoughton, 1932).

Mazzini's views on the relationship between democracy and international peace, although undoubtedly quite speculative, anticipated several key elements of the current scholarly debate concerning the hypothesis of a separate "democratic peace." Contemporary international relations scholars have sought to explain why over the past two centuries consolidated liberal democracies have never engaged in war with one another, although they have been involved in numerous wars with nondemocracies. Michael Doyle, in particular, has traced his explanation of a separate peace among liberal democracies back to Kant's essay "Perpetual Peace."[57] But the hypothesis that liberal democracies are peacefully inclined only in their mutual relations, while they will continue to fight against despotic regimes, is based on an original reconstruction of the Kantian argument.

Kant requires in his famous Second Definitive Article of Perpetual Peace that "*each nation, for the sake of its own security,*" enter along with all other nations into a voluntary and loosely institutionalized international federation.[58] He nowhere implies that membership in this pacific federation (*foedus pacificum*) shall be limited to republics. Indeed, Kant scholars have emphasized that he probably "did not sanction a rigid dichotomization of the world between (peaceful) interliberal and (warring) liberal-nonliberal zones."[59] Kant revealingly thought that most nonrepublican states would first have to overcome the international state of war, by joining the *foedus pacificum* and thus morally committing to nonaggression, before they could develop a republican constitution that would in turn further consolidate international peace: "*The problem of establishing a perfect civil constitution is subordinate to the problem of a law-governed external relationship with other states, and cannot be solved un-*

[57]Michael W. Doyle, "Kant, Liberal Legacies, and Foreign Affairs," *Philosophy and Public Affairs* 12 (3) (1983): 213. Following Doyle's seminal research, several contemporary political scientists have based their arguments concerning a putative separate, or "dyadic," peace among democracies on a reconstruction of Kant's political thought. See especially Bruce Russett and John Oneal, *Triangulating Peace: Democracy, Interdependence, and International Organizations* (New York: Norton, 2001). For a concise discussion, see also Michael Doyle and Stefano Recchia, "Liberalism and International Relations," in *International Encyclopedia of Political Science* (London: Sage, 2010).

[58]Kant, "Perpetual Peace," 102, emphasis added. Kant recognizes that the initial establishment of such a federation could be facilitated if one powerful republic were to take the lead: "For if by good fortune one powerful and enlightened nation can form a republic (which by its nature is inclined to seek peace), this will provide a focal point for federal association among other states" (104). Yet he nowhere suggests that further membership in the foedus pacificum would be limited to *republics*.

[59]John MacMillan, "Immanuel Kant and the Democratic Peace," in *Classical Theory in International Relations*, ed. Beate Jahn (Cambridge, UK: Cambridge University Press, 2006), 58; see also Georg Cavallar, "Kantian Perspectives on Democratic Peace: Alternatives to Doyle," *Review of International Studies* 27 (2001), esp. 243-6.

less the latter is also solved."[60] Hence for Kant, perpetual peace can be achieved only after virtually all states have joined the *foedus pacificum*, thus formally renouncing war as an instrument of foreign policy, and set up a republican constitution.[61]

The first to explicitly outline the possibility of a separate peace among democratic nations was not Kant, but Mazzini. It should be noted that Mazzini had probably never read Kant's political writings and was only superficially familiar with the latter's ethics.[62] Moreover, although writing more than half a century after Kant, Mazzini did not have significantly more empirical evidence on which to base his expectation. By the mid nineteenth century, Great Britain, Switzerland, and France (from 1830 to 1848), as well as the United States, were broadly liberal-constitutional nations, although none of them was a full-fledged democracy according to Mazzini's ideal. Yet Mazzini boldly foresaw that established constitutional democracies would not engage in war with one another and would indeed establish friendly, cooperative relations among themselves, although for defensive reasons they might still have to fight against despotic states.[63]

THE ROCKY ROAD TO PERPETUAL PEACE: INSURGENCY, INSURRECTION, AND INTERNATIONAL INTERVENTION

Mazzini clearly believed that the spread of democracy and national self-determination would lay solid foundations for the achievement of global peace in the long run. However, his primary intellectual as well as practical concerns had to do more with the *means* by which independent democratic nations could be brought about. Mazzini was no liberal pacifist who believed in a natural "harmony of interests," like his contemporaries Richard Cobden and John Bright. His fundamental reasoning was that where despotic oppression and foreign domination made peaceful political contestation all but impossible, violent insurrections might be justified in the short run to establish free and self-determining democracies in the future. These conditions applied to mid-nineteenth-century Italy, in the face of harsh repression by the Austrian and Bour-

---

[60] Kant, "Idea for a Universal History with a Cosmopolitan Purpose" [1784], in *Kant: Political Writings*, 47; emphasis in original.

[61] For Kant, as for Mazzini, progress toward peace is ultimately contingent on the moral progress of individuals, and republican government provides the framework within which such progress is possible. For an excellent discussion of Kant's international theory, see Andrew Hurrell, "Kant and the Kantian Paradigm in International Relations," *Review of International Studies* 16 (1990): 196–97.

[62] Wight, *Four Seminal Thinkers in International Theory*, 97; Mack Smith, *Mazzini*, 229.

[63] Most wars, he pointed out, would continue to be "but the result of mutual fear." Cf. Mazzini, "Nationality and Cosmopolitanism," chapter 3 of this book, 61.

bon despots and their local puppet principalities.[64] Yet Mazzini was neither a warmonger who invariably called for violent insurrection, nor a crusading liberal who blindly invoked international military interventions for the sake of freedom and democracy. His often inflammatory rhetoric and his repeated calls on established liberal nations to "support" foreign peoples in their struggle against despotic oppression have misled several Anglo-American readers and especially international relations scholars in this regard.[65]

Throughout his life, Mazzini insisted that national liberation and the establishment of democratic governments would have to be achieved through primarily *domestic political struggles*. Wherever possible, those struggles ought to be peaceful. Public opinion and its mobilization for the national cause always remained central to Mazzini's republican project.[66] Even when brutal governmental oppression made violence the only means available, wanton destruction should always be avoided and violence should be used with as much circumspection as the circumstances allowed:

> We disagree with those dreamers who preach peace at any cost, even that of dishonor, and who do not strive to make Justice the sole basis of any lasting peace. We believe war to be sacred under certain circumstances. But war must always be fought within the limits of necessity, when there is no other way to achieve the good. . . . No war must ever be contaminated by the spirit of vengeance, or by the brutal ferocity of a boundless egoism.[67]

[64] Mazzini's international thought is thus quite compatible with the recent empirical finding that while consolidated liberal democracies appear indeed to have established a separate peace among themselves, *transitions* to democracy are often rocky and violent. See Edward D. Mansfield and Jack Snyder, *Electing to Fight: Why Emerging Democracies Go to War* (Cambridge, MA: MIT Press, 2005).

[65] For instance, Kenneth Waltz suggests that Mazzini unabashedly called for interventionist "crusades to establish the conditions under which all states can coexist in perpetual peace." Cf. Kenneth N. Waltz, *Man, the State, and War: A Theoretical Analysis* (New York: Columbia University Press, 2001 [1959]), 3, 111. Martin Wight and John Vincent similarly claim that the Italian revolutionary was advocating a liberal crusade in support of democracy and "international intervention against despotic governments." Martin Wight, *Four Seminal Thinkers in International Theory*, 107; and John R. Vincent, *Nonintervention and International Order* (Princeton, NJ: Princeton University Press, 1974), 60–61.

[66] Among the available means to rally public opinion behind the cause of national liberation, Mazzini mentions politically active associations, public meetings, and perhaps most important, the press and popular newspapers. Cf. Mazzini, "Letters on the State and Prospects of Italy" [1839], in *Scritti Editi ed Inediti*, 22:166. See also Gaetano Salvemini, *Mazzini*, trans. I. M. Rawson (Stanford, CA: Stanford University Press, 1961), 70; and Mack Smith, *Mazzini*, 51.

[67] Mazzini, "Neither Pacifism nor Terror: Considerations on the Paris Commune and the French National Assembly," chapter 13 of this book, 157.

Mazzini always strongly opposed terrorist activity against civilians, although he supported guerrilla warfare against the members of regular armies. "We do not want terror," he insisted, and then went on to "reject terror as both cowardly and immoral."[68] In the long run, any revolutionary struggle would lack legitimacy and be doomed to failure, unless a majority of the population was clearly willing to support it.[69]

Historically, his views on political violence reflected the experience of the French revolution and subsequent Napoleonic wars. The older generation of Italian patriots had fought for Napoleon's army in Spain between 1808 and 1814, where they had experienced a fierce and highly effective guerrilla-type resistance by the local population. In the 1820s and 1830s, it was quite natural for those Italian patriots to suggest the formation of similar guerrilla bands for the fight against despotism in Italy, given the country's rough and mountainous terrain. Mazzini quickly made their arguments his own.[70] He also crucially theorized how guerrilla-type resistance could become part of a broader strategy of national emancipation: guerrilla bands, he argued in one of his earliest essays, are the "precursors of the nation," and they should "attempt to rouse the nation into insurrection."[71]

Mazzini always thought of the Italian struggle for national unification as part of a broader European battle aimed at the emancipation of oppressed nationalities all over Central and Southeastern Europe, from Poland to the Balkans. In his writings, he therefore repeatedly called for the organization of a "Holy Alliance of the Peoples," a transnational association of European revolutionary leaders who would coordinate resistance movements and popular insurrections against the Holy Alliance of despotic monarchs. Throughout his decade-long exile, he repeatedly tried to put this idea into practice, seeking to establish an organization of revolutionaries from various European countries. He was convinced that only if the oppressed peoples rose up against their despotic oppressors all at once could their national emancipation have a realistic chance of success.[72]

[68] Mazzini, "Against the Foreign Imposition of Domestic Institutions" [1851], chapter 9 of this book, 138; see also Mack Smith, *Mazzini*, 9.

[69] The motto of revolutionary guerrilla bands should thus be: "Respect for women, for property, for the rights of individuals, and for the crops." Mazzini, "Rules for the Conduct of Guerrilla Bands" [1832], chapter 6 of this book, 111.

[70] Franco della Peruta, "La guerra di liberazione spagnola e la teoria della guerra per bande nel Risorgimento," in della Peruta, *L'Italia del Risorgimento: Problemi, momenti e figure* (Milan: Franco Angeli, 1997), 11–29.

[71] Mazzini, "Rules for the Conduct of Guerrilla Bands," chapter 6 of this book, 111.

[72] "What we need [is] . . . a single union of all the European peoples who are striving toward the same goal. . . . When we will rise up simultaneously in every country where our movement is currently active, we will win. Foreign intervention [by the despots] will then become impossible." Cf. Mazzini, "Toward a Holy Alliance of the Peoples," chapter 7 of this book, 121.

But for all his insistence on the need for a pan-European revolutionary alliance, he believed that the forces of despotism in each country would have to be essentially defeated by domestic revolutionaries on their own. Mazzini unequivocally stressed that liberty and democracy could never be delivered to an oppressed population from the outside. Subject peoples should "not look for liberty at the hands of the foreigner."[73] Each people should find their own path to liberty and collective emancipation, relying on their own memories of political oppression and their broader cultural and historical background. "The nation alone has the inviolable right to *choose* its own institutions, to *correct* them and *change* them when they no longer correspond to its needs."[74] Moreover, if liberty did not grow domestically, it could hardly be sustained. Mazzini's republicanism requires that each people develop their own *ethos* of liberty, by fighting for it if necessary and actively participating in its sustenance and progress day after day. Even if democratic revolutions were unsuccessful in the short run, they would instill a widespread love of liberty and country and thereby prepare the ground for democracy in the long run.

The view that democracy achieved with the help of foreign armies would either not last, or would otherwise not be worthy of its name, is today most closely associated with J. S. Mill. The most famous articulation of Mill's views on the legitimacy of popular insurrections for the sake of national self-determination, and his related rejection of foreign-imposed regime change, can be found in his 1859 essay *A Few Words on Non-Intervention*.[75] Yet Mill's views on these issues had already been outlined by Mazzini over the previous three decades. Mill and Mazzini were acquaintances; they met several times during the latter's exile in London, and their relationship was characterized by mutual admiration.[76]

Mazzini's views on the conditions that justify international military intervention were ultimately quite conservative. He believed that if a

[73] Mazzini, "Manifesto of Young Italy" [1831], chapter 1 of this book, 36.

[74] Mazzini, "On the Superiority of Representative Government," chapter 2 of this book, 50; emphasis in original. Elsewhere, Mazzini insists that "if a people were to impose their own solution to the specific social problems of another country, they would thereby commit an act of usurpation." Cf. Mazzini, "Against the Foreign Imposition of Domestic Institutions," chapter 9 of this book, 140.

[75] John Stuart Mill, "A Few Words on Nonintervention" [1859], in *Essays on Politics and Culture*, ed. Gertrude Himmelfarb (Gloucester, MA: Peter Smith, 1973).

[76] Mill openly acknowledged his "highest admiration for Mazzini," although he did not always sympathize with the latter's revolutionary mode of working. Cf. J.S. Mill, "Letter to Peter Alfred Taylor," in *Collected Works of John Stuart Mill*, vol. 17 (Toronto: University of Toronto Press, 1963 [1870]), 1759. See also Maria Teresa Pichetto, "Alcune note su Mazzini, Mill e l'ambiente politico inglese di metà ottocento," in *Giuseppe Mazzini e John Stuart Mill*, ed. Andrea Bocchi and Claudio Palazzolo (Pisa: Plus Edizioni, 2004).

people genuinely wanted to be free, under most circumstances they would be able to throw off any native despotism on their own, supported by a transnational alliance of republican solidarity. Only when the local despot was being actively supported by foreign armies and foreign money could patriotic insurgents no longer succeed. In the face of such "cooperation of despots against peoples," the liberal powers and especially Great Britain should in turn abandon their policy of nonintervention.[77]

Mazzini was making a case for *counterintervention* aimed at neutralizing any previous intervention in support of the despots. If the rule of nonintervention is to mean anything, he insisted, "it must mean that in every state the government must deal directly and alone with its own people."[78] Mazzini was again developing his normative arguments against the backdrop of the European political reality of his time. Since the defeat of Napoleon in 1815, the conservative great powers had been openly supporting each other, sometimes intervening militarily on each other's behalf to crush popular uprisings that threatened to overturn the status quo.[79]

In Mazzini's view, as soon as a foreign power had intervened militarily to crush an ongoing democratic insurrection, liberal-constitutional states would acquire a right and indeed a prima facie duty of counterintervention:

> If the government of a state is despotic and if the people . . . resist that government, carry on a war of the press against it, and at last, in spite of police and military force, defeat it; then . . . the decision is final. . . . But should the government of a neighboring despotic state, either invited by the vanquished party or fearing the contagion of liberal ideas in its own territory, militarily invade the convulsed state and so interrupt or repeal the revolution, then the principle of Nonintervention is at an end, and all moral obligation on other states to observe it is from that moment annulled.[80]

The only legitimate goal of counterintervention would be to rebalance the situation on the ground, so as "to make good all prior infrac-

---

[77] Mazzini, "On Nonintervention," chapter 19 of this book, 217.

[78] Ibid., 216.

[79] For instance, in June 1849 Russia had sent its imperial army into Hungary at Austria's request to crush a nationalist uprising there. Earlier that same year, France and Austria had answered a call for military assistance by the pope, dispatching an expeditionary force to crush the revolutionary Roman Republic led by Mazzini himself. And since the early 1820s, Austria had repeatedly intervened on the Italian Peninsula to support its local vassal states in the face of frequent popular uprisings.

[80] Mazzini, "On Nonintervention," chapter 19 of this book, 216.

tions of the law of Noninterference" and leave the patriotic insurgents with a realistic chance of success.[81] Thus for instance, the British should have first threatened and then actually executed a counterintervention on Italian soil in the spring of 1849, when the French had sent a military expedition to crush the revolutionary Roman republic. As Mazzini later recalled in a letter addressed to a British friend: "Ah! If you had in England, condescended to see that the *glorious* declaration of non-interference ought to have begun by taking away the French interference in Rome! How many troubles and sacrifices you would have saved us."[82] But in most instances, he believed, the credible *threat* of counterintervention by a powerful liberal nation would be sufficient to deter despotic states from intervening in the first place. Hence it would certainly not be necessary for the British "government to plunge itself into a revolutionary crusade, which no one dreams of invoking.'"[83] Mazzini's argument on counterintervention was again closely echoed by J. S. Mill, who similarly argued that in the case of a native despotism upheld by foreign armies, the reasons for nonintervention would cease to exist.[84]

More than anything else, Mazzini was seeking diplomatic assistance, or, as he liked to put it, "moral support" from other liberal nations and from Great Britain in particular. Toward the end of his life, he also increasingly hoped that significant help for the cause of democracy and national self-determination in Europe might be forthcoming from the United States of America. He believed that after the victory of Union forces in the American Civil War, the United States could—and should indeed—help European republicans to successfully face the many challenges that still confronted them:

> You [the United States] have become a *leading* Nation. Now you must act as such. . . . you must feel that to stand aloof would be a sin; . . . You must then help your republican brothers, mainly morally, and

[81] Ibid., 216. Mazzini never explicitly suggested that foreign imperial rule over a subject population, such as Austria's domination over northern Italy, constituted a sufficient cause for military intervention by the liberal great powers.

[82] Mazzini, "Extract from a Letter to Peter Taylor" [1860], in *Mazzini's Letters to an English Family, 1855–1860*, ed. E. F. Richards (London: John Lane, 1922), 236.

[83] Mazzini, "The European Question: Foreign Intervention and National Self-Determination" [1847], chapter 16 of this book, 195.

[84] The similarity between Mazzini's and Mill's reasoning is again striking: "A people the most attached to freedom, the most capable of defending and making a good use of free institutions, may be unable to contend successfully for them against the military strength of another nation much more powerful. To assist a people thus kept down is not to disturb the balance of forces on which the permanent balance of freedom in a country depends, but to redress that balance when it is already unfairly and violently disturbed." Cf. John S. Mill, "A Few Words on Nonintervention," 383.

materially if needed, whenever the sacred battle is being fought and you have the ability to effectively inspire and support those who toil and bleed for truth and for justice.[85]

When writing for British and American audiences, Mazzini sometimes conceded that in the short run, supporting his revolutionary movement would have led to increased political turmoil on the European continent. But he insisted that patriotic insurrections against despotic governments and foreign rule were a natural expression of people's desires and indeed part of God's "providential design." Lack of international support for those movements would have merely prolonged a bloody European conflict, which the forces of democracy would have finally won no matter what. Hence, even setting moral considerations aside, it would be in the enlightened self-interest of the liberal great powers to openly back Mazzini's revolutionary leadership, so that the conflict could be swiftly brought to an end and everyone might look forward to an epoch of international peace and prosperity.

Mazzini thought that foreign military intervention would be justified only in one additional instance beyond counterintervention—namely, to rescue populations abroad from systematic slaughter. His thinking on this matter remained quite tentative, yet he was in fact putting forward one of the earliest justifications for humanitarian intervention. He envisaged an international society in which liberal nations might combine as a matter of moral duty to counter egregious human rights violations committed within an independent state:

> People begin to feel that . . . there are bonds of international duty binding all the nations of this earth together. Hence, the conviction is gaining ground that if on any spot of the world, even within the limits of an independent nation, some glaring wrong should be done, . . .
> —if, for example, there should be, as there has been in our time, a massacre of Christians within the dominions of the Turks—then other nations are not absolved from all concern in the matter simply because of the large distance between them and the scene of the wrong.[86]

Mazzini's reflections on humanitarian intervention were probably spurred by repeated instances of European military interference in the Ottoman Empire, which ostensibly sought to protect local Christian populations from religiously motivated violence. As early as 1827, Russia, Great Britain, and France had intervened militarily in the Greek war

---

[85] Mazzini, "America as a Leading Nation in the Cause of Liberty," chapter 20 of this book, 221. See also Howard R. Marraro, "Mazzini on American Intervention in European Affairs," *Journal of Modern History* 21 (2) (1949): 109–14.

[86] Mazzini, "On Nonintervention," chapter 19 of this book, 218.

of independence, inflicting a decisive defeat to the Ottoman army (although humanitarian considerations were at best secondary in this context). Most significantly, in the summer of 1860 France dispatched six thousand troops to Lebanon to stop ongoing massacres of the local Christian Maronite population in the context of a bloody civil war; and the intervention had been collectively authorized by most of the European great powers.[87]

Mazzini was certainly a progressive and in many regards a revolutionary; yet his intellectual frame of reference was that of a thoroughly nineteenth-century figure. Hence he also shared his contemporaries' attitude toward colonialism. Most fundamentally, he shared with them a philosophy of progress that portrayed most non-European peoples as backward, in need of being "educated" and trained to become ready for self-government. As he wrote to his mother in 1845, he believed "that Europe has been providentially called to conquer the rest of the world to progressive civilization."[88] Mazzini's paternalistic endorsement of colonialism as an instrument of Europe's "civilizing mission" echoed Mill's idea that "Nations which are still barbarous . . . should be conquered and held in subjection by foreigners."[89] More generally, nineteenth-century reformist thinking was marked by Saint-Simon's stage theory of social evolution (which played an important role in Mazzini's own political thought) and by continental philosophy of history, particularly idealism (Mazzini welcomed the revival of Giambattista Vico's historicism). This led to a backlash against Enlightenment natural-rights theories in favor of the idea that civil and political liberties were historically contingent and required the achievement of a certain stage of social and moral development before they could be sustained. Distinguished nineteenth-century liberals, democrats, and revolutionaries therefore justified colonialism as a painful but neces-

[87] See Martha Finnemore, *The Purpose of Intervention: Changing Beliefs about the Use of Force* (Ithaca, NY: Cornell University Press, 2003), 58–62; and for a more detailed historical analysis, Gary Bass, *Freedom's Battle: The Origins of Humanitarian Intervention* (New York: Knopf, 2008).

[88] Mazzini, *Letters*, 98. Several years later, he repeated the same basic point in a longer essay on international politics: a newly unified Italy should follow other European nations and "contribute to the great civilizing mission suggested by our times." An integral part of this mission would be for Italy to "invade and colonize the Tunisian lands when the opportunity presents itself." Mazzini, "Principles of International Politics," chapter 22 of this book, 238–39.

[89] Mill, "A Few Words on Nonintervention," 377. In his classical treatise, *Considerations on Representative Government*, Mill similarly insisted that "subjection to a foreign government . . . , notwithstanding its inevitable evils, is often of the greatest advantage to a people, carrying them rapidly through several stages of progress." Cf. Mill, *On Liberty and Other Essays*, ed. John Gray (Oxford: Oxford University Press, 1998), 264.

sary school of modernization and/or self-government for "backward" peoples.[90] Mazzini was no exception, although his insistence on popular consent as the primary criterion of political legitimacy suggests that he would have been invariably sympathetic to all movements of national self-determination, wherever they emerged.

In conclusion, Mazzini made a seminal contribution to the development of modern democratic republicanism, as well as to liberal-internationalist thinking on national self-determination and international politics more broadly. He developed an original, democratic conception of the nation as a political association of equals, and he crucially anticipated that democracy within states would create the conditions for lasting international peace.

Mazzini was a visionary and undoubtedly an idealist, in the sense that he deeply believed in the power of ideas to effect lasting political change. But he was also a sophisticated political thinker who based his normative arguments and passionate calls to action on a solid grasp of the actual political forces and emerging ideological trends that characterized his time. He understood that in mid-nineteenth-century Europe, as the industrial revolution took off in the aftermath of the Napoleonic Wars, the people were yearning for deep-cutting social and political change, and the time had become ripe for an overthrow of the imperial and authoritarian structures of the *ancien régime*. Following Rousseau, he took human beings as they are and laws as they might be: the former as free and equal individuals with their own interests and passions, endowed with the ability to learn to live and associate peacefully with others; the latter as conditions that should channel the people's energies and aspirations toward genuine moral and political emancipation.

---

[90] See William Bain, *Between Anarchy and Society: Trusteeship and the Obligations of Power* (Oxford: Oxford University Press, 2003).

PART 1

Democracy and the Nation: A Republican Creed

CHAPTER ONE

Manifesto of Young Italy (1831)

Too MUCH TIME has hitherto been spent in words among us, too little in acts.[1] Were we simply to consider the suggestions of our individual tendencies, silence would appear the fittest reply to undeserved calumny and overwhelming misfortune; the silence of the indignant soul burning for the moment of solemn justification. But in consideration of the actual state of things and the desire expressed by our Italian brothers, we feel it a duty to disregard our individual inclinations for the sake of the general good. We feel it urgent to speak out frankly and freely, addressing some words of severe truth to our fellow countrymen and to the peoples who have witnessed our misfortune.

Great revolutions are the work of principles rather than of bayonets. They are first achieved in the moral, and then in the material sphere. Bayonets are truly powerful only when they assert or maintain a right. Now, the rights and duties of society spring from a profound moral sense that has taken root in the majority. Blind, brute force may create victors, victims, and martyrs, but the triumph of force always results in tyranny if it is achieved in antagonism to the will of the majority. Only the diffusion and propagation of *principles* among the peoples makes their right to liberty manifest. By creating the desire and need of liberty, it invests mere force with the vigor and justice of law.

There is only one truth. But the principles of which it is composed are manifold. The human intellect cannot embrace them all at once; and even after it has comprehended them, it cannot organize and combine

---

[1] Original title: "Manifesto della Giovine Italia." Mazzini founded the political organization "Young Italy" (*Giovine Italia*) during his first exile in Marseille in 1831. His immediate goal was to secretly prepare and coordinate revolutionary activities in Italy. Mazzini was well aware that the revolutionary effort could succeed only by winning over a large segment of the Italian population to its cause. Hence, a sustained public propaganda effort would be needed to inform the Italian population about Young Italy's ultimate goal: the liberation of the Italian Peninsula from foreign domination and its political unification under a popular, republican government. To support the propaganda effort, a periodical publication with the same name was circulated among Italian sympathizers and followers. The movement was immediately popular, but an attempted uprising in 1834 failed miserably. The present manifesto was originally translated into English under Mazzini's oversight. For the present edition, language and sentence structure have been partially updated.

them all in a single intelligible and absolute form. Men of great genius who are also endowed with a large heart sow the seeds of a new degree of progress in the world. But those seeds bear fruit only after many years and through the labors of many men. The education of humanity does not proceed by fits and starts. The beliefs of humanity are the result of a long and patient application of principles, the study of details, and related attempts to identify the causes of different facts and events.

Therefore a journal appears to be the method of popular instruction most in harmony with the impatient rapidity and multiplicity of events in our present day. It will be a gradual, successive, and progressive enterprise of wide and vast proportions; the work of many men who share the same goal. It will reject no fact but rather observe them all in their true order and various bearings, tracing in each the action of the immutable first principles of things.

In Italy, as in every country aspiring toward a new life, there is a clash of opposing elements, of passions assuming a variety of forms, and of desires tending toward one sole aim, although through almost infinite modifications. There are many men in Italy who are full of indignant hatred of the foreigner, who shout for liberty simply because it is the foreigner who withholds it. There are others who have at heart the unification of Italy before anything else and would gladly unite her divided children under any strong will, whether of a native or foreign tyrant. Others again are fearful of all violent upheavals; they doubt the possibility of controlling the sudden shock of private interests and the jealousies of different provinces, and thus they shrink from the idea of absolute union and are ready to accept any new territorial organization that diminishes the number of sections into which the country is currently divided.

Few appear to understand that any true progress will be fatally impossible in Italy, until every effort at emancipation shall proceed along the three inseparable bases of unity, liberty, and independence. But the number of those who do understand this is increasing daily, and this conviction will rapidly absorb every other variety of opinion. Love of country, abhorrence of Austria, and a burning desire to throw off her yoke, are now universally diffused passions. There will no longer be *compromises* inculcated by fear. Long-held misleading notions of tactics and diplomacy will be abandoned, vanishing before the authority of the national will. There will be a decisive struggle between tyranny, driven to its final and most desperate resistance, and those bravely resolved to dare its overthrow.

The question as to the means by which to reach our aim, and convert the insurrection into a lasting and fruitful victory, is by no means simple. There is a class of men, endowed with civic ability and influence, who imagine that revolutions are to be conducted with diplomatic caution and reserve, rather than with the energy of an irrevocable faith and will. They accept our principles but reject their consequences; they shrink from extreme remedies to extreme evils; and they believe that the peoples can be led to liberty by adopting the same cunning and artifice of the tyrants who enslave them. Born and educated at a time when the conscience of a free man was a thing almost unknown in Italy, they have no faith in the power of a people rising in the name of their rights, their past glories, and their very existence. They have no faith in enthusiasm, nor indeed in anything whatever beyond the calculations of that diplomacy by which we have a thousand times been bought and sold, and the foreign bayonets by which we have been a thousand times betrayed.

They know nothing of the elements of regeneration that have been fermenting for the last half century in Italy; they know nothing of that yearning for betterment that our masses desire from the deepest of their hearts at the present day. They do not understand that, after many centuries of slavery, a nation can only be regenerated through virtue, or through death. They do not understand that 26 million men, made strong by their pursuit of a good cause and by an inflexible will, are practically invincible. They do not believe in the possibility of uniting the masses behind a single aim and purpose. But have they ever earnestly attempted this? Have they shown themselves ready to die for this? Have they ever proclaimed an Italian crusade? Have they ever taught the people that there is but one path to salvation, that a movement made in their cause must be upheld and sustained by themselves, that war is inevitable—a desperate and determined war that knows no truce save in victory or the grave? No; they have either stood aloof, dismayed by the greatness of the enterprise, or advanced doubtfully and timidly, as if the glorious path they trod were the path of illegality or crime.

They deluded the people by teaching them to hope in the observance of principles inferred from the records of diplomatic congresses or ministerial cabinets; they extinguished the ardor of those ready for fruitful sacrifice by promising that foreign aid would be forthcoming soon; and they wasted the time that should have been wholly devoted to forceful action or battle in inertia. Afterward, when deceived in their calculations and betrayed by diplomacy, with the enemy at their gates and terror in their hearts, when they could only have expiated their wrongdoing by honorably dying at their post, they shrank even from that and fled. Now, they deny all power of faith in the nation—they who never sought to arouse it by their example—and scoff at the enthusiasm they extinguished by their cowardice and hesitation. Peace be with them, for their errors sprang from weakness rather than baseness. But what right do they have to assume the leadership of an enterprise they cannot even grasp in its vastness and unity?

In the progress of revolutions, every error committed serves as a step toward the truth. Recent events have been a better lesson to the rising generation than whole volumes of theory. Indeed, we affirm that the events of 1821 have consummated and concluded the separation of Young Italy from the men of the past.[2] Perhaps this most recent example, where the solemn oath sworn over the corpses of seven thousand of their countrymen ultimately resulted in infamy and delusion, was needed to convince the Italians that God and fortune protect the brave, that victory lies at the point of a sword and not in the artifices of protocols.

Perhaps the lessons of ten centuries and the curses of their vanquished fathers were insufficient to convince the people that they may not look for liberty at the hands of the foreigner. But now, in this nineteenth century, Italy knows that unity of enterprise is a condition without which there is no salvation, that every true revolution is a declaration of war unto death between two opposing principles, that the fate of Italy must be decided on the plains of Lombardy.

Italy knows that there is no true war without the masses. The secret of raising the masses lies in the hands of those who show themselves ready to fight and promise to lead the people to victory. New circumstances call for new men—men untrammeled by old habits and systems, their souls free from petty interests or greed and moved by the Idea alone. Italy knows all this, and it knows that the secret of power is faith, that true virtue is sacrifice, and true policy to prove oneself strong.

Young Italy knows these things. It feels the greatness of its mission and will fulfill it. We swear it by the thousands of victims that have fallen over the last ten years, and who have shown that persecutions do not crush but rather fortify conviction. We swear it by the human soul that aspires to progress, by the youthful combatants of Rimini, by the

---

[2] In 1820 there was an insurrection in Spain over constitutional matters, which spurred a similar movement in the Kingdom of Two Sicilies (in southern Italy). The ruling monarch there, Ferdinand I of Bourbon, first agreed to enact a new constitution, but then repressed the insurrection and abolished the constitution with the help of Austrian troops that had intervened under the auspices of the Holy Alliance. In 1821 similar constitutional insurrections occurred in other Italian states and particularly in Piedmont, but they were once again put down by the rulers with foreign assistance. The "men of the past" that Mazzini refers to are the members of the *Carboneria*, a secret association with Masonic roots that had been founded in Italy in 1814. Mazzini was a *carbonaro* for a short time, before realizing that a national self-determination movement would require open popular mobilization rather than a secret society; hence he founded *Young Italy* as an alternative popular organization.

blood of the martyrs of Modena.[3] There is a religious faith that transpires from that blood. No power can destroy the seed of liberty once it has begun to grow in the blood of brave men. Today our religion is still that of martyrdom; tomorrow it will be the religion of victory.

And for us, the young—for all those of us who share the same creed—it is a duty to further the sacred cause by all available means. Since present circumstances make the use of arms impossible, we will write. The ideas and aspirations now scattered and disseminated among our ranks need to be organized into a system. This new and powerful element of life, which is leading young Italy toward her regeneration, needs to be purified from every servile habit and every unworthy affection.

And we will undertake this task, with the help of the Italians. We will strive to make ourselves the true interpreters of the various desires, sufferings, and aspirations that constitute Italy in the nineteenth century. It is our intention to publish, in a specific form and under certain conditions, a series of writings directed toward this goal. Those writings will be governed by the principles we have indicated.

We shall not abstain from dealing with philosophical or literary subjects. Unity is the first law of the mind. The reformation of a people rests on no certain foundation, unless it is based on agreement in religious belief and on the harmonious union of the entire sum of human faculties. The role of literature, viewed as a moral priesthood, is to give form and expression to the principles of truth; as such, it is a powerful engine of civilization.

Italy is our chief object. Hence, we shall not deal with foreign affairs or events elsewhere in Europe, except insofar as it may be useful to educate the Italians, or to heap infamy on the oppressors of mankind, and to strengthen those feelings of sympathy that should unite the freemen of all nations in a brotherly bond of hope and action.

There is a voice that loudly tells us: the religion of humanity is love. We certainly know that whenever two hearts beat with the same pulse and two souls commune in virtue, there is a country. Nor will we deny the noblest aspiration of our epoch, the aspiration toward the universal association of good men. But we must not forget the blood that is still flowing from the wounds caused by trust in the foreigner. The last cries of those who were betrayed still lie between us and the nations that have sold, neglected, or despised us. Pardon is a virtue that only the victorious can afford. And love demands equality, both of power and esteem.

---

[3] Popular revolts were launched unsuccessfully in Rimini, then part of the Papal States, and Modena, then ruled by Duke Francis IV of Este, between 1820 and 1821.

We reject both the assistance and the pity of foreign nations. But we will help to enlighten the European mind by showing how Italians really are: neither blind nor cowardly, but merely unfortunate. Thus we will lay the foundations of future international friendship based on mutual esteem.

Italy is little known abroad. Vanity, thoughtlessness, and the necessity felt by other nations of seeking excuses for crimes committed toward her have all contributed to misrepresent facts, passions, habits, and customs. Now we will uncover our wounds. We will show to foreign nations our blood being spilled as the price of that peace [the Vienna settlement of 1815] for which we have been sacrificed by the fears of diplomats. We will proclaim the duties of other nations toward us and unveil the falsehoods by which we have been overcome.

We will drag forth from the prisons and the darkness of despotism documentary evidence of the wrongs committed against us, of our sorrows, and our virtues. We will descend into the dust of our graves and display to the eyes of foreign nations the bones of our martyrs and the names of our unknown great men, mute witnesses of our sufferings, our steadfastness, and their guilty indifference. A cry of fearful anguish emerges from those Italian ruins on which Europe gazes in cold indifference, forgetful that they have twice shed the light of liberty and civilization on her. We listen to that cry, and we will repeat it to Europe until she learns the greatness of the wrong that has been committed thus far. We will tell the peoples: such are the souls you have bought and sold; such is the land you have condemned to isolation and eternal slavery.

On the Superiority of Representative Government (1832)

Ora e sempre.
Fais ce que dois, advienne que pourra.
[Now and forever.
Do what you must, and whatever is possible shall be
accomplished.]

OUR NEWSPAPER, *Giovine Italia* [*Young Italy*], has now been in existence for more than three months.[1] We thus feel the need to look back at what we have accomplished and at the debates that our writings have stimulated among those Italians who desire an improvement of their country's conditions. In addition, we feel the need to respond once and for all to some objections that have been raised against us. We want to state the principles that govern our work and the intentions that guide us in the choice of our means, so that we can quickly get back on track, free from any worries that our doctrine may be misinterpreted, and with no other care but the future, our consistency, and victory. We want to identify our friends and our enemies alike, and they should get to know us in turn. . . .

Strength in political matters results from the concentration of homogenous elements and forces toward a single purpose; it cannot result from the merely temporary agreement of many heterogeneous agents that lack any harmony among them. In other words: strength is measured by the level of cohesion, much more than by number or size. . . .

The axiom that guided Napoleon to victory, and Alexander the Great before him, was *to concentrate the greatest number of forces on a single goal.* And this is an inescapable law for anybody who attempts a revolution. During great campaigns of military conquest, a sense of unity can be

---

[1] Original title: "I collaboratori della Giovine Italia ai loro concittadini." In this essay Mazzini clearly lays out his revolutionary republican creed: he challenges paternalistic arguments for monarchical government, including constitutional monarchy. He then argues for the introduction of a truly republican government, based on universal suffrage, social justice, and the abolition of all hereditary privilege. He discusses the benefits of representative government and opts for *mandatory*, or representative, democracy.

instilled by a single man. But during great revolutions, it can only descend from a principle, which needs to be clear, certain, and sensible. Now, strictly speaking, of course, the liberty to which we aspire is not a principle, but rather that state in which a people can develop their own principle. Liberty is not itself an *end*, but rather a *means* to achieve it. The question, then, is: How can we achieve and organize the means, or even just fight openly for it, without actually knowing the end itself?

This extremely simple thought leads us to the central political question: *How to coordinate the means toward a given end*? Different ends require different means. Whoever wants to set liberty on a constitutional throne had better proceed by a different avenue than whoever wants to establish it on republican foundations. A people aspiring only to gain independence from foreign rule will be able to take advantage of several elements that will be precluded to other peoples, who seek to gain both independence and liberty [i.e., democratic government] at once. And a different principle necessarily produces different consequences: the history of revolutions provides us with ample evidence of this, and it is the only maxim by which to directly judge political events and their causes.

In every epoch and in every nation, those who want to entrust the people's destiny to a king will have to find a man of truly regal breeding, who can constitute a unitary nation. First, that man should be able to gain the favor of a certain class of men who will form the country's aristocracy, because a throne without an aristocracy cannot be sustained.[2] Second, he will have to rely on the popular element and its support, as much as necessary, to achieve successful political change; but the people should not be mobilized too much, because otherwise they get accustomed to it, and that usually results in troubles and restlessness and is a perpetual obstacle to monarchical power, no matter how organized. Third, once such a princely ruler is found and has been established, he needs to be surrounded with a permanent army, while the citizen's militia ought to submit itself, as much as possible, to the manners and spirit of the army. Fourth, the king should be given riches, courtly honors, and plenty of luxury. Fifth, he will have to be recognized and accepted by other kings through the granting of privileges and the signing of treaties, because everyone loves to be close to his fellows in rank. To keep it short: whoever wants to establish a kingdom should behave like the supporters of the monarchical constitution in France. It seems to us that all those who have been protesting against

---

[2] *See Montesquieu—and the examples of England, France, and all the other constitutional monarchies that currently exist or have ever existed. Whether the aristocracy be based on blood or on riches is hardly relevant. [This footnote is part of Mazzini's original essay].*

the French rulers' behavior thus far, but without wanting to change the actual form of government there, are utterly inconsistent.

Meanwhile, whoever wishes to found a republic should follow a different path. In the first case, the central question consists in finding a man, or princely ruler; in the second case it is necessary to create a people. *The first law of every revolution is to know exactly what you want to achieve.* The question of how to achieve your goal naturally follows from this initial consideration. It was therefore necessary for us to first of all choose a symbol, a belief, and a goal from among the many we had before us. And we have chosen the republican symbol.

There are many reasons for which we have embraced what our heart suggested: the existence of a few timeless principles, from which the republican form necessarily and inevitably descends; the impossibility of reconciling true liberty and the dogma of equality with the monarchical form, as the history of half a century has now shown; thousands of disappointments over time and some recent shameful events; the difficulty for a single throne to resolve all local conflicts and overcome all local competition; and the lack of a man with suitable reputation, virtue, and genius to direct our Italian regeneration. Further reasons that have guided our decision are: the existence of powerful republican memories among our people [from the time of Renaissance city-states]; the need to become active to convince a people, which has so many times been betrayed and sold off, that the freedom-loving patriots are truly working on its behalf; the absence in our lands of many elements that would be necessary to constitute a monarchy; the European trajectory that manifests itself by actual events day after day; and finally our desire to cut short the question with a single revolution. But I do not intend to elaborate on all these reasons in the present article. I may elaborate on several of them in the future; but for now I only want to lay out our principles and deduce their consequences.

We have chosen the republican symbol. All differences between ourselves and those who preceded us on the political scene can be traced back to this principle. The revolutions in Naples [1820] and the Piedmont [1821] simply aimed to promote the establishment of one or several constitutional monarchies in Italy. But these uprisings could not move beyond the narrow confines of their underlying political objectives. A few among the leaders of those uprisings have continued to insist that constitutional monarchy is the most perfect form of government. Most, however, merely regarded the establishment of constitutional monarchy as a transitional arrangement, as only a first step on the path toward future progress. Thereby they implicitly suggested that the Italian people might not yet be mature enough for a complete emancipation, that the tutelage of a king combined with that of an intermediary aristocracy remained necessary for the time being, and that opening the path to complete freedom, unleashing the people, would result in many perils that needed to be avoided at any cost. Accepting a king at the head of the social edifice, they also implicitly recognized a need for international balancing, for some agreement between their own *government* and foreign monarchical *governments*. By accepting a king at the head of the social edifice, they necessarily gave him all the rights and powers of kingship: authority to decide over peace and war, choice of ministers, immunity, and all those legal fictions that make up the essence of a mixed monarchical government.

Hence in 1820–21, no arms were distributed to the youth and those among the multitude who asked for them. The word *equality*, which could have roused the people, was barely uttered at all. And the decision was made not to promote and not even to consider a guerrilla war, which I do not hesitate to say, is the only kind of struggle able to regenerate those nations that have been held in slavery for many centuries. There were no instructions and no declarations of liberty addressed to the lower classes. The reasons for all this are clear: Had the people been mobilized and truly taught their own force, who would then have been able to restrain them within the shabby confines of mixed monarchical government?

Hence, nobody seriously challenged the existing aristocracy, because an aristocracy is an indispensable intermediary between the throne and the people. The command of the army was entrusted to suspect and inept men, who were known for past betrayals, because the constitution gave the king the right of appointment, and to refuse him that right would have meant to create institutions only to tear them down on the next day, thereby creating anarchy. The revolution itself was managed with a slowness and secrecy characteristic of the official diplomacy, and concessions were sought from the cabinets by offering an equal amount of concessions in return. And while the revolution was ongoing, the king was allowed to expatriate and attend international congresses, because it would indeed have been a contradiction to first approve of a leader and then forbid him to exercise his authority, or to openly mistrust every one of his moves without very good reasons.

I believe that these are all legitimate consequences of a given principle, and I do not blame the men of 1821 when they consistently followed their principle. Perhaps in those days Italy was not yet mature enough for better solutions; perhaps the multitudes can indeed only be trained through many failed attempts and ensuing disappointments. Perhaps it was necessary, to entrench the republican ideal in the people's souls, for the Italians to observe the joint spectacle of two princes [the Neapolitan and the Piedmontese] advancing liberty and then solemnly betraying it; and then to see the degree of ferocity displayed by those kings, whom the people had offended but not extinguished. And if all that can exculpate the leaders of those failed revolutionary attempts, for which Italy paid with eleven years of misery, then so be it. But today the experience has been completed. A simple truth can be inferred from studying those events, and other similar ones that subsequently took place in Europe: hereditary kingship and true liberty for the people cannot be reconciled. Therefore we have chosen the republican symbol as our revolutionary principle, and we will rely on a wholly different set of norms to guide our movement.

We will raise up high the banner of the Italian people, and we will call on the people to fight. We will place our greatest hopes in them. We will teach them their rights; we will try not to hamper their action, even while trying to channel it in a better direction. We will promote as zealously as possible a truly popular and national guerrilla war, against which there can be no equal enemy. We will seek to abolish all privilege, which is today at the core of the social question; and we will raise to the level of religion the dogma of equality. We will bring down and fuse within a great national unity all the various castes that have so far kept aloof from the mass of the people, because in founding a republic we do not need any intermediary aristocracies between two conflicting powers.

We will not attempt any alliances with the kings. We will not delude ourselves that we can remain free by relying on international treaties and diplomatic tricks. We will not beg for our well-being via the protocols of conferences or the promises of monarchic cabinet ministers. We will refuse to deal with the kings, because in raising ourselves to a republic, we know that we are entering into an irreconcilable conflict with the principle that still predominates among most European governments. We will refuse to negotiate with the princes, because given the present state of European affairs, we cannot expect any tolerance from them or any mutually beneficial agreements, except for short-term, mendacious compromises that would only prepare a boundless war and along the way would require that we give up at least part of the implications of our principles. We will not seek any agreement with the princes, because there is only one meaningful difference between wholehearted animosity and hidden plots: the first gets you either a rapid and decisive victory, or else an honorable ruin; the second may allow you to continue a worried and painful existence for the time being, but only at the cost of letting you fail miserably and be derided by all in the not-so-distant future. And finally, we will refuse to negotiate with the princes, because revolutions cannot be ratified except at the point of a bayonet. Therefore listen, Italian people: we will deal only with other peoples, never with kings; and the peoples will thankfully listen to us.

We will advance decisively and forcefully; we will be generous with those who accept their defeat and relentless with those who try to hold us up. We will entrust our destiny to the few strong, virtuous, and steadfast revolutionary leaders whom the revolution itself will generate. But we will keep an eye on those leaders and make sure that they are not led astray, because the only power in which we trust is the people, and they do not recognize any God in politics except for action. They follow only the strong, and they move ahead only when their back is secure. We will rely on a few virtuous leaders, because new things require new men, and revolutionary leaders must be created and inspired by actual revolutions. One cannot blindly entrust the destiny of a nation to any single man, even if he had the spirit of a George Washington or the genius of a Bonaparte. Any people that seek self-regeneration must keep on fighting for as long as the battle lasts.

These ideas were fermenting in our heart, when the uprisings of 1831 [in central Italy] confirmed to us the necessity of expressing them, of propagating them through hard work, and condensing them into one. In 1831 the progress was obvious: from its very beginning, the revolution had broken off from the old path and from the transitional order that had prevailed until then.[3] The word *republic* was uttered, and no one opposed it. At first political change spread rapidly, conceived and executed by young men who already felt the breath of new ideas and the spirit of a new century. Perhaps this change could indeed have triumphed, if they had not been so inexperienced in political matters; if a man who identified himself with the revolution had risen up resolutely, completely unfurling his banner; if they had not been so mistrustful of their own powers, and had not entrusted all leadership to men who perhaps had a heart for the needs of Italy, but who lacked the mind, the energy, and the endurance to satisfy those needs.

The men of 1831 caught a glimpse of the new theory, yet they clung to the old ways. They called themselves men of the republic, but they sought to found it relying on the same methods typically used by those who found a constitutional monarchy. Those men spoke of the people,

---

[3] Following the July revolution of 1830 and the proclamation of Louis Philippe as king of the French, a series of popular insurrections broke out in the states of central Italy at the beginning of 1831. While the uprisings of 1820–21 had been led primarily by former military officers who had served in Napoleon's army, the 1831 uprisings were supported by enlightened elements of the bourgeoisie and the aristocracy, with some instances of broader popular mobilization. However, both the 1820–21 and the 1831 uprisings still lacked any clear national inspiration and were largely constitutionalist in character.

but they did not attempt to either arouse them or truly emancipate them. They spoke of Italy, but they did not attempt to step even one foot outside of their own circle [i.e. their regional statelets], within which the magic formula of *nonintervention* bound them. Those men constituted a tie between the past and the future; they were the last point of transition between two generations and two systems. Hence they wandered fearfully, without fully withdrawing from the old, and without fully advancing to the new possibilities that were then arising. They were isolated like those Angels to whom Dante denied both Heaven and Hell, and thus reduced themselves to adopting as the goal and principle of their revolution the establishment of a form of government [constitutional monarchy] developed abroad. But what revolution can there be without its *own* principle? A revolution is the ultimate proof that a higher level of development has been achieved. It is the expression of a new need and a new thought; it is the triumph of a new social principle. But those men did not understand this axiom, which constitutes the basis of our own doctrine. . . .

There are backward-looking men in Italy today who would want to force the multitudes, with their desire for a genuine *social* revolution, to accept instead a meager reform. There are opportunistic men who want to exploit the ruin of one privileged class, the aristocracy, to simply elevate another class into privilege. There are the so-called "moderates" who continue to preach the principle of hereditary monarchy, after so many unhappy attempts, and ask that thousands of our brothers fling themselves into martyrdom, only so that their corpses can serve as the foundation of a new tyranny after three years, after three months, or even after three days. There are men who demand the abolition of privileges and the institution of political equality, any yet they place at the head of their constitution an inviolable king, joined by a hereditary chamber and a class of electors, all of whom symbolize the dogma of privilege and inequality. There are those who want to destroy an old principle while intending to tolerate its consequences, and those who preach a new principle but do not dare to accept its consequences. There are those arrogant weaklings who claim for themselves the right to change a people's destiny, and yet they tremble in the face of death, of dangers, and fear the people more than anything. And then there are those who believe that they can change a State without using all the means on which the State itself relies; those who would like 26 million people [the estimated population of Italy at the time] to revolt without telling them why and for what positive purpose; those who boast an ardently Italian soul and profess to hate everything foreign, regardless of how good it may be, and then rely on the plots of foreign cabinets and invoke foreign interventions for the sake of their own country, because they think that any home-grown revolutionary attempt would be imprudent. And finally there are those who are willing to grant the right of political liberty, while they continue to deny basic freedom in the sphere of religion, philosophy, and literary studies. For all those men of the past, with their dangerous and backward-looking attitudes, but only for *them*, I suggest the name *Old Italy*, regardless of their age, their condition, and the place where they live. We, the members of *Young Italy*, declare ourselves separate from the aforementioned men forever. We are men of progress; we look toward the future and aim at independence, regardless of our age, our condition, or the place where we live.

Our symbol, our movement and our undertaking can be summarized as follows: *LIBERTY in all things and for everyone. EQUALITY of rights and duties, both social and political. Association of all the peoples, of all free men in a mission of progress that embraces HUMANITY as a whole.* Whoever can suggest a better enterprise should come forward; he ought to proclaim it. Those who can think of no better undertaking should be our brothers and our comrades. And finally, those who do not want to associate with us shall languish in isolation, but they should not pretend to condemn us to inertia or to silence. . . .

In politics, in economics, in the sciences, and in all things that matter, progress can only be achieved by discovering a *principle* and then generalizing it and elevating it to a widely held belief. Once the *principle* has been identified that must underlie all social phenomena constituting an epoch of civilization, its consequences and practical applications are easily derived from it, clear and indisputable. The epoch itself and every small event suggest how the principle ought to be applied in practice.

But whenever reforms are implemented that do not cohere with a single, sovereign *principle*, that are merely the confused result of an instinct for the better, or of an emotional impulse unfiltered by reason, they are not harbingers of true civilizational progress. Such reforms, carried out in isolation, are always precarious and inefficient, because there is no certain standard for judging them and no guarantee of their duration, apart from the arbitrary will of the reformer. In addition, different reforms are frequently in conflict with each other. So long as there is no unifying bond that reconciles and coordinates them, they merely transfer unwarranted political privileges from one social class to another, from one branch of the civil order to another, without ever completely overcoming them. Incomplete reforms do not satisfy any needs, but instead let them emerge more starkly. So, for instance, the many efforts undertaken by England to combat mendicancy have borne no fruit. Mendicancy there continues to grow like a gaping and devouring wound, before the eyes of those who delude themselves that they can overcome it with mere charity and other isolated measures, without eliminating its actual causes: that is, boundless inequality and the concentration of property in the hands of the few. Similarly, the abolition of the death penalty, which is an absolute priority for our future civilization, could be very damaging unless the principle that currently underpins the entire penal system were not also changed. Or think of the mixed [monarchical] systems of France and England, with their endless troubles and disagreements that make them so unstable: any attempt at political reform there will invariably fail, unless it also tackles the electoral law, the true *principle* of all liberty.

If we have so far insisted on the principles on which Italy's regeneration must rely, and have been somewhat hesitant to move further down to the issue of practical applications, it is only because we believe that the first cause of all past disappointments has been exactly the absence of a solemnly agreed-upon *principle*. The greatest obstacle faced by all those who want to change conditions for the better in Italy is in fact the all-too widespread *individualism*. This individualism undermines all common faith: it may at best be able to advance personal liberty among a people where the exercise of rights is not denied, but it can only generate skepticism among an oppressed and abased people. But we are confident that once the regenerating *principle* [i.e. the principle of republican, popular government] becomes widely accepted, the ingenuity and strength of our Italian people will make it possible to swiftly move forward to the domain of practical applications.

We insist on the question of principles, because we are firmly convinced that Italy's well-being can only be advanced by means of our principles. But we feel the need to proceed slowly and more cautiously when it comes to developing concrete applications of those principles to the diverse branches of the civil constitution. It would be quite impossible to infer all the consequences of a principle at once, and announcing them prematurely would only put the principle itself at risk. The secret of successful politics does not lie in rapidly exhausting all possible applications of a principle, but rather in never flouting or contradicting the principle itself: the particular circumstances of time and place will then suggest to what degree and how fast the principle should be implemented. Or could anyone possibly foresee all viable applications and then calculate precisely the necessary time to get there, without any fear of error? Would anybody be able to do this, without first having closely experienced the actual needs and feelings of his fellow citizens under revolutionary circumstances? Nobody can predict exactly how much the passions and abilities of our fellow Italians will be strengthened by the course of the revolutionary upheaval itself.

It may well be that we, as exiles [Mazzini was living in France at the time], believe today in the necessity and feasibility of certain reforms, which tomorrow, when luck will have brought us back among our fellow brothers, we will recognize as useless, impossible, and perhaps even inappropriate given the needs and wants of the people. Exile in foreign countries does not suit us well to lay out precise constitutional proposals for our homeland. We would first need to breathe the Italian breeze; we would need to purify ourselves, to renew our soul and clear up our mind under the rays of the Italian sun. What I mean by this is that Italy's legislators can only arise within Italy itself, from a revived people, among the relics of ancient Rome and the first signs of our future Rome. Our primary role as exiles is to exhort our fellow citizens to learn from our errors and failures. We need to spread and hold up high the regenerative *principle* whose neglect led us to ruin. That principle is innate to Humanity, as history and the current conditions of Europe suggest, and it reveals itself to man wherever he lives, whatever his needs.

However, a few consequences can indeed be so tightly derived from the principle we propose, that we will briefly mention them here. Their detailed enunciation will be postponed until a later time. By roughly expressing our fundamental political ideals, without a wealth of proof and without all the details that might perfect the system, we will if nothing else alert our fellow citizens to the vital questions that shall emerge during the first days of our national *risorgimento* [reawakening].

THE PEOPLE: this is our *principle,* as we have said. It constitutes the basis of the social pyramid. The *people* is what unites us; it is the collective entity that inspires us any time we think and speak about regeneration, or about the Italian revolution.

By *people* we mean the ENTIRETY OF HUMAN BEINGS THAT MAKE UP THE NATION. However, a multitude of individuals does not yet constitute a *Nation*, unless it is directed by common principles, governed by the same laws, and united in a fraternal bond. *Nation* is a word that stands for *Unity*: *Unity of principles*, of *purpose,* and of *rights*. That is the only kind of unity able to associate a multitude of men and transform them into a homogenous whole. Without it there is no *nation*, but only a *crowd*. The barbarians [Germanic tribes], who came down from the North and slaughtered each other after having conquered what remained of the Roman Empire, were a *crowd*. The Italians, too, have so far remained a *crowd*, given that for centuries they have not been allowed to express any principle or purpose or to enjoy any rights.

But let me point out that unity by itself is not sufficient: a society of men who are united by a principle of egoism in the pursuit of an exclusively material goal cannot be a *nation*. A gang of bandits, a crowd that temporarily joins together for the sake of conquest, is not a *nation*. In order for a nation to exist, the principles, purposes, and rights that constitute it have to rest on solid, lasting foundations. The principle on which the nation relies must therefore be inviolable and *progressive*, so that neither time nor the whims of men can wear it out. The underlying purpose must be radically *moral*, because a merely material purpose will quickly exhaust itself and thus cannot constitute the basis of a truly perpetual union. And finally the nation's laws must be derived from human nature, which is the only thing that the centuries do not erase.

One can hardly think of a genuine *unity of principles* that is not *free* and spontaneous. Under such circumstances, every human being pursues one's own perfection, and the *ordered development of one's own faculties*. At the same time, the nation pursues the *perfection and progressive development of all social activities and capabilities*. The means towards this is *Association*.

Every association of forces multiplies those very forces. In other words: any increase or decrease in forces, and thus of moral and material accomplishments, is directly proportional to the strength of the *associational bond*. Historically, any serious weakening of the associational bond signaled the decadence of nations, and it could only be revived by means of a revolution. At the time when the Roman Empire fell, most of its provinces were fighting against each other. Few, or perhaps none at all, were following orders from the capital. Meanwhile praetorians were fighting against senators; plebeians were fighting against patricians; Christians against pagan priests, and philosophers against both. Everywhere, before great revolutions occur, history reveals this pattern of *disassociation* and of conflicting interests among the social classes and the various orders of a State.

True association is only possible among equals in rights and duties. When equal distribution of *rights* is not a universal law, there are castes, domination, privileges, superiority, helotism, and dependence. But there can be neither social balance, nor liberty, nor association, since they all require a society based on free consent. Men are born morally equal. They are endowed with the same faculties and the same organs, and they will develop the same tendency toward progress if exposed to the same principles. The only types of inequality existing among men are that of the intellect and that which derives from the greater or lesser exertion of their faculties: the first is a de facto or natural inequality, more than a matter of right, and it is neither hereditary nor tyrannical, because men spontaneously accept it. This kind of inequality can be advantageous to those nations that know how to use it well; indeed it can be a highly effective element of progress. The second kind of inequality is susceptible to continuous change and needs to be regulated by the law. It can be gradually diminished by means of a more just distribution of *labor* and of *compensations;* that is, by making the latter more *proportional to one's actual labor*. But it is crucial that all the laws apply equally to every human being who makes up the *nation*, and that everyone enjoy the same civil and political rights. Whoever asserts the contrary does great harm to humanity. In that case it might be better to do like the ancients, who at least acted in a consistently unjust manner: they decreed the existence of two natures, namely one of free men and one of slaves. In Sparta the slaves were *Helots*; in Rome they were *things* (*res*), and not *men*.

Equality, Liberty, Association: only these three elements together can constitute a genuine *Nation*. By NATION we mean THE ENTIRETY OF CITIZENS WHO SPEAK THE SAME LANGUAGE AND ARE ASSOCIATED, UNDER EQUAL ENJOYMENT OF CIVIL AND POLITICAL RIGHTS, FOR THE COMMON PURPOSE OF DEVELOPING AND PROGRESSIVELY PERFECTING ALL SOCIAL FORCES AND THEIR ACTIVITY. This kind of *Association*, based on the *Equality* of all the associates, entails several consequences: first, no family or individual can assume the power of *exclusive rule* over the entirety, or even just over a portion, of the social forces and their activity; second, no single *class* and no individual may legitimately take over the *administration* of the social forces and their activity, without a *direct mandate* from the *nation*. The final result is that all hereditary privilege must be abolished. Those individuals who form the ruling hierarchy are not invested with the powers they hold by virtue of some inherent right or authority; instead they are merely the *revocable representatives* of the nation.

THE NATION IS THE ONLY SOVEREIGN. Any *power* that is not derived from it results in usurpation. Any representative who oversteps his electoral mandate by even an inch becomes guilty of treason. The nation alone has the inviolable right to *choose* its own institutions, to *correct* them and *change* them, when they no longer correspond to its needs and no longer contribute to social and intellectual *progress*. But since it is not possible for the entire Nation to come together in an assembly to discuss and vote on its institutions, it elects a certain number of trustworthy representatives and delegates that task to them. These elected men will then follow the Nation's expression of its *needs* and its *will* in establishing the *law*. THE WILL OF THE NATION, EXPRESSED BY DEPUTIES WHO ARE CHOSEN BY IT IN ORDER TO REPRESENT IT, SHALL BE THE LAW FOR ALL CITIZENS.

The Nation's representatives must therefore reflect the full diversity of conditions that characterize the nation itself.

ONE NATION, ONE NATIONAL REPRESENTATION. The cohesion of the former brings about the unity of the latter. The nation brings together different elements and social forces in a vast *association*. The representative body must therefore include deputies who speak for all these different elements and *forces*, if it is to be truly *national*. Wherever just one of these *forces* is neglected, there is no truly national representation. The forces that remain excluded will be eager to achieve their own representation, thus generating the need for radical political change. Under certain conditions, such change cannot be achieved through quiet, peaceful progress, but only by means of active struggle and revolution. For instance, in France and England, where only the property holders are currently represented, there is an ongoing struggle between the class of property holders and the proletarians, who own nothing at all. The latter threaten to rebel, and indeed they will rise.

NATIONAL REPRESENTATION NEEDS TO BE FOUNDED not on wealth and census requirements, but rather ON THE POPULATION AS A WHOLE. For representation to be truly *national*, every citizen needs to participate in the election of deputies through his vote. If a man is prevented from exercising his *right to vote* for some reason, he ceases to be a citizen and becomes a subject. Unless he expresses his will on the occasion of elections, the pact of *association* remains incomplete for him, and he might experience every law as tyrannical. Therefore when elections are to be held, it is necessary to ensure that every single district will be represented. The representatives, for their part, must be compensated by the nation. They must be excluded from every other public office during the exercise of their mandate. Their number must be the greatest possible, for this will make corruption more difficult. Suffice it to mention that every decrease of liberty among the French in recent times was preceded by a decrease in the number of deputies.

When the representatives convene, they take the place of the nation. And since the nation's power is unlimited, any restrictions brought to the exercise of its power and to the deputies' ultimate choice would contradict the principle of national sovereignty. Once national representation has been established according to the aforementioned guidelines, it becomes inviolable and is entrusted to the nation's custody. Its mission and its duties derive directly from the definition of its social purpose.

As already mentioned, the fundamental law that guides all nations consists in *the development and progressive perfection of the social forces and their activity*—this is the basis that underpins every national association. THE NATIONAL REPRESENTATIVES ARE ENTRUSTED WITH DIRECTING AND PERFECTING THESE SOCIAL FORCES, IN VIEW OF PROMOTING THE COMMON GOOD. Hence, the representatives must ensure that all subsequently created institutions advance *social equality*, without undermining *political equality*. This implies that a great part of their efforts needs to be directed toward the improvement of the largest social class, which is also the poorest. Specific laws must be enacted with regard to wills and inheritance issues, as well as donations, to prevent the excessive accumulation of wealth and property in the hands of a tiny minority of families. The explicit goal of all legislation should be to compensate people for their work according to their contribution to the Common Good. A system of public welfare must be established, which shall be based on the principle of progressive taxation of all income, except for subsistence wages. Finally, the maxim that every man has a right to be judged by his peers should lead to the introduction of a *jury system* for the administration of justice.

The Nation's Representatives will be the guardians of *Liberty*, and as such they must always seek to reconcile the greatest possible degree of individual freedom with the greatest possible degree of social improvement. Personal liberty must be guaranteed, and any violation of individual rights shall be severely punished. Important freedoms and administrative autonomy shall be conceded to local municipalities and departments. Freedom of conscience must be inviolable, and thus all questions of religion ought to be left to the judgment of individual reason and personal belief. Finally, complete freedom of the press must always be guaranteed.

However, what the nation really aspires to is to perfect the *Association* on which it rests. In other words, it seeks not just to *preserve*, but rather to *improve*, the potential of its social forces. Our National Representatives will therefore have to proceed with an eye to the future, moving beyond what appears to be the most progressive goal at present and aiming at a yet superior level of civilization. To support this constant progress, freedom of association must become an inviolable law. The level of public education must be improved by all possible means. There shall be a universally applied plan of elementary education, various encouragements shall be offered to the arts and sciences, and all scientific bodies will be protected. Public administrators, employees, and all those who govern some part of the social forces will be chosen according to their intellectual capacities, their personal integrity, and the purity of their intentions. The corrupt principle that has guided the penal system so far will have to be reformed and improved. Finally, the founding of public libraries, newspapers, prizes, and universities should be actively encouraged.

We believe that these are the necessary foundations of any state that wants to call itself free and well-ordered. We are confident that if these foundations are developed in due time and are organized into a coherent system, they will open up the path to genuine progress for Italy in coming years, which we so ardently desire. If a truly Italian government can be established that enjoys the support of a popular majority and openly agrees to pursue the aforementioned goals, we will welcome it happily and faithfully. . . .

Three Essays on Cosmopolitan Ideals and National Sentiment

I. HUMANITY AND COUNTRY (1836)

The goal of every rejuvenation effort that is taking place in the world and every movement of European renewal that characterizes our epoch should be one: to establish a general social organization that will have Humanity as its ultimate objective and the Country [*Patrie*] as its starting point.[1] We believe that these two terms need to be harmonized within the European system, like the two terms *individuality* and *association* need to be harmonized within every state. This is the real problem for which the nineteenth century has been seeking a solution. Every political doctrine that departs from this approach to pursue its own path, and every organization that suppresses one of these two concepts for the sake of the other, will sooner or later result in either anarchy or tyranny.

Virtually every idea that has inspired the work of politicians so far is marred by significant flaws. For this reason, it has been impossible to develop any plan for the future based on these ideas. The watchword of our age is composed of two terms, and whoever neglects one of them will not be able to revive the peoples. But precisely this mistake has been frequently committed in recent times. On the one hand, there are those who have sought to rouse the people in the name of *Humanity* without teaching them about their *Country*. On the other hand, there are those who have been speaking of *nationality* without any reference to *humanity's* law. In the first case, the movement lacked both a starting point and a means of support; in the second, it lacked an ultimate purpose. The peoples have not responded to the call, and for good reasons.

In our opinion, to revive the nationality of different peoples is an indispensable condition for the progressive advancement of our epoch. It must be the immediate objective of all our efforts, the cry of the press, the flag under which we shall march forward.... Since we are ourselves working for the principle of *nationality*, we should be careful to pin down the meaning of this term. What does nationality mean in

---

[1] The original title of this essay is "Humanité et Patrie."

the nineteenth century? Where does it come from? What needs to be done in order to revitalize it? How should it be organized in Europe? These are all questions in search of a solution. If the questions are well put and well understood to begin with, they may themselves contribute to shaping our future. So let us first look at this problem of nationality in isolation. Does there not appear to be something reactionary, incomplete, and selfish about it that contrasts with the younger generation's need for fusion, harmony, and unity? Does not the very word *nationality* seem too narrow and restricted for this century, next to the great ideas and the beams of light that higher minds are projecting over all of Europe?

Some will indeed say: on the one hand, you speak of a great initiative to be achieved for the benefit of this century. You declare a bitter war on individualism. You proclaim *Humanity* to be the sole thought and synthesis of the new era, the mother-concept, the soul of the European world. You want to renew Humanity by organizing it as a whole and transmitting to it the enthusiasm of a vast and unique belief. You then wish to launch this great and powerful ideal along the path of progress. But then, amidst these thoughts of a higher and universal order, you come to cast this word—*nationality*—like a seed of discord. Isn't it a manifestation of the past, a medieval concept that has caused much bloodshed, and that continues to fractionalize God's thinking on earth? We have some clearly more advanced solutions, those critics may say: we embrace all races with a single spurt of our intelligence. Our point of reference is the globe's entire surface and our faith lies in unity. Let the diplomats, those agents of a waning power, debate the final consequences of the national spirit. But you, apostles of renewal, should not attempt to revive it in the name of the power that will characterize our future....

My answer to those critics is that we are practical people above anything else, and so we aim toward the possible. We believe that it is not just a matter of expressing ideas but also of making them bear fruit. Now, an idea can only bear fruit on fertile ground. We want to think and then act, because thought can only be completed through action. We therefore need to study our epoch and adapt to it: we need to understand what is feasible and should not demand of our epoch more than it can give. It may well be that sometimes, during those dreamlike moments where our soul listens to the future and senses the secrets of the world, we can venture into the realms of absolute thought. Yet we are placed on earth amidst people who suffer and struggle to satisfy their basic needs day after day. Hence we must stay and fight here, among our fellow soldiers: we cannot choose our battlefield. Those who elevate themselves too much lose sight of the people and their interests; by isolating themselves in an ivory tower, they become useless. Also, sometimes people think they are elevating themselves, while in fact they are straying from their ultimate purpose.

We do not believe in the timelessness of races. We do not believe in the timelessness of languages. We do not believe in the timeless and powerful influence of climate on the development of human activity. We do not believe in the timeless impact of any given cause on human affairs, especially when that cause is partial and thus affects only a tiny fraction of the human race or just a single aspect of human life. But we do believe in a single agent that embraces within its vast activity the entire family of possible phenomena, an agent that constantly affects our moral and physical environment by means of an immutable and verifiable law.

We believe in a sole and constant general law. Therefore we also believe in a sole and constant general objective, and we believe in progressive development toward this given objective, which can only be achieved by means of coming closer together—that is, through *association*. All human faculties and strengths are affected by this development. Finally, we believe that the combined work of all these human faculties, once they are fully developed and can thus be converted into active forces, will lead to the fusion of all members of Humanity in the awareness of a common origin, a common law, and a common goal. In this way, the great edifice that the centuries and the peoples are called to erect will vaguely resemble a pyramid whose top can touch the sky and whose base embraces Humanity as a whole. God's eye will radiate from the peak of this pyramid.

The word that will scientifically define all this is: Unity. And we mean unity in the widest, most comprehensive, and most profound possible sense. Unity in heaven and on earth, unity in every single part of this earth, unity in Humanity, and finally unity inside every human being. We believe that our Universe must necessarily be organized in a concentric manner. Everything in existence is thus only a more or less extensive, civilized, or perfect manifestation of the same principle. Every part of this grand whole and every being, no matter how small, exists and lives by virtue of a single and constant law. Every living being thus embodies the same law of the Universe, and what varies is just the scale. Each man is a miniature version of humanity, like the earth is a miniature version of the universe. If this were not the case, there could be no progress, no humanity, and no harmony. There would be nothing.

But all this cannot be accomplished at once, by a single people, or even within a single epoch. Every epoch has its own assigned task. There should be no confusion about these tasks, for the result might be utter lack of effectiveness. . . . For this reason, you should not attempt to superimpose a world whose time has not yet come on the world that you can presently observe at your feet; *forget* about that. You should instead take inspiration from what actually surrounds you. This can be done by walking amongst the people, who at this very time are attempting to become masters of their own destiny before your eyes.

We clearly believe in the future unity of the human species and in the fusion of all existing races. Indeed, the latter represent nothing but different stages in the progressive development of a special civilization. We also believe in the sacred family of humanity, which can only be realized by following one path and one law; that family of humanity that has only one altar, one thought, one poem as its hymn, and one language to sing it. However, we believe that this time of ultimate unity has not yet arrived.

We believe that for us today, the challenge consists in *harmonizing* things, not in *blending* them together. It seems to us that the plan of action for this epoch is to manage the instrument of progress and direct it toward a newly determined goal. As history advances, the ultimate *goal* of a given epoch serves as the point of departure for the epoch that follows. The epoch that is today coming to an end has sought to achieve the emancipation of the *individual* as its mission: *man* was this epoch's instrument and the *people* were its ultimate goal, though this was often poorly understood. The epoch that has just begun will have the *peoples* as its instrument and humanity as its goal—that is, its mission—and whoever seeks to move beyond this goal risks committing fateful mistakes.

God and *Humanity*, as we have said, is the ultimate horizon that we can foresee. But just because we envision these two concepts as the ultimate benchmarks of a future synthesis, do we have to suppress all intermediary terms and thereby undermine the only means that can actually get us there? Look around you. Look to the North, to the South, to the East. Everywhere there are peoples in motion that are asking to live. What will you do about them? Will you dip your finger in ink, like Catherine [of Russia], and seek to erase them?[2] But nothing can be erased from this earth, as the Greeks and the Poles will testify. Life is sacred. Now, life consists in constant development, and progress is a mission to be accomplished. Have the peoples so far accomplished their mission? Have they achieved their fullest development? Has the vitality of languages perhaps already begun to decline? Are the peoples' different languages indeed already so complete, so refined, and so fixed that there is nothing more for them but immobility? Language expresses a people's thought. It embodies a people's idea and it symbolizes their mission.

---

[2] Catherine II, known as "The Great," empress of Russia from 1762 until her death in 1796. During her reign, she extended the borders of the Russian Empire southward and westward. She also took a leading role in the partitions of Poland in the 1790s and thus "erased" the Polish nation from the map.

We are far from having reached that final stage of development. Indeed, for most of the peoples their mission has not even been defined yet. There are some races, such as the Slavs, for instance, whose lives thus far have been but a vague anticipation of things to come. There are some languages that have yet to be clearly structured according to the logic of prose; their voice still wavers naively, poetic and imprecise like a lullaby. We are well aware that time wears out the different races, but not before the fulfillment of their mission on earth. We have seen ten races become extinct on the Roman soil in less than ten centuries, to make room for the Italian element. But indeed, once they had fulfilled their mission and achieved the goal of their existence, what else remained for them to do? Those races had emerged in the wake of the Roman Empire. They had picked up and hoped to develop further the Empire's belief in unity; yet as they died so did the belief in unity. Those older races had emerged quickly like a rising tide, and then like the falling tide they had waned, carrying away with them some segments detached from the shore. But that stage has been hardly achieved yet by the different races that ask for their place within the Europe of peoples that our epoch needs to organize. Or does anybody seriously believe that the peoples have already been able to accomplish their assigned task in the Europe of kings, subjugated and divided as they have been due to the interests of some ruling families?

II. Nationality and Cosmopolitanism (1847)

I do often use the word *Nationality*; it is the ground on which the cause of all the oppressed Peoples is pleaded in our present time.[3] And it may be useful, first of all, to clarify the value we attach to this word.

I have heard many honorable men, animated by the best intentions, declare this standard of *Nationality* that we cherish to be dangerous and retrograde. They told me: "We are more advanced than you," and they continued: "We no longer believe in the *nation*; we believe in humanity: we are *Cosmopolitans.*" Now, I am not like Ugo Foscolo, that voluntary exile from Italy, who whenever he heard anyone declare himself a Cosmopolitan, got his hat and left.[4] But I do believe that this word, *cosmopolitanism*, implies a somewhat outdated idea, which is much more

[3] This essay was first published in English, in the London *People's Journal*. For the present edition, language and sentence structure have been partially updated.

[4] Ugo Foscolo (1778–1827), poet and patriotic novelist who spent many years in England as an exile. His poems and works articulate the feelings of many Italians during the turbulent epoch of the Napoleonic Wars and the subsequent restoration of Austrian rule; they rank among the masterpieces of Italian literature.

vague and difficult to realize than that of Nationality. I believe that those who adopt it yield to a barren sentiment of reaction against a past that is forever dead in our own hearts and draw their definition of Nationality from a state of things that can never again be reproduced, regardless of what may happen.

We are all Cosmopolitans, if by Cosmopolitanism we understand the love and brotherhood of all, and the destruction of all barriers that separate the Peoples and provide them with opposite interests. But can that be all? Is it sufficient just to proclaim these sacred truths, in order to secure their triumph over the obstacles that the league of unlawful powers present to them in Europe? Our work aims at transforming ideas into reality; we have to *organize,* if I may say so, not thought, but *action.*

Now, every organization that is to concretely affect reality requires a starting point and a goal. To operate effectively, every lever needs both a pivot on which to rest and an object to be raised or moved. For us, the end is humanity; the pivot, or point of support, is the country. I freely admit that for Cosmopolitans, the end is also humanity; but their pivot or point of support is man, the isolated *individual.* Therein lies almost all the difference between us and the Cosmopolitans, but it is a major difference. It is the same difference as that which separates the partisans of association from those who think that the belief in individual liberty, alone and unaided, can promote social change.

The Cosmopolitan stands alone at the center of an immense circle that extends itself around him, and whose limits are beyond his grasp. He has no other aid on which to rely than the consciousness of his unfulfilled rights and of his individual capabilities, which however powerful they may be, cannot by themselves move the whole sphere of practical application placed before them. Hence the Cosmopolitan can choose between only two paths: inaction or despotism. Is he consistent with his own beliefs? Not being able to emancipate the world on his own, the Cosmopolitan ends up believing that the task of emancipation is not really his. Not being able to attain the desired end through the mere exercise of his individual rights, and actually not even being able to obtain the free exercise of those rights, he ends up believing that his own individual rights are the means and the end at the same time. But whenever those rights remain unfulfilled, he does not struggle and is not willing to die; quite the opposite, he just steps back and looks away. He utters the egoists' maxim: "Ubi bene, ibi patria" (Where my interest is, there is my country); and he drags his country along with him, attached to the soles of his shoes. He is already beginning to put this axiom into practice. Let him just have the slightest suspicion that he may be unable to successfully improve social conditions, and he resigns himself at once without even attempting to struggle. He just hopes that progress will eventually be achieved through the natural course of things. He becomes an optimist, and he contents himself with accomplishing his mission as an individual to the best of his abilities, that is, he exercises *charity*. But I think it is beginning to be felt that it is not from charity alone that we can expect a solution to the social problems that occupy our attention today. The cause of the People, which we plead, is far more important than mere almsgiving.

Is the Cosmopolitan perhaps not consistent with his own beliefs? He desires above anything else to achieve some progress and hopes to be able to rely for that purpose on a pivot, or point of support, proportioned to the vastness of his end. Hence he seeks such a point of support wherever he can: he attempts to replace real personal strength, which he lacks, with a borrowed and usurped strength. He either develops or simply adopts from others the idea of a social Utopia, and he thinks that by relying on logical deduction and a priori reasoning alone, he can lead humanity toward this goal. Now, by relying on exactly this type of reasoning, Saint-Simonianism and communism have reached the following conclusion: namely, that the liberty of each should be violated in the name of the well-being of all. Several French political and philosophical schools have recently attained the same conclusion: they began by denying the mission of peoples, by disdainfully shrugging their shoulder at the very words *Nationality* or *country*; and so, as soon as a plan of action was demanded from them, they ended up placing *their own* country, and even in *their own* town, at the center of their theoretical edifice. Such schools of thought do not destroy Nationalities; rather they condemn all the rest for the sake of a single one. Each of them has its own chosen people, a sort of "Napoleonic" people; and so while formally negating the very idea of Nationality, in fact their own Nationality ends up usurping all the others, if not by arms, which thank God is no longer possible, then certainly with the pretentious claim of a permanent and exclusive moral and intellectual leadership. So our future would look quite bleak indeed, were the Peoples to be misled into adopting such theories and persuaded to actually put them into practice.

The adversaries of Nationality draw their definition of this word from the past. But they should rather seek their definition in the future, and in all the signs that anticipate what it will look like. All their current arguments and their apparent aversion to our ideas would then disappear at once. When we speak of Nationality, it is of Nationality such as the *Peoples*, free and brotherly associated, will conceive it. Now, this Nationality of the *Peoples* has never existed so far. In the past, Nationality existed only as absolute kings conceived of it and as it was systematized by treaties among governments. But those kings had only their own personal interests in mind, without any concern for the peoples, whose very existence they denied. Hence the existing treaties, too, have been drawn up by individuals without a mission, in the obscurity of cabinets, without any popular intervention and without any collective inspiration. Of course, no good whatsoever could result from all this.

The old despotic rulers relied on their family, their race, and their dynasty as the basis of their *nation*. Their permanent end consisted in aggrandizement at the expense of others and encroachment on the rights of others. Their theory could be summarized in a single sentence: everyone should be weakened and exploited for the sake of the ruler's own narrow interests. Their treaties were nothing but the result of necessary concessions; peace was never more for them than a mere cessation of hostilities; their pursuit of a *balance of power* was an attempt to equalize their strength, always having future wars in mind and always mistrusting each other.

Such is the predominant understanding of the "Nation" that underlies every diplomatic alliance. In particular, this understanding constitutes the basis of the Treaty of Westphalia, which still rules in great measure international right in Europe, and which entrenched the idea of established and unquestionable legitimacy of the monarchic rulers. It could indeed not be otherwise. Any peaceful organization of Nationalities would have been impossible for a system of diplomacy that failed to recognize any superior principle, beyond all those partial and secondary interests, and which was thus unable to put forward a common faith as a foundation and guarantee for its princely agreements. It could thus only give rise to a parody of what is perhaps the most beautiful sentiment that God has placed in the heart of man; it led to a narrow and mean *Nationalism*, which was jealous of everything that surrounded it.

It was in those times, and with good reason, that the Cosmopolitan ideal appeared. It forcefully reacted against this state of things, be it through its underlying political creed, which preaches that the rights of all men are equal, regardless of their country, or through its conceptions of political economy, which preached freedom of industry and commerce. But then it ended up like every purely reactive ideal: sacred at first, it ended up going beyond what its actual principle implies. It looked around itself and saw only monarchical Nationalities, as well as countries without a people. As a consequence, it denied both country and Nationality; it ended up recognizing only our common planet and the individual. Thus the cosmopolitans have been wholly unable to even conceive of the future nation, which will be the workshop of all those who labor for the sake of humanity. In the future, different nations will signify the *special* vocation and contribution of each member toward accomplishing a great common enterprise within the human family. But in the days when cosmopolitan theories used to be widespread, the people had not yet transformed the nation's character by reconstructing it.

Now the danger against which cosmopolitanism was reacting no longer exists. Today, most men no longer believe in the selfish Nationalism of the absolute powers. Those despotic regimes continue to survive only by relying on brute force; but any power that does not ultimately rest on a shared faith bears within itself the seeds of its own destruction. Hence the old-fashioned *Nationalism* is rapidly dying out among the Peoples. The alliances contracted by their masters have taught them that the secret of power lies in unity. Likewise, the numerous setbacks that each one of those Peoples has had to experience, every time they attempted to regenerate themselves in isolation, must have served them a lesson. They have learned that no future victory will be possible except by recognizing the necessity of association. Cosmopolitanism has thus completed its task.

Another task now lies ahead of us: that of promoting the association of different Countries, an alliance of Nations that will make it possible for them to accomplish their mission on earth in peace and love. Free and equal Peoples will help one another; each will be able to benefit from the resources that others possess in the pursuit of their common civilization and progress. Having thrown off all chains, each People will march forward in freedom toward the realization of that part of God's providence that has been set aside for their native land, and that appears inscribed in their traditions, their national language, and the shape of their territory. And as each People advances toward the accomplishment of their special mission, the law of recognized duty will take the place of that policy of encroachment on the rights of others which has until now ruled over all international affairs, and which is in reality but the result of mutual fear. The guiding principle underpinning all domestic or international law will no longer be the *weakening of everything that does not promote one's narrow self-interest*, but rather the *improvement of all through everyone's contribution, the progress of each for the benefit of all*.

In conclusion, it makes no sense to seek to efface all patriotic sentiment from the Peoples' hearts, or to seek to suppress at once all Nationalities. It would indeed be vain to desire to confound the special destinies of countries and to attempt to force all human beings, which God has placed into different peoples to facilitate their progress, into the uniformity of I do not know what abstract Cosmopolitanism. It is impossible to falsify the character of our epoch, which aims at instilling again in everyone's hearts the love of country and seeks to bring it into agreement with the progress of Humanity as a whole. The only thing that our enemies can achieve today is to delay perhaps for some Peoples the moment of their regeneration.

It is not *individuals* who must sign the new pact; it is rather the free Peoples, with their own name, their ideal, and their moral conscience. To pretend that the Peoples can actually get there without first speaking to them of country, without making them fully aware of their existence and of their Nationality, is to pretend that the lever may act without a pivot; it is to ask the Peoples to work without assigning a part to them; it is to demand that the work be done while actually *breaking the instrument* necessary for its fulfillment. No human being can erase what God has written down. Only God himself could do so, with his power over life and death. But a Nationality can die only once it has borne all its fruits, and never before. Those among our contemporaries who wish to suppress it, even in good faith like the Cosmopolitans, will thus not succeed, although unfortunately they could well delay for a long time the fraternal and peaceful organization toward which we aspire.

III. Nationalism and Nationality (1871)

. . . Yes, we are concerned with *human beings*; but with human beings in the full and active development of all their faculties and all their strength.[5] We look to man as an intelligent, loving, and willing creature who is capable of leading himself and others ahead on the path toward Progress. We look to man as the embodiment of the concept of harmony that God has infused in the universe, man as the incarnation of the Moral Law. Yet for this man to exist will require the long work of centuries, as it is summarized and expressed by Tradition, that ever-growing repository of human achievements in time and space. It will require the help of all his fellow human beings and an intimate bond with the faculties and the strength of others. It will require *association* and agreed-upon tasks and therefore a division of labor. It may be worth insisting on this point: the *division* of labor is an essential condition of all labor. How could one recognize this principle in the smallest industrial undertaking and at the same time be oblivious to it in a much greater enterprise that embraces past and future generations? The end of our current enterprise is to unify the human family under a common Law that must direct it, and in a mutual sentiment of Love that shall stimulate it to fulfill its purpose. Now, what is nationality if not exactly a *division of labor* at the level of Humanity as a whole? Are not the peoples the

---

[5] Original title: "Nazionalismo e nazionalità."

actual laborers of Humanity? Is not what we call *nationality* simply a special ability, confirmed by the tradition of a people, to complete better than anybody else a given task within the common project?

Yes, our final goal is the establishment of a United States of Europe, a Republican Alliance among the Peoples. It is truly sad that some of our youth today present this idea, which was first uttered by Italian lips some forty years ago, as a foreign invention.[6] But most of those who are not part of our movement continue to underestimate the crucial question of *how to achieve* this goal, and that further strengthens us in our own faith. In particular, we believe that without first establishing our own Country [*patria*], we can hardly contribute to the future organization of Humanity. Without Peoples there can be no Alliance of Peoples. Furthermore, to establish a lasting Alliance based on mutual trust, the peoples must be free and equal; they need to be aware of and affirm their own individuality and their own *principle*; in other words, they must be *nations*. Humanity constitutes the *end* and the nation the *means*. Without the nation you will be able to worship Humanity in idle contemplation, but you will not be able to actually help it or even seriously attempt to do so.

When placed before this immense problem, the isolated individual becomes aware of his own powerlessness and withdraws. What forces and what elements can he put forth that might benefit the organization of Humanity as a whole? The individual's means and his thirty or forty years of adult life are but a tiny drop in the vast Ocean of Existence. As soon as he becomes aware of this, he ends up discouraged and abandons the entire undertaking. If he is a good man, he will now and again engage in simple charity. If he is evil, he will isolate himself in complete selfishness. But give this man a Country [patria] and establish a link of solidarity between his individual efforts and the efforts of all subsequent generations; place him in association with the labors of 25 to 30 million men who speak the same language, have similar habits and beliefs, profess faith in the same *goal*, and have developed specific tools for their work as required by the general conditions of their land, and the problem will change for him at once: his strengths will be greatly multiplied, allowing him to feel up to the task. The national tradition and his own intellect, revitalized by a communal bond with the intellects of millions, reveal to him a *special* goal, placed along the way towards the *general* goal. This special goal is not out of reach if he combines his own

[6] Mazzini himself had anticipated the possibility of a United States of Europe in some of his earlier writings (see, for example, "From a Revolutionary Alliance to the United States of Europe"). The most forceful advocate of a United States of Europe in the late 1830s and early 1840s had been Carlo Cattaneo, the leading figure of liberal and reformist republicanism within the Italian Risorgimento.

strength with the strength of all his countrymen. He can be confident that the tiny grain of sand which he adds to the great pyramid that we have committed to erect from the earth to the sky is placed on millions of similar grains and will be followed by millions more. If well organized, a Nation is like a factory, dedicated to a specific branch of production toward general moral, intellectual, and economic development. Each single Nation's contribution is therefore necessary to a proper functioning of the whole.

These truths seem so obvious to us that we almost feel uncomfortable in writing them down. Yet unfortunately the champions of an abstract cosmopolitanism, who oppose the organic concept of the *nation*, continue to disregard these simple truths. Too often, the actual subject of discussion is not properly defined, although doing so could save the opponents in a controversy valuable time and effort, as well as costly mistakes. Our opponents' materialism condemns them to look at each single fact in isolation, without any comprehensive analysis. They are thus incapable of rising to the level of general principles, which alone can organize the facts sequentially and assign them to specific times and spaces, in order to identify their actual meaning and value. Our opponents' materialism misunderstands the idea of the Nation, as it misunderstands life more generally. Hence, the materialists stutter the word *progress* without properly understanding its meaning. They are incapable of grasping either what links different historical epochs together, or what distinguishes them in terms of their characteristic principles. The materialists confuse the *nationalism* of feudal and dynastic Europe with the *nationality* of republican Europe; hence they fear identical consequences from two radically contrasting principles.

Dynastic *nationalism* was founded on the absolute negation of our current beliefs. There was no concept of Progress: political doctrines merely theorized the circular movement of nations and the ebb and flow of time. Thinkers at the time were unaware of the idea of a Moral Law that triumphs above everything else. The kings were seen as intermediaries between God and the subjects; the Law was simply an expression their arbitrary will. Likewise, nobody knew of the idea of a people. For most thinkers in the age of dynastic nationalism, a "people" was nothing but a collection of men who had to eke out a living as best they could, born to serve and nurture the splendor of the nobility and the monarchy. When Louis XIV said, "I am the State," he summarized the political doctrine of all those of his kind who had preceded and would follow him. A "Nation" was thus an ill-defined territory, of varying size, which could quite easily be dismembered or enlarged, including by means of royal marriages and female succession. More typically, "Nations" were created by conquest and maintained by force.

And force long remained effective mainly because of the weakness of others: for indeed, the most powerful and secure States were those surrounded by small and weaker neighbors. Wars were caused by anger, jealousy, greed, or the fears of single states.

Today the peoples are becoming aware of their Rights and their own power. The fundamental idea of our times is Progress, and the principle of *association* is an indispensable means to achieve it. Meanwhile the idea of Nationality is expressed by our common purpose and our common *goal*, and it comes alive in the belief that all peoples ought to work together toward the unity of the human family, according to the Moral Law. The Nation is not simply a territory that ought to be strengthened by enlarging its size. Nor is it just a collection of men who speak the same language and follow the initiative of a single leader. It is instead an organic whole held together by a unity of *goals* and common efforts. Each nation derives its vitality from its own faith and traditions. It is kept strong and distinguishes itself from others by its specific ability to accomplish its own secondary mission, which constitutes an intermediary step toward the overarching mission of Humanity.

Language, territory, and race are just indications of *nationality*. They remain unstable when they are not all combined. More than anything, they need to be supported by a specific historical tradition and by the long development of a collective life that results in a common character. After all, Rome was the most powerful nationality of the ancient world, although the sheer diversity of its constitutive elements (both Italian and foreign) largely overshadowed the original Roman element. Likewise, France, the most powerful nationality of the modern world, emerged out of a mixture of Germanic, Celtic, Roman, and Frankish elements that were united by Christianity around a common *goal*. In matters of nationality, as in all others, the ultimate *goal* matters more than anything else. And the ultimate goal of popularly constituted nations is intimately connected with the goal of Humanity. The cry for Nationality that today inspires all the most important European movements did in fact emerge shortly before 1815, precisely when the French initiative was falling and a distinct desire for human unity and fraternal alliance among the peoples began to be widely felt. The progressive education of the human race has thus revealed to us both our ultimate *goal* and the *means* to achieve it. The history of humankind has constantly displayed a twofold tendency, toward, on the one hand, an overarching *moral* unity, and on the other, the organization of peoples into *nationalities* as a means to achieve the former. . . .

CHAPTER FOUR

In Defense of Democracy:
A Reply to Mr. Guizot (1839)

MR. GUIZOT'S[1] CONTRIBUTION has had the honor of being twice translated into English, the one quoted by us being the second and best translation.[2] It has also been translated into German, and here in London it has been praised and quoted by both Whig and Tory journals, which pointed it out to the public as an important tract on an important subject.

The importance of the subject we are by no means disposed to deny. It is immense and urgent: immense, for the safety of generations depends on it; urgent, for a time is approaching when the solution of the problem may, here in England, as throughout all of Europe, be called for as a matter of necessity. Too long the power of this word, *democracy*, dazzling us here on the first page, has been despised. Branded not long ago as the watchword of certain obscure fanatics, now it meets us as if by enchantment; it is central to all questions of any weight; it has become the burden of all writers, even the most quiet loving, to whatever rank they may belong. Whatever else may be said, we largely attribute the attention that Mr. Guizot's pamphlet seems to have excited to a widespread interest in its subject characteristic of our present epoch. For the pamphlet's intrinsic importance is, in our opinion (may we be pardoned by our Whig and Tory contemporaries?), none, or next to none. Perhaps the most evident lesson it teaches is twofold: first, the *Doctrinaire* or *Juste-Milieu* school is unable to properly understand today's central political question; and second, superior intellectual talents

[1] Original title: "Guizot on Democracy." François Pierre Guillaume Guizot (1787–1874), moderate liberal intellectual, played an important role in French politics between the July revolution of 1830 and the Revolution of 1848. His unwavering support for the policies of King Louis Philippe, and his opposition to any further expansion of the political franchise, earned him the scorn of more progressive liberals and republicans. The present essay is a polemical review of Guizot's pamphlet, *Democracy in Modern Communities*. Mazzini develops a sustained critique of Guizot's preference for census democracy, which he views as a form of aristocracy, and puts forward a passionate defense of universal suffrage against paternal rule.

[2] François Guizot, *Democracy in Modern Communities* (London: Senior, 1838).

inevitably degrade themselves whenever they undertake, like in this case, to defend an unjust cause.[3]

The abilities of Mr. Guizot are really superior and have destined him for something better than the part he has played since 1830.[4] We are certainly willing to do justice to his volumes on European history, though they hardly provide any insight into the future. We recognize the gravity and the conscientiousness of his disquisition on our own revolution, though the light in which he compares it with the French Revolution appears to us totally false. And we are ready to acknowledge that there is much excellence in his character, provided it be also acknowledged that the love of power has modified it considerably. Hence, we do not challenge his right to hold a position of leadership among the men who compose the Doctrinaire phalanx. Alone, perhaps, among them, does he possess the qualities required to be the chief of a party; for he alone has a definite system and a resolute purpose; he alone knows from where he is setting out and where he wants to go. The middle-class aristocracy which has replaced the aristocracy of blood could not have a more able supporter and a more faithful representative than Mr. Guizot. But what can we say of a party that relies on intelligence to slay its best friends; that forces men who have become wise through searching historical study to break the law of progress, which is the very foundation of history? What can we say of those sturdy spirits who speak in misty and unintelligible phrases; those hardy and choleric politicians who recoil before the competing *Idea* and attack it through byways, never daring to confront it bravely and honorably?

All this is reflected in the pamphlet of Mr. Guizot. All this and, what is worse, nothing but this. We should thus not have cared to write these few pages had we not perceived some danger stemming from the exaggerated reputation that Mr. Guizot enjoys as a statesman (a reputation that has been promoted, not without design perhaps, by certain persons), and had we not found in this little essay a concise expression of

[3] The *doctrinaires* were the French liberals of the Restoration age, as for instance Royer-Collard and Guizot. The term denoted a kind of bourgeois liberalism that claimed to be moderate (of the *Juste-Milieu*) and was essentially antidemocratic and antiegalitarian.

[4] Guizot was elected to the French Chamber of Deputies in 1830. He was named minister of the interior after the July revolution but resigned in November. Subsequently he served as minister of education (1832), of foreign affairs (1840–46), and prime minister (1846–48). He had to flee France when the revolution fully erupted in late February 1848 and spent a year in exile in England. Some of his major works are *Mémoires pour servir à l'histoire de mon temps; Histoire parlementaire de la France; Histoire de la civilisation en Europe; Histoire de la révolution d'Angleterre depuis Charles I à Charles II; Histoire des origines du gouvernerment représentatif, 1821–1822.*

the general tactics that govern the operations and discussions, parliamentary or otherwise, of his entire party.

More precisely, the danger we refer to is that of being sold back—brushed, smartened, trimmed, and disguised by a continental cut—the very clothes that Mr. Guizot bought from us some fifteen years ago. It is the danger of falling in love with a translation; the danger of rejecting the road to progress, fancying ourselves all the while on the march forward. We can now only point out this danger, without further explanation. But we promise to return to it, should the occasion present itself.

The Doctrinaire's tactics and ideas, summed up in as few words as possible, are these: whenever you desire to refute a principle and prevent it from having any future impact, begin by approving everything it has achieved in the past. You risk nothing by accepting what is an accomplished fact. Moreover, you give yourself an appearance of impartiality and moderation, which will create a bias in your favor among the majority of readers. The business of the past thus settled, you have nothing further to do with it. All your efforts can now be directed to the perversion of the principle itself; by misrepresenting it you can practically destroy it. Take a purely formal manifestation of the principle, focus on its most mechanical elements, and then constantly substitute this latter, narrow conception of the principle for a broader and more appropriate conception. Analyze the principle; then take the elements that make it up, separately and *one by one,* and show how each of them is incomplete. Never look at the whole; never provide any precise definitions—nothing is more dangerous—just talk in catchy phrases and be positive. If you succeed in getting your approach to the question accepted, victory is yours. Now, working deductively from your premises you may play the logician at your ease.

We would be surprised if among all the political works of the school to which Guizot, Cousin,[5] and others belong, there was to be found a single one that does not in some way betray the influence of the aforementioned system. The little sample before us is quite instructive in this regard.

The democratic *fact* exists. It exists and is actually quite powerful: it has fought, conquered, and destroyed other rival political principles. Like the ghost in Hamlet, it reveals itself here, there, and everywhere. Some look at it hopefully, others fear it, but nobody denies it. Of the two writers who furnished Mr. Guizot with the occasion for his article, the first, Mr. Billiard, shares our republican creed: in his "Essay on the Dem-

[5] Victor Cousin (1792–1867) was a leading philosopher of Doctrinaire liberalism and stood close to Guizot's politics.

ocratic Organization of France," he maintains that the existing condition of society "must inevitably tend to establish an equality of political rights, universal suffrage, and, in fact, end in a republic."[6] The other, Mr. Alletz, used to side with the Carlists and now sides with the Doctrinaires: in his book *On the New Democracy, or the Habits and Influence of the Middle Classes*, he asserts that "the natural result of this condition is the consolidation of a constitutional monarchy (as established by the Revolution of 1830), in the spirit of the charter, and in the persons of the present dynasty."[7] Mr. Alletz's analysis would be perfectly compelling if democracy were indeed nothing more than the aristocracy of the middle classes, as his title seems to suggest. But then he goes on to assert that "all unanimously concur in admitting that the present state of society is thoroughly democratic, and that the democratic principle will ultimately triumph over every other."

Let us not suppose that Mr. Guizot is mistaken to such a degree as to abjure the democratic principle entirely. Far from it, he takes it under his protection. "Certainly," Guizot writes, "there must be truth, considerable truth, in this opinion." Is there not, as it were, a shade of sadness hovering over these words? Mr. Guizot performs his part with tolerable grace. He presents himself as a historian of democracy; he recounts and confirms its advances. "It has destroyed"—these admissions are significant—"the feudal system, or the personal power of one man over another, by virtue of the right of property; it has destroyed the system of castes, or the immovable and perpetual concentration of social privileges and power in the hands of a few; and the system of divine right, lay or ecclesiastical, that is, the presumption of representing God on earth. These are the victories of modern democracy. They are at once glorious and legitimate victories " (p. 16).

Now, should we not expect that Mr. Guizot would go on to deduce the law of future developments from a principle endowed with so much vitality? Should we not expect that, while trying to systematically identify those future developments, he would also predict democracy's future achievements? Should we not suppose that, having described that prophetic series of successive emancipations so logically accomplished, he would go on to cry in the ear of all the retrograde and stationary members of our societies: "Forward movement is the law of the world. All your efforts will only transform that force into something violent and dangerous, while it could evolve mildly and productively if it were to encounter no obstacles. In the past, you were unable to prevent the

[6] Auguste Billiard, *De l'organisation de la République Française* (Paris: Pagnerre, 1848).

[7] Edouard Alletz, *De la démocratie nouvelle, ou, Des mœurs et de la puissance des classes moyennes en France* (Paris: F. Lequien, 1838).

evolution of the slave into the serf, and then of the serf into the peasant and craftsman. Likewise, you will now not be able to prevent the transformation of the peasant and craftsman into a citizen."

Alas, no! This would be logical enough for us, since we have no reason for halting our march. But not so for Mr. Guizot. He has two systems of logic: one for the past, the other for the future, or rather for the existing state of things, which he intends to maintain as long as possible. Mr. Guizot is a revolutionary—but only to the year 1830. He is progressive—but only to the amended charter of the fourth of August. In his view, on that day democracy should have sent in her resignation. In destroying the aristocracy of blood, she did well—Mr. Guizot is not noble. But as far as the moneyed or middle-class aristocracy is concerned, beware of touching it—Mr. Guizot is of the middle class. If democracy has overturned the eldest branch of the Bourbons, so far so right; but for the youngest, it ought to be immortal. [8] And so with the rest. Why do you talk of the eternal rights of humanity, of the incessant hard work going on in its midst? All of humanity has worked only to achieve the charter of 1830; and perhaps the laws of September went just far enough to attain the system preferred by Mr. Guizot. Humanity is truly fortunate, for she has now only to repose in quiet. By a legislative effort of seven hours, on the seventh of August those Pillars of Hercules, those ultimate boundaries, were raised, and beyond them there can be no progress.

What if someone should tell Mr. Guizot:

There are no known Pillars of Hercules that limit progress. God alone has fixed those limits; and we can't see how he should have revealed his secret to you. In virtue of what right, of what criterion, of what principle, then, do you dare to determine their place? On what law do you base yourself, in pronouncing that certain advances of the human mind are lawful, while others are not so? How do you dare to approve of the past, if not in virtue of a principle derived from God himself, and legitimating the progress thus far achieved? If you possess any knowledge of this principle, why not proclaim it boldly? Can it be that this principle would be inconvenient to you? Instead of accepting only the material fact of already consolidated advances, you

[8] Guizot was a supporter of monarchical government, but he had been a strong critic of the ineptitude and oppressive rule of Charles X. He supported Louis Philippe in the July revolution of 1830 and thus favored a change in the hereditary line of succession, in conflict with his monarchic sentiment. In August 1830 Guizot was named minister of the interior by the new king, but he resigned in November. With that move, he joined the conservative camp. During the next twenty years he became a determined adversary of democracy, the unyielding champion of "a monarchy limited by a limited number of bourgeois."

should recognize in this very fact a manifestation of God's will—the eternal source of the life of humanity. Then you would also be compelled to ratify every advance that humanity may accomplish in the future. These consolidated advances, which you have just approved of, are either merely the fruit of chance, or of a capricious revolt crowned with success. But if the latter is true, how can they appear *glorious* to you? How can you declare them *legitimate*—that is to say, in conformity with the law of humanity's existence?

Perhaps those advances are indeed the effect of a divine impulse, in accordance with which men unceasingly strive to develop, associate, and perfect themselves, and to approach that *unity* willed by God when he caused humanity to proceed from a single man? Perhaps those advances have emerged from the same impulse which leads men to pursue that *Liberty* willed by God when he placed before them good and evil, right and wrong, and thus made them responsible for their choice? The same impulse which leads men to pursue that *Equality* (which is, at bottom, but liberty for all, and without which liberty is but a bitter deception) willed by God when he gave everybody an immortal soul? The same impulse which leads them to pursue that *Association* willed by God when he made man an essentially social being, unable to exist where there is no common law and no common aim, no consent and no cooperation? If all the advances you mention stem from this same impulse, then how dare you fix an arbitrary limit to its activity? How dare you hinder the forward march of the People? How dare you prevent them from overturning successively all the obstacles that ambition and selfishness may place on their path?

The People first confronted the aristocracy of the nobles and overturned it. The People did well, you say. True—but why should they not do equally well in overturning everything else that should hamper their progress? France has overthrown Louis XVI and Charles X. She did well, you still say. But was it because Louis XVI and Charles X carried these particular names that France did well; or is it that France would do well to overthrow every influence, whatever its name, which threatens to strike at her nationality, her honor, her freedom of progress? Quite evidently, it cannot be from a *detail*, but from a *principle*, that we must deduce the legitimacy of humanity's undertakings. Humanity's goal cannot be the overthrow of the aristocracy of *nobility*, or of any particular man who may encroach on the rights of the mass. Rather, its goal lies in the overthrow of Aristocracy as such, by whatever term of privilege and exclusiveness it may be called, whether it presents itself as a single man or as a caste, as a king or as a tribune, as an individual, or as an assembly. By claiming that democracy should not oppose the aristocracy of the *middle* classes, while you are lauding its conflict with the *higher* classes, you are renouncing every rational basis for the appreciation of events, and you are mistaking for general law the caprices of your own individual impressions.

Judging from his pamphlet, Mr. Guizot has little to offer in reply to these criticisms, at least not directly. But, by suddenly changing his ground, he takes the question in another direction. "You can," he tells the proponents of genuine Democracy, "only reject, overthrow, and destroy; but you cannot build anything; you do not possess a single positive principle able to organize anything." Of course, the world cannot be built on ruins, it cannot live on negations. But it is actually not us who desire to arrest progress; it is rather you, Mr. Guizot, who are utterly unable to produce it. There is a great deal of deception in Mr. Guizot's argument, and we shall be content to meet it by a series of interrogations.

First, we would ask Mr. Guizot: What is it that ought to be destroyed, and what should be built instead? Is not to reject anything, to affirm its contrary? When the religion of Christ superseded the pagan belief of two nations, producing the abolition of slavery in Europe, did it not accomplish for humanity the first essential step toward its union? When Democracy rejected the feudal power, did it not affirm human *liberty*? When it overthrew the influence of castes, did it not proclaim the *equality* of men among each other? Have not the Americans relied on these two fundamental principles of every association—liberty and equality—to build something that, though far from being faultless in our eyes, nevertheless lives, proceeds, and prospers, at least as much as any of the governments now existing in Europe? Coherently understood, Mr. Guizot's critique should apply to democracy from its earliest stages, and not just at the present day. Now, if indeed his critique had been applied and accepted early on, we would probably have been deprived of those two aforementioned advances (the successive overthrow of slavery and feudalism), which Mr. Guizot himself proclaims to be glorious and legitimate.

Would it not have been far more natural to affirm that no principle can successfully work toward a new organization until it has annihilated the opposing principle in all its manifestations?—And that since the aristocratic principle has not yet been vanquished (given its existence in the middle classes, which lies at the heart of our present question), we have no right to chastise Democracy for its organizational ineptitude? When we have asked all this, we shall have done but one half of our questioning. But it is our wish to meet Mr. Guizot on his own ground.

"Democracy," says Mr. Guizot, "has only two principles on which to rely for its reorganization of society. These are: first, personal sovereignty, or the right of every individual over himself; and second, the sovereignty of the number—which its partisans call the sovereignty of the People in order to disguise it—that is, the right of the majority over the minority. Whoever considers modern Democracy closely will discover that all its ideas, all its attempts at social organization, issue from and finally return to these principles." Mr. Guizot then goes on to examine these principles *one by one,* that is separately, and thus he wants to prove the impotence of these two principles. But these principles should never be allowed to work separately; they should on the contrary be harmonized within a true Democratic constitution. This should be particularly remarked. For all the force of Mr. Guizot's pamphlet rests in the separate consideration of two elements, which are equally sacred in our eyes, but which are only complete if they mutually support each other. We do not have the space here to discuss in much detail our author's errors in what he says about personal sovereignty. Besides, no one maintains that the sovereignty of the *individual* over himself can alone furnish the basis of a [constitutional] charter for any social system. Every association has a common end, and this is not expressed by the right of each over himself. To keep it short, we shall then only observe that Mr. Guizot's assault on this principle stems, on his part, from a logical error. Curiously enough, it is Mr. Guizot's own philosophy which, like all eclectic philosophy, ultimately rests on no other basis than this very sovereignty of the *Ego.*

But we have much to observe on Mr. Guizot's analysis of the sovereignty of the People (in accordance with the tactics explained above, Mr. Guizot abandons the notion of popular sovereignty and speaks instead of the sovereignty of the number).

First: on a close examination of the argument, we find that all of Mr. Guizot's declamation on the oppression of the minority by the majority—the inevitable consequence, he says, of the sovereignty of the People—raises against the consent of the greatest number that same right of each individual over himself, which he has condemned just a moment before. The right of the minority can indeed not be anything else than the right of a part against the whole—that is, of *individuality* against *association.*

Second: What is the meaning of all this argument coming from a constitutional writer and ex-minister? What is a constitutional government, such as the one that now exists, if not a government of the majority? Who decides on the proceeding of the State, if not a majority of Parliament? And who determines the nature and bias of a majority of Parliament, if not a majority of electors? Only, as in ancient states there was a mass of slaves excluded from all institutions, political and social, so now there are unrepresented People who are excluded from the sphere of political power. But how does this change the question?

In the system that Mr. Guizot attacks, parliamentary majorities would represent the majority of the nation. Now, they only represent the majority of a small fraction. Is that perhaps an advantage of the present system? Following Mr. Guizot's own reasoning, there are now two oppressions in place of one: first, the Parliamentary majority oppresses the parliamentary minority, that is, the minority of those who are actually represented; and then there is a much wider oppression of the whole mass of the unrepresented. In our system there would be but one—the first. The inconvenience pointed out, then, belongs to both systems, but to his much more than to ours. To fully overcome this problem, Mr. Guizot would have but one remedy—that of divine right and the infallibility of power. Perhaps he has understood this: perhaps his constant choice of examples from the constitution of the family hides an instinctive predilection for a government of *paternal despotism*. He does not dare to be always logical. Perhaps it also occurs to him that France might choose him as its savior for a second time; after all it is by the aid of some parliamentary majority that his friends strive to get him back into office. Moreover, this is not the real question. All this concern for minorities, pleasant enough from the mouth of somebody who declared as a minister that it was necessary to govern by fear, tends but to misrepresent his argument.

With regard to society, there is oppression only where there is injustice. Whenever an action is taken in view of the good, of duty, of the ultimate goal, and of the principle of association, there is on the one side a right to impose, and on the other a duty to submit. Selfishness alone can then complain. But are the chances that this may happen greater under the system to which Mr. Guizot subscribes, or under our own? In other words: Is it easier to find the expression of a love of the general good, which is the goal of association, in the universality of the elements composing the Nation—that is, in the People—or rather in a class—that is, in some narrow elements with their specific interests, no matter whether patrician or territorial?

This, and only this, is the question that really matters, and the ex-minister has not even hinted at it. To be in a position to judge it, or even to throw some light on it, one must begin with a sound, rational, and complete definition of the words *people* and *sovereignty*. Mr. Guizot has done nothing of the like. He has simply taken the material fact for the principle; the sign for the idea; the effect for the cause. In the People, he sees but an agglomeration of a certain number of individual interests; in sovereignty, some number greater than another; in the will of the national majority, a caprice.

It is not true that the People are but the sum, the agglomeration of the interests of all *individuals*. A *People* is not a class: it includes everybody, and they are not a mob drawn together by chance. They are an association of men in a given territory and with a given language; they are one country, one law, a moral and material unity, a common interest, a common aim: all this it is what constitutes a nationality. And in this there is nothing obscure, or abstrusely theoretical. The first among us who, being asked, "Who are you?" shall proudly reply, "I am a Briton," will express everything that we have just said. By these words, he will express that he has a country; that he is attached to it; that he seeks not only the satisfaction of his moral and physical wants as a man and an individual, but also as an Englishman and a citizen; that he not only cherishes his own honor, but that he feels himself bound also to that of his country; that he not only likes to carry his head proudly amidst his family and in his personal transactions, but also before the children of other nations; that he desires that his country's flag should be loved at home and welcomed with respect and sympathy abroad; that it is his wish that the rank and the mission marked out for his nation by her situation, her strength, and the principles of her constitution should be faithfully preserved. In a word, he will make it clear that he recognizes within himself a double existence, personal and social.

Likewise it is not true that the sovereignty of the People is but a number, large or small. For sovereignty is not power, but rather the legitimacy of power. Any association can only be legitimate if it tends to exercise its functions instead of, and for the good of, the entire body—that is, in view of a common end, a common interest, and common progress. Whenever this is not the case, power merely results in usurpation. Hence sovereignty of the People implies sovereignty of the national aim, sovereignty of a tendency to the progressive welfare of the association. Now, this tendency on which the legitimacy of power depends should manifest itself by acts. And one should establish the means to verify whether power is indeed legitimate, based on the actions it takes. So the legitimacy of power could be contested if necessary. Likewise, the submission and cooperation of all could be guaranteed, once it had been shown that the exercise of power is legitimate. Only at this point does the question of numbers—if we may so call it—become relevant.

Democratic opinion holds that only the nation in its entirety, for whose good power ought to be exercised in order to be legitimate, is able to judge whether what has been done is indeed for its common good. And the only possible means of expressing this judgment is national, universal suffrage. Conversely, it is the opinion of people like Mr. Guizot that the right of suffrage, and the right of judging whether power is employed for the common good, belongs to only a fraction of the nation.

But regardless of the solution that may be ultimately adopted, how, after this brief analysis, should we assess Mr. Guizot's language? How should we best describe the cunning with which he attempts to terrify our consciences, by likening the exercise of national sovereignty to that of a brutal and capricious force, and by constantly talking of the aggregate and the number without properly explaining what they represent? What arguments does he pretend to refute, when he cries—in the tone of an alarmed moralist—that the will alone is not the legitimate law of man, that it cannot declare what is just to be unjust, and that "reason and justice are completely supreme over all will"? Democracy accepts this supremacy of the moral law as fully as Mr. Guizot himself; indeed she admits it so fully that she is looking for the best method to interpret and apply it. But Mr. Guizot does not have the moral law in his pocket, since it is written only in the history and experience of generations. Also, it has not yet been proved that either Mr. Guizot, or his friends, or the doctrine he preaches are universal history and the living embodiment of experience. Hence one wonders whether the moral law would be more likely to be effectively interpreted and applied by relying on society as a whole or only on a minority. In discussing the existence or nonexistence of the law, Mr. Guizot has brought up a question that nobody has asked. And while it is certainly permitted to discuss the value of democracy, nobody ought to calumniate it.

If Mr. Guizot really meant well, and therefore conscientiously studied the opinions and progress of our age, he could not simply ignore the background against which the democrats of the present day pursue their labors. As a continental writer, he could not ignore that the formula *Sovereignty of the People* is much better understood today than it was in Rousseau's time; he could not ignore that really existing democracy has far outpaced the narrow and reactionary idea of *individual right*; that democracy is no longer about material interests and that indeed she raises the flag of *God and the People*; that the whole question is aggrandized by an awareness of *duty*, which endows it with all the sanctity of a religious source. He could not be ignorant of La Mennais, of the principal political schools of his own country, and of all those associations in other countries that have as their point of departure the ideas we have set forth.[9]

Neither can we allow, as we have already remarked, a separation, one by one, of the elements of a complex idea, for the purpose of refuting them. One also needs to take into account what may proceed from the combination of those elements; for it is not by analyzing the individual substances composing a medicine, and discovering each to be

[9] Hughes Felicité Robert de Lamennais (also known as Frédéric de La Mennais) (1782–1854), a French priest and philosopher who, after beginning as an early supporter of royalist principles, became the prophet of a kind of theocratic democracy, an idea that inspired both conservative and republican movements. Lamennais's works, and specifically his idea of society as a harmonic unity, had a decisive influence on Mazzini's own thinking.

pernicious or inefficacious on its own, that we form our opinion of its value.

The sovereignty of the individual is legitimate. For there is a sphere of action, springing entirely from the individual, which lives in him and concerns the personal wants of his physical and moral life; and for this it is necessary that individual sovereignty exercise itself freely. But the sovereignty of the people is equally legitimate. For there is a sphere of social action, springing from the ideas of country and nationality; from a common aim; from the vital principle of association, internally and externally applied; and for these it is necessary that social sovereignty be admitted and exercised without obstacle. Now, social sovereignty cannot reside in a fraction of society; it must reside in the whole. These two spheres—individual and social—are linked by a common principle, a superior law, which is reflected in the conscience of the individual, as far as individual acts are concerned, and in the conscience of the united nation, concerning social acts.

Hence, with regard to the acts of individual life, it is desirable that the individual himself intervene to ensure, as far as possible, the amelioration of the means necessary to his accomplishing them unfettered. But with regard to the acts of social life, it is desirable that society as a whole intervene to ensure that they be accomplished with the least possible departure from the superior moral law, which is the ultimate source of all sovereignty. Or would it perhaps be better that a very small minority, chosen by the hazard of birth or fortune, be entrusted to fulfill this oversight function, without any superior requirement or control save that of violence? Save, we say, that of violence. For, in fact, no minority can abolish violence: it is used in revolutions, and it is often the only option that the adversaries of Democracy, by we know not what fatal blindness, leave open to the people; indeed they even approve of it, for every revolution accomplished they regard as legitimate, and a passage is to be found in Mr. Guizot's pamphlet admitting it as a right.[10]

Every conscientious writer should formulate the question in the aforementioned way, when about to deal with universal suffrage and "Democracy in Modern Communities." To state the question as Mr. Guizot does is to deceive the reader and to condemn oneself to say nothing useful.

When the question shall have been thus stated and resolved, we can move on to examine what is the best political organization to bring the

---

[10] *"Permanent and universal rights are all centered in the right of obeying only such rules as are just and wise. Variable rights are all comprised in the right of suffrage—that is to say, in the right of passing judgment, directly or indirectly, on the wisdom of laws and government" (42). Thus, disobedience itself is placed in a more favorable condition than the expression of the reasons for which we find ourselves compelled to disobey [Mazzini's own footnote].*

two spheres into harmony and agreement; and subsequently we can ask which is the speediest and most efficacious path for progressively illuminating the souls of men with the light of the sovereign moral law, so that the People may diverge from it as little and as seldom as possible. The solution of the first question will result in a plan of political organization; that of the second in a plan of general education. We are not going to deal with these complex issues at the present moment. We only wanted to prove that Mr. Guizot has not even thought of it, and that consequently his pamphlet, translated, retranslated, and praised, cannot furnish a single idea, abstract or practical, to advance the discussion by a single step.

We shall now proceed to Mr. Guizot's conclusions, and we may then ask what could be learned from them:

1. "Permanent unity of social opinion represented by the government!" Who does not desire this? But a few questions necessarily follow: Does this unity exist at present? Did it exist in France eight years ago, when a revolution exploded that you applaud? What guarantee do you give us, other than the *individual sovereignty* of your own intelligence, that it exists at the present hour? Does a government represent the unity of social tendencies when it is in a state of permanent struggle and when millions proclaim the contrary? Who guarantees this representation, when the majority is deprived of all means to do so? What protection do you offer the nation against the emergence of political monopoly, against the substitution of the general good, and the advancement of the general interest, with private interests and the wishes of a privileged class? Does the ex-minister successfully deal with even one of these questions?

2. "Respect for public authorities!" Again, who does not desire this? But isn't it first necessary to ascertain that all their *decisions are just and wise*?

3. "Subordination of individual inclinations to the law!" Sure; who does not desire this? But is it not first of all necessary to see whether the law-making power is actually legitimate? Isn't the law a prerogative of sovereignty? And is not the source of sovereignty the very question at issue?

4. "Distribution of rights according to capacity!" Well, very well. But here a series of questions arise: What is capacity? Is it intelligence? Is it morality? Who is to measure capacity? What is to be the standard? Perhaps success in public and social life? But then there must be a law to assess the value of different achievements. Can we just take the tax-collector's list as a correct valuation of human faculties and translate intellect into money?

To all these questions Mr. Guizot offers no answer. The oracle utters only thus much, and the meaning of his words may be divined by those who can:

> The capacity here spoken of, is not merely that of intellectual development, or the possession of *this* or *that* particular *faculty*; it is a *complex* and *profound* whole, comprising *spontaneous authority*, habitual situation, and *natural* acquaintance with the different interests to be regulated. It is in fact a certain aggregate of faculties, knowledge, and *methods* of *action*, which animate the whole man, and which decide with more certainty than his spirit alone on his course of conduct and the use which he will make of power (p.43).

What a precise definition of the capacity to be an elector! What a foundation for an improved system of government! And a page later he writes: "Its (rights of suffrage) legitimate limit is a *concealed* principle which unfolds itself in a ratio with the material and moral development of society. And in a free community, in proportion as this principle is well or badly defined in its laws, so that community is well or ill governed, and becomes steady or unsteady, under the hand of its government" (p.44). What a splendid discovery! We will take our leave of Mr. Guizot with one further quote, to which our readers will this time heartily assent: "It cannot be that truth imposes on man so much confusion, impossibility, and incoherence" (p. 23).

CHAPTER FIVE

On the Duties of Man (1841–60)

To the Italian workingmen.

1. INTRODUCTION

I intend to speak to you of your duties. I intend to speak to you, according to the dictates of my heart, of the holiest things we know—of God, of Humanity, of our Country, and of the Family.[1] Listen to me in love, as I shall speak to you in love. My words are words of conviction matured by long years of study, of experience, and of sorrow. The duties that I am going to point out to you I have striven and will strive to fulfill to the utmost of my power, as long as I live. I may err, but my error is not of the heart. I may deceive myself, but I will not deceive you. So listen to me as brothers; judge freely among yourselves whether it seems to you that I speak the truth. Abandon me if you think that I preach what is false; but follow me and act according to my teachings if you believe me an apostle of the truth. To err is a misfortune to be pitied; but to know the truth and fail to conform one's actions to it is a crime that both Heaven and Earth condemn.

Why do I speak to you of your *duties* before speaking to you of your *rights?* Why—in a society where all, voluntarily or involuntarily, oppress you; where the exercise of so many of the rights that belong to man is constantly denied to you; where misery is your lot, and what is called happiness is only for other classes of men—why do I speak to you of *self-sacrifice* rather than of *conquest?* Why do I speak to you of virtue, moral improvement and education, rather than of material well-being? This is a question I must answer clearly before going further, because here precisely lies the difference between our school and many

---

[1] In this pamphlet, reprinted here in an abridged version, Mazzini came closest to a systematic exposition of his political creed. The pamphlet is explicitly addressed to the Italian working class: Mazzini wanted to educate it and stimulate it to action, helping it to move beyond its wretched position, yet without launching what he thought would be a dangerous class conflict. Of the seven chapters reprinted here, the first three were originally published in the weekly newspaper *Apostolato Popolare* between 1841 and 1842; chapters 4 and 5 originally appeared in the periodical newspaper *Pensiero e Azione* in 1859; finally chapters 6 and 7 were first published in the daily paper *L'Unità d'Italia* in 1860. The text has been adapted from previous translations.

others now existing in Europe; and also because this is a question that naturally arises in the vexed mind of the suffering workingman.

"We are the slaves of labor—poor and unhappy; speak to us of material improvement, of liberty, of happiness. Tell us if we are doomed to suffer forever; if we are never to enjoy in turn. Preach Duty to our employers, to the classes above us, which treat us like machines and monopolize the sources of well-being that belong to all. Speak to us of our rights and tell us how to gain them; speak to us of our strength. Let us first obtain a recognized social and political existence; then indeed you may speak to us of our duties." This is what many of our [Italian] workingmen say. Stimulated by such thoughts and desires, they follow political doctrines and join associations. But they forget one thing, namely, that the doctrines that they invoke have been preached for the last fifty years without producing the slightest material improvement in the condition of the working people.

All that has been done for the cause of progress in Europe over the last fifty years, whether against absolute governments or hereditary aristocracies, has been done in the name of the *Rights of man*, in the name of Liberty as the means, and of well-being as the end of life. All the achievements of the French Revolution and of the revolutions that followed and imitated it were a consequence of the Declaration of the Rights of Man. All the works of the philosophers who prepared the way for that revolution were founded on a theory of Liberty, and on the need of making known to every individual his own Rights. The revolutionary schools preached that man is born for *happiness*; that he has the right to seek happiness by all the means in his power; and that no one has the right to obstruct him in that search, while he has the right to overthrow whatever obstacles he may encounter on his path. And the obstacles were indeed overthrown; individual liberty was achieved. In many countries it lasted for years; in some it still exists. Has the social condition of the people improved? Have the millions who live by the daily labor of their hands gained even the smallest fraction of the promised and desired well-being? No; the social condition of the people has not improved. On the contrary, in most countries it has rather deteriorated. Especially here where I write [in England], the price of the necessaries of life has continued to rise, the wages of the workingmen in many branches of industry have fallen, and the population has increased. In almost all countries the condition of workers has become more uncertain and more precarious, while the labor crises that condemn thousands of workingmen to idleness for a certain period have become more frequent. . . .

Why has the fresh impulse given to industry and commerce produced, not the well-being of the many, but the luxury of the few? The answer is clear to those who look closely into things. Men are the creatures of education, and they act only according to the principle of education given to them. All revolutions and political transformations have thus far been founded on one idea; the idea of the *Rights* of the individual. Those revolutions achieved Liberty: individual liberty, liberty of education, liberty of belief, liberty of commerce, liberty in all things and for all men. But of what use was the recognition of rights to those who lacked the means of exercising them? Of what use was mere liberty of education to those who had neither time nor means to benefit from it? Of what use was mere liberty of commerce to those who possessed neither merchandise, nor capital, or credit?

In all the countries where these principles were proclaimed, society was composed of a small number of individuals who possessed all the land, the capital, and the credit, and of vast multitudes of men who possessed nothing but the labor of their own hands and were forced to sell that labor to the former class, on any terms, in order to survive. For such men, forced to spend the whole day in material and monotonous toil, and condemned to a perpetual struggle against hunger and want, what was liberty but an illusion and a bitter irony? The only way to prevent this state of things would have been for the upper classes voluntarily to reduce the hours of labor while increasing its remuneration; to offer a uniform and free education to the masses; to make the instruments of labor accessible to all; and offer credit to all workers of good capacity and of good intentions. But why should they have done this? Was not *well-being* the supreme end and aim of life? Was not material prosperity desired above anything else? Why should they diminish their own enjoyment in favor of others? "Let those who can help themselves. When society has secured to everybody the free exercise of the Rights inherent in human nature, it has done all that it is bound to do. If there is anybody who from the fatality of his own circumstances is unable to exercise any of these rights, he must resign himself to his fate and not blame others." It was natural that they should speak in this way, and this is exactly what they did. And this attitude of the privileged classes toward the poor soon became the attitude of every individual toward every other. Each man looked after his own rights and the improvement of his own position, without seeking to provide for others. . . .

The theory of Rights may suffice to arouse men to overthrow the obstacles placed in their path by tyranny, but it is impotent where the goal is to create a strong and lasting harmony between the various elements that compose the Nation. With the theory of happiness as the primary aim of existence, we shall only produce egoistic men who will carry the old passions and desires into the new order of things and corrupt it in a few months. We have therefore to find a principle of Education superior to any such theory, which shall guide men toward their own improvement, teach them constancy and self-sacrifice, and unite them with their fellow men without making them dependent either on the ideas of a single man or the force of the majority. And this principle is Duty. We must convince men that as children of the same God, they must obey one sole law here on earth; that each of them must live not for himself but for others; that the aim of existence is not to be more or less happy, but to make themselves and others more virtuous; that to struggle against injustice and error for the benefit of one's brothers is not only a *right* but a Duty; a duty which may not be neglected without sin—the duty of their whole life.

Workingmen, brothers—understand me well. When I say that the consciousness of your rights will never suffice to produce an important and lasting progress, I do not ask you to renounce those rights. I merely say that such rights can only exist as a consequence of duties fulfilled, and that we must begin with the latter in order to achieve the former. And when I say that in proposing happiness, well-being, or material interest as the aim of existence, we run the risk of producing egoists, I do not say that you should never strive for all these things. But I do say that the exclusive pursuit of material interests, not as a *means,* but as an *end,* always leads to disastrous and deplorable results. . . .

Hence, when you hear those who preach the necessity of a social transformation declare that they can accomplish it by invoking only your rights, be grateful to them for their good intentions, but distrustful of the outcome. The sufferings of the poor are at least partially known to the wealthier classes; *known* but not *felt.* In the general indifference resulting from the absence of a common faith, in the egoism that is the inevitable consequence of so many years spent in preaching material well-being, those who do not suffer themselves have little by little grown accustomed to regard the sufferings of others as a sorrowful necessity of social order and to leave the remedy to the generations to come. The difficulty is not so much to convince them, but to shake them from their inertia and, once they have been convinced, to induce them to *act,* to associate, and unite with you in brotherly fellowship, for the purpose of creating a social organization capable of putting an end, as far as humanly possible, to your sufferings and their own fears. . . .

Workingmen! We live in an epoch similar to that of Christ. We live in the midst of a society as corrupt as that of the Roman Empire. We feel in our inmost soul the need of reviving and transforming it; of uniting all its various members in a single faith, under a single Law, and for a single purpose: the free and progressive development of all the faculties with which God has endowed his creatures. We seek the kingdom of God on earth as it is in heaven; or rather, that earth may become a preparation for heaven, and society an attempt to progressively realize the

Divine Idea. . . . A few among you, once imbued with the true principles on which the moral, social, and political education of a People depends, will suffice to spread them among the millions, as a guide for their behavior and a protection against the sophisms and false doctrines that might otherwise lead the masses astray. . . .

2. The Law

You live; therefore you have a Law of life. There is no life without its law. Whatever exists, does exist in a certain manner, according to certain conditions, and is governed by a certain law. The mineral world is governed by a law of aggregation; the world of vegetables by a law of growth; the stars are ruled by a law of motion. Your life is governed by a law higher and nobler than these, since you are superior to all other created things on earth. To develop yourselves, to act and live according to your law, is your first, or rather your sole, Duty.

God gave you life; God therefore gave you the Law. God is the only Lawgiver to the human race. His law is the only law you are bound to obey. Human laws are only good and valid insofar as they conform to, explain, and apply the Law of God. They are evil whenever they contrast with or oppose it, and it is then not only your right, but your duty to disobey and abolish them. He who shall best explain the law of God, and best apply it to human things, is your legitimate ruler. Love him and follow him. But you do not have, and cannot have, any Master save God Himself. To accept any other is to be unfaithful and rebellious to Him.

Hence, the foundation of all morality, the rule of all your actions and duties, and the measure of your responsibility, is to be found in the knowledge of your law of life, of the Law of God. It is also your defense against the unjust laws that the arbitrary will of one man, or many men, may seek to impose on you. Unless you know this Law, you cannot pretend to the name or the rights of men. All rights have their origin in a law, and as long as you are unable to invoke this law you may be tyrants or slaves, but nothing else: tyrants if you are strong, slaves of the stronger if you are weak.

In order to be *men*, you must know the Law, which distinguishes human nature from that of animals, plants, and minerals, and you must conform your actions to it. Now, how are you to know this Law? This is the question which Humanity has in all times addressed to those who have pronounced the word *Duty*, and there have always been several different answers. Some have answered by pointing to a code or a book, saying: *the whole moral law is comprised in this book.* Others have said: *let every man interrogate his own conscience; he will find the definition of good and evil there.* Others again, rejecting the judgment of the individual, invoke universal opinion and declare: *whenever Humanity agrees in a belief, that belief is the true one.* But they are all wrong. And the history of the human race has proved by unassailable evidence the shortcomings of all these answers.

Those who declare that the whole moral law is to be found in a book, or in the words of a single man, forget that there is no moral code that Humanity has not abandoned, after believing in it for some centuries, in order to seek and preach a better one. And there is no special reason for believing that Humanity will alter its course today. It will be sufficient to remind those who declare that individual conscience is an adequate criterion of the just and true, that no Religion, however holy, has ever existed without heretics and dissenters who were ready to endure martyrdom for the sake of their conscience. Protestantism is today divided and subdivided into a thousand sects, all founded on the right of individual conscience; all eager to make war on each other and perpetuating that anarchy of beliefs that is the only true cause of the social and political disturbances that torment the peoples of Europe. On the other hand, those who reject the testimony of individual conscience, and appeal only to the common opinion of Humanity, should be reminded that all the great ideas that have contributed to the progress of Humanity began by being opposed to the beliefs then accepted by Humanity and were preached by individuals whom Humanity derided, persecuted, and crucified.

Each of these rules, then, is insufficient to gain knowledge of the Law of God, of Truth. Yet nevertheless, individual conscience is sacred; the common opinion of Humanity is sacred; and everyone who refuses to interrogate either of them deprives himself of an essential means of knowing the Truth. The common error until now has been the desire to reach the truth by one of these means alone, an error most fatal and decisive in its consequences: it is in fact impossible to elevate individual conscience into the sole judge of truth without falling into anarchy; and it is impossible to rely exclusively on the general opinion of Humanity at any given moment without crushing human liberty and producing tyranny.

Thus—and I quote these examples to show how much more than is generally assumed the entire social edifice rests on these primary foundations—some men have fallen into the error of organizing society only with respect to the rights of the individual, forgetting altogether the educational mission of society; meanwhile others have based their organization exclusively on the rights of society, sacrificing the free action and liberty of the individual.[2] France after her great revolution, and still

[2] *I speak, of course, of those countries governed by a constitutional monarchy, where a certain organization of society has been attempted. In countries governed despotically there is no society, individual and social rights being equally sacrificed.* [Footnote from original Mazzini chapter.]

more conspicuously England, have provided us with ample evidence that the first system results in inequality and the oppression of the many. Communism, if it were ever to become a fact, would show us how the second condemns society to petrifaction, by depriving it of all mobility and opportunity for progress.

Thus some, considering only the rights of the individual, have organized, or rather disorganized, society by founding it solely on the theory of unlimited freedom of competition; while others, thinking only of social unity, would give the government the monopoly of all the productive forces of the state. The first of these theories has resulted in all the evils of anarchy; the second would lead to immobility and all the evils of tyranny.

God has given you both the opinion of your fellow men and your own conscience, like two wings with which to elevate yourselves toward Him. Why should you persist in cutting off one of them? Why should you isolate yourselves, or let the world absorb you altogether? Why should you seek to stifle the voice of the individual or that of the human race? Both are sacred; God speaks through each of them. *Whenever they agree,* whenever the voice of your own conscience is ratified by the general opinion of Humanity, God is there. Then you are certain of having found the truth, for the one confirms the other.

If your duties were merely negative, if they merely consisted in not doing evil, in not harming your fellow men, then perhaps even at the stage of development which the least educated among you have reached, the voice of conscience might suffice to guide you. You are born with a tendency toward good, and every time you act in direct contrast to the moral Law, every time you commit a crime, there is something within you that condemns you, some voice of reproval that you may conceal from others, but not from yourselves. However, your most important duties are *positive.* It is not enough *not to do;* you must *act.* It is not enough to limit yourselves not to act contrary to the Law; you must act according to the Law. It is not enough not to do harm to your brothers; you must do good to them. Up to now morality has too often been presented to mankind in a negative, rather than an affirmative form. The interpreters of the law have typically said: "Thou shalt not kill; thou shalt not steal." But few, or none, have taught us the active duties of man: how we may be useful to our fellow creatures and further God's design on earth. Yet this is the primary aim of morality, and no individual can reach that aim by consulting his conscience alone.

Individual conscience speaks in accordance with man's education, tendencies, habits, and passions. The conscience of the savage Iroquois speaks a different language from that of the nineteenth-century European. The conscience of the free man suggests to him duties that the conscience of the slave does not even imagine. . . .

Evidently the voice of individual conscience is not sufficient, without any other guide to reveal the law to us. Conscience alone may teach us that a law exists; it cannot teach us the duties derived from it. For this reason, martyrdom has never been extinguished among men, however great the predominance of egoism; but how many martyrs have sacrificed their existence for imaginary duties, or for what appear to all of us today as errors! Conscience is in need of a guide, of a torch to illuminate the darkness by which it is surrounded, of a rule by which to direct and confirm its instincts. This rule is the *Reason of Humanity*.

God has given reason to each of you, so that you may educate yourselves to know His law. At present, poverty and the deep-rooted errors of centuries deprive you of the possibility to fully educate yourselves. Hence the obstacles to education are the first you need to overthrow. But even when all these obstacles are removed, the individual man's reason would still be insufficient to gain knowledge of the law of God, unless aided and supported by the combined reason of Humanity. Your life is short, your individual faculties are weak, uncertain, and in need of support. Now, God has placed beside you a being whose life is continuous, whose faculties are the result and sum of all the individual faculties that have existed over several ages; a being who amidst the errors and flaws of individuals steadily advances in wisdom and morality; a being whose development and progress expresses in every epoch a line of God's law. This being is Humanity.

Humanity, as a thinker of the past century has put it, is *a man that lives and learns forever*. Individuals die, but the truth they have gained knowledge of, and the good they have done, does not die with them. Humanity gathers it all, and the men who pass over the graves of the dead reap the benefit of it. Each of us is born today in an atmosphere of ideas and beliefs that has been previously elaborated by Humanity, and each of us contributes, even without knowing it, a more or less important element to the life of Humanity that is to come. The education of Humanity grows step by step, like those Eastern pyramids to which every passing traveler added a stone. We pass along, travelers of a day, destined to complete our individual education elsewhere. The education of Humanity shows itself by glimpses in each of us, but it is revealed progressively and continuously in Humanity as a whole.

Humanity is the living word of God. The spirit of God makes it fruitful and manifests itself in it more purely age after age, now by means of an individual, now by means of a people. From labor to labor, from belief to belief, Humanity gradually acquires a clearer perception of its own life, of its own mission, of God and His law. God manifests himself progressively in Humanity. The law of God is one, as God is one; but we only discover it article by article, line by line, through the accumulated experience of preceding generations, and according to the growing intensity of *association* among races, peoples, and individuals. No man, no people, and no age may pretend to have discovered the whole of the Law. The Moral Law, the Law of Life of Humanity, can only be discovered in its entirety by the whole of Humanity united in association, when all the powers and all the faculties that constitute our human nature shall be developed and in action. But meanwhile, that part of Humanity that is most advanced in education reveals to us through its progress and development a part of the Law that we seek to know. The history of that most advanced part of humanity reveals to us God's design, and its needs teach us about our duties, because our first duty is to cooperate in lifting Humanity to that stage of education and improvement to which God and the times have prepared it.

Hence, to know the Law of God you must interrogate not only *your own* conscience, but also the conscience and general opinion of Humanity. In order to know your own duties you must ask yourself what are the present needs of Humanity. Morality is progressive, as is your education and that of the entire human race. The morality of early Christianity was different from that of Paganism; and the morality of our own age differs from the morality of eighteen hundred years ago. . . .

God, the Father and Educator of Humanity, reveals His Law to Humanity through time and space. Interrogate the opinion of Humanity, as expressed by all your fellow men, not just in the restricted circle of one age or one school of thought, but as it has accumulated throughout the ages, in the majority of men past and present. *Whenever that opinion of Humanity corresponds with the teachings of your own conscience, you are certain of the Truth*; certain, that is, of knowing one line of the Law of God. *I believe in Humanity, sole interpreter of God's law on earth.* And from the agreement between my own individual conscience and the general opinion of Humanity, I deduce what I am now about to tell you with regard to your duties.

3. DUTIES TOWARD HUMANITY

Your first duties, first not in point of time but of importance, are toward Humanity. Unless you understand these primary duties, you can only imperfectly fulfill the rest. You have duties as citizens, as sons, as husbands, and as fathers; and all these duties are sacred and inviolable. But what constitutes the sacredness and inviolability of these latter duties is the mission, the supreme *duty* that results from your *human* nature. You are fathers so that you may educate men to worship and fulfill God's Law. You are citizens and you have a Country so that in a limited sphere of action, and with the cooperation of a certain number of men who are already related to you by language, tendencies, and customs, you may work more effectively for the benefit of *all men*, present and future. Without the cooperation of your fellow countrymen, your solitary effort would be lost amid the immense multitude of your fellow human beings. Those who pretend to teach you about morality by limiting your duties to those you owe to your family and Country do in fact teach you a more or less narrow egoism that harms both others and yourself. Family and Country are like two circles, drawn within a larger circle that contains them both; they are two steps of the ladder without which your ascent would be impossible, but it is forbidden to rest on them.

You are *men*; that is, rational and social creatures *capable of intellectual progress only by means of association*. Nobody may assign a limit to your progress. This is all we know with regard to Humanity's Law of Life. These characteristics constitute your *human nature*, which distinguishes you from the other beings around you and is given to each of you as the seed to bring to fruit. Your entire life should tend to the regular development and exercise of these fundamental faculties of your nature. Whenever you suppress one of these faculties or allow it to be suppressed, in whole or in part, you descend from the rank of men to that of the inferior animals and violate your Law of Life, the Law of God.

You descend to the level of brutes whenever you suppress, or allow to be suppressed, any of the faculties that constitute human nature, either in yourself or in others. God wants you to fulfill His Law not only as individuals, for had he intended this, he would have created you as solitary beings. He wants the Law to be fulfilled all over the earth, among all the beings He created after His own image. God wants the Divine Idea of perfectibility and love that he has given to the world to be revealed in ever-increasing brightness, and worshipped by His creatures. In your earthly existence as individuals, with your limited capacities and education, you can only realize this Divine Idea most imperfectly. Only Humanity, continually in existence through the generations, and with the accumulated intellect of all its successive members, is capable of gradually achieving, applying, and glorifying the Divine Idea.

Hence life was given to you by God so that you might employ it for the benefit of Humanity; that you might direct your individual faculties to aid the development of the faculties of your fellow men, and contribute by your labor to the collective work of progress and the discovery of the truth that the generations are destined slowly but continuously to pursue. You must educate yourselves and educate others; strive to perfect yourselves and others. . . .

The first men *felt* God, but without understanding or even seeking to understand Him and His Law. They felt Him in His power, not in His love. They had a confused conception of some sort of relation between Him and their own individuality, but nothing more. Able to detach themselves but little from the sphere of visible objects, they embodied Him in one of these: in the tree they had seen struck by the thunderbolt, the rock beside which they had raised their tent, the animal that first presented itself to their eyes. This was the kind of worship that in the history of religions is termed *fetishism*. In those days men knew of no bond beyond the *Family*, the reproduction in a certain sense of their own individuality. Beyond the circle of the family there were strangers, or more often enemies; to preserve themselves and their families was to them the sole foundation of morality.

In later days the idea of God was expanded. From visible objects men timidly raised their thoughts to abstractions; they learned to generalize. God was no longer regarded as the Protector of the family alone, but of the association of many families, of cities, of peoples. Thus *fetishism* was succeeded by *polytheism*, the worship of many gods. The sphere of action of morality was also enlarged: men recognized the existence of more extended duties than those due to the family alone; they strove for the advancement of their *people*, their *Nation*. Yet nevertheless Humanity was still ignored. Each nation called foreigners *barbarians*, regarded them as such, and sought to conquer or oppress them by force or fraud. Each nation also had foreigners or barbarians in its own midst; millions of men not admitted to the religious rites of citizenship and believed to be of an inferior nature—slaves among the free.

The idea of the Unity of the human race could only be conceived as a consequence of the Unity of God. And the Unity of God, though anticipated by a few rare thinkers of antiquity and openly declared by Moses (but with the fatal restriction of believing that a single people was His elect), was not widely recognized until toward the fall of the Roman Empire, through the teachings of Christianity. Foremost amid the teachings of Christ were these two inseparable truths: *there is but one God; all men are children of God.* The diffusion of these two truths changed the face of the world and enlarged the moral circle to the confines of the inhabited earth. Duties toward Humanity were now added to the duties of men toward Family and Country. Then man learned that wherever there was a fellow human being, there was a brother; a brother with a soul immortal like his own, called to ascend toward Heaven; a brother whom he owed love, help, and counsel when needed. . . .

We have to teach mankind that humanity is one single body that must be governed by a single law, and that the first article of this law is *Progress*; progress here, on this earth, where we are to accomplish God's design to the best of our abilities and educate ourselves for higher destinies. We have to teach mankind that, as humanity is one single body, we are all as members of that body bound to work for its development and to make its life more harmonious, active, and strong. We have to convince ourselves that we can only rise toward God through the souls of our fellow human beings, and that it is our duty to improve and purify them even when they do not ask for it themselves. Finally, we have to substitute a work of *association*, tending to improve the masses, to the exercise of charity toward individuals and to organize both the family and the country for this purpose. For it is only through the cooperation of humanity as a whole that God's design can be fully accomplished here below on earth. Other and greater duties will be revealed to us in the future, as we gradually acquire a clearer and less imperfect understanding of our law of life. . . .

In a country that is governed despotically, where taxes and restrictions are imposed at the sole caprice of the ruler, the cost of whose armies, spies, agents, and pensioners grows constantly as the necessity of securing the regime against overthrow increases, no sustained development of industry and manufactures is possible. But do you think that it will be enough for you to improve the government and social condition of *your own* country? No, it will not be enough. No nation lives exclusively on its own produce today. You live by exchanges, by imports and exports. An impoverished foreign nation, where the number of consumers diminishes, is one market less for you. A foreign business ruined in consequence of a bad administration produces mischief and crises in your own business. Failures in England and America bring about Italian failures. Credit nowadays is no longer a national but a European institution. Moreover, so long as you focus only on your own country, all other governments will be hostile to your national improvements, for there is an alliance today among the princes, who were among the first to understand that the social question has become a general question.

The only lasting hope for you lies in the general amelioration, improvement, and brotherhood of all the peoples of Europe, and through Europe of all Humanity. Therefore, my brothers, in the name of your duty and for the sake of your interest, never forget that your first duties are toward Humanity. Without fulfilling those latter duties, you cannot hope to fulfill those owed to family and country. Let your words and your actions be for all, since God is for all, in His Love and His Law. In whatever land you may be, wherever a man is fighting for right, for justice, for truth—that man is your brother. Wherever a man suffers from error, injustice, or tyranny—that man is your brother. Free men or slaves, you are all brothers.

You all have one common origin, you are governed by the same law, and you are destined to attain the same the goal. Let your faith, your action, and the flag under which you fight likewise be one. Don't say,

The language we speak is different; because acts, tears, and martyrdom are a language common to all men, and which all understand. Don't say, *Humanity is too vast, and we are too weak*; because God does not judge your power but your intention. Love Humanity. Always ask yourselves, when you act within the sphere of your family or country: *If what I am now doing were done by all men, would it be beneficial or harmful to Humanity?* And if your conscience tells you it would be harmful, desist from acting; desist even though it might seem that an immediate advantage to your country or family would be the result. May you be the champions of this faith: champions of the brotherhood of nations, and of the Unity of the human race, which though admitted in principle, is today still denied in practice. May you promote this faith, wherever you are, to the best of your abilities. Neither God nor man can demand more of you than this. But I tell you that by promoting this faith, even if you should convince only yourselves, you will serve Humanity well. God determines the steps of education he permits the human race to ascend by the number and purity of the believers. When the pure among you are many, God, having counted you, will disclose to you the way to action.

4. Duties toward Your Country

Your first duties, first with regard to their importance, are toward Humanity, as I have already told you. You are *human beings* before you are either citizens or parents. If you don't embrace the whole human family in your love; if you don't provide evidence of your belief in the Unity of that family, which follows from the Unity of God, and in the brotherhood of peoples, which alone can realize that Unity; if wherever one of your fellow men suffers, wherever the dignity of human nature is violated by falsehood or tyranny, you are not willing to help the unhappy to the best of your abilities, and do not feel called on to combat for the redemption of the betrayed or oppressed—you violate your Law of life and don't understand that religion which will be the guide and blessing of our future.

But what can each of you *individually* do for the moral improvement and progress of Humanity? You can, from time to time, express your belief in a sterile manner that will have little or no consequence; you may, on some rare occasions, perform some act of *charity* toward a brother from a foreign land; but no more. Charity is not the watchword of the Faith of the future. The watchword of the Faith of the future is *association*; fraternal cooperation of all toward a common aim. This is far superior to all charity, as the building which all of you could raise united would be superior to the humble hut that each of you could build alone. But distinct and divided as you are in language, customs, tendencies, and capacity, you cannot attempt such united action. The individual is too insignificant, and Humanity too vast. The sailor from Brittany prays to God as he puts to sea: *Help me, my God; my boat is so small and Thy ocean so wide!* This prayer sums up the condition of each one of you, as long as you don't find the means of multiplying your forces and powers indefinitely.

God provided you with the means to multiply your forces when he gave you a country, when like a wise supervisor of labor who assigns different tasks according to the different capacities of the workmen, he divided Humanity into distinct groups on the face of our earth, thus planting the seeds of Nationalities. Evil governments have tampered with God's design and have disfigured it by their conquests, their greed, and their jealousy of the just sovereignty of others; they have disfigured it to such an extent that, with the exception of England and France, there is perhaps not a single country whose present borders correspond to that Design. These evil governments did not, and do not, recognize any country except their own families or dynasty and the egoism of caste. Nonetheless, you may still trace God's design, distinctly marked out—at least as far as Europe is concerned—by the course of the great rivers, the direction of the higher mountains, and other geographical conditions. And God's design will infallibly be realized. Natural divisions and the innate spontaneous tendencies of the peoples will replace the arbitrary divisions sanctioned by evil governments. The map of Europe will be redrawn. Free nations, defined by the vote of free men, will arise on the ruins of monarchic privilege. Between these new countries there will be harmony and brotherhood. And the common work of Humanity for general improvement, and for the gradual discovery and application of the Law of Life, will be accomplished by peaceful and progressive development, with different tasks being assigned according to local capacities. Then each of you, strengthened by the affection and the cooperation of many millions, all speaking the same language, endowed with the same tendencies, and educated by the same historical tradition, may hope by your personal effort to benefit the whole of Humanity. . . .

Oh my brothers, love your Country! Our country is our Home, the House that God has given us, placing therein a numerous family that loves us, and which we love in turn; a family with which we sympathize more readily and which we understand more quickly than others; a family which, by its concentration on a given spot and the homogeneous nature of its elements, is destined for a special kind of activity. Our Country is our own workshop, from where the products of our activity are sent forth for the benefit of the entire world. The tools and instruments of labor that we can most usefully employ are gathered there, and we may not reject them without being unfaithful to God's purpose and diminishing our own strength. In laboring for our own country according to the right principle, we labor for Humanity. Our country is the pivot of the lever we have to wield for the common good. If we abandon that pivot, we run the risk of rendering ourselves useless not only to humanity but to our country itself. Before we can *associate* with the other nations that compose humanity, we must ourselves have a National existence. There can be no true association except among equals.

Humanity is a great army that advances to the conquest of unknown lands, against powerful and shrewd enemies. The Peoples are the different units and divisions of that army. Each of them has its specific post assigned to it and a special operation to perform; their common victory depends on how precisely the different operations are carried out. Do not disturb the order of battle. Do not abandon the flag that God has given you. Whereever you may be, in the midst of whatever people circumstances may have placed you, be always ready to fight for the liberty of that people, should it be necessary. And fight in such a way that the blood you shed may reflect glory, not on yourself alone, but on your entire Country. Don't say *I*; say *we*. May each of you strive to embody his country in himself. May each of you regard himself as responsible for his fellow countrymen and learn to act in such a way that his country will be loved and respected through him. Your Country is one and indivisible. As the members of a family cannot rejoice at the common table if one of their number is far away, snatched from the affection of his brothers, so you should have no joy or repose as long as a portion of the territory on which your language is spoken remains separated from the Nation.

Your country is proof of the mission that God has given you to fulfill toward humanity. The faculties and forces of *all* its children should be united in the pursuit of that mission. A certain number of common duties and rights belong to every man who answers the "Who are you?" of other peoples by claiming: "I am Italian." Those duties and rights cannot be represented except by a *single* authority resulting from your votes. Each Country must therefore have a single government. Those politicians who call themselves federalists, and who would like to make Italy into an association of different states, would dismember the Country, not understanding the idea of Unity. . . .

A true Country is a community of free and equal human beings, bound together in brotherly concord to work toward a common end. You must make it and maintain it as such. A Country is not an *aggrega-*

tion, but an *association.* There is therefore no true country without a uniform Right. There is no true country where the uniformity of that Right is violated by the existence of castes, privilege, and inequality. Wherever the powers and faculties of a large number of individuals are either cancelled or dormant; wherever there is not a common Principle recognized, accepted, and developed by all, there is no true Nation, no People, but only a multitude, a fortuitous agglomeration of men whom circumstances have brought together and whom circumstances will again separate. In the name of the love you owe your country, you must peacefully but untiringly combat the existence of privilege and inequality in the land that gave you life. There is but one legitimate privilege, the privilege of Genius when it reveals itself united with virtue. But this is a privilege given by God, and when you acknowledge it and follow its inspiration, you do so freely, exercising your own reason and your own choice. Every privilege that demands your submission in virtue of power, inheritance, or any right that is not the Right common to all, is a usurpation and a tyranny that you are bound to resist and destroy. Your Country should be your Temple. God at the summit; a People of equals at the base. Accept no other formula, no other moral law, if you do not want to dishonor both your Country and yourselves. All secondary laws should aim at the gradual regulation of your existence through the progressive application of this supreme law.

And for secondary laws to fulfill this purpose—to progressively apply the supreme moral law—it is necessary that *all* of you should aid in framing them. Laws framed only by a fraction of the citizens can never, by the very nature of things, be anything else than a mere expression of the thoughts, aspirations, and desires of that fraction; they represent not the Country, but a third or fourth part, a class or a region of the Country. The secondary laws should express a people's general aspirations and promote the universal good; they should reflect the beat of the Nation's heart. The entire Nation should legislate, either directly or indirectly. By yielding this mission into the hands of a few, you put the egoism of a single class in place of the Country, which is the Union of *all* classes. A Country is not a mere territory; the particular territory is only its foundation. A true Country is the Idea to which it gives birth; it is the sentiment of love, the sense of fellowship that binds together all the sons of that territory.

So long as a single one of your brothers is not represented by his own vote in the development of the National life, so long as there is a single one left to vegetate in ignorance while others are educated, so long as a single man who is able and willing to work languishes in poverty for want of work—there is no Country in the sense in which a Country ought to exist, a Country of all and for all. Education, work, and the franchise are the three main pillars of the Nation. Do not rest until you have solidly erected those pillars with your own hands. And when you have erected them; when you have secured food for the body and soul for every one of you; when freely united, you advance in beautiful concord toward the development of your faculties and the fulfillment of the Italian mission—keep in mind that this mission is the moral unity of Europe—then remember the immense duties that remain for you to fulfill. . . .

There are countries in Europe that consider liberty to be sacred domestically but systematically violate it internationally. There are peoples who say: "Truth is one thing, utility another; theory is one thing, practice another." These countries will inevitably have to pay for their egoism with long isolation, oppression, and anarchy. . . . Never disavow your sister Nations. The Life of your Country shall grow through your efforts in beauty and strength, free from servile fears and the hesitations of doubt; keeping as its *foundation* the People; as its *guide* the consequences of its principles, logically deduced and energetically applied; as its *strength* the united strength of all; as its *goal* the fulfillment of the mission that God has given it. And as long as you are ready to die for Humanity, the Life of your Country will be immortal. . . .

5. LIBERTY

Without liberty you cannot fulfill any of your duties. Therefore you have a right to liberty and a duty to obtain it at any cost from whatever Power shall seek to withhold or deny it. Without liberty there is no true Morality, because if there is no free choice between good and evil, between devotion to the common good and the spirit of egoism, there can be no responsibility. Without liberty there is no true society, because any association between free men and slaves is impossible; there can only be the rule of the one over the others. Liberty is sacred, as the individual whose life it expresses is sacred. Where there is no liberty, life is reduced to a mere organic function. When a man allows the violation of his liberty, he betrays his own nature and rebels against God's law. There is no true liberty whenever a caste, a family, or a single man pretend to rule over others in virtue of an alleged divine right or of any other inherited privilege. In short, liberty must be visibly granted to all human beings.

God does not delegate the Sovereign power to any individual. That degree of Sovereign power that can be justly represented on this earth has been entrusted by God to humanity and to the different nations and societies. But the different parts of Humanity lose even this degree of Sovereignty when they cease to employ it for the common good and in accordance with God's design. Nobody therefore holds Sovereignty *as a right*. True Sovereignty consists in the ultimate *goal*, and in all those acts that bring us closer to it. These acts, and the goal toward which we are advancing, must be submitted to the judgment of all. Hence there is not, and there cannot be, any permanent Sovereignty. The institution we call Government is merely a directorate entrusted to a few in order to more speedily attain the National goal; and should the Government betray its mandate, the power of direction entrusted to those few ought to cease. Every man who becomes a member of the Government is an administrator who should facilitate the pursuit of the common Idea. He should be elected and be subject to have his election revoked whenever he misconceives or deliberately opposes that Idea.

Therefore, I repeat, no family or caste can possess the governing power of its own right, without a violation of your liberty. How could you call yourselves free in the face of men possessing the power to command you without your consent? The Republic is thus the only logical and truly legitimate form of Government. You have no master save God in heaven and the People on earth. Whenever you discover a line of the Law, of God's will, you are bound to obey it. Whenever the people, the Collective Unity of your fellow men, shall express their preference, you are bound to lower your head and abstain from any act of rebellion. But there are certain things that are constitutive of your very individuality and are essential elements of human life. Over these, not even the People have any right. No majority may establish a tyrannical regime, thereby destroying or alienating its own freedom. While foreigners do not have a right to forcibly intervene against a People that were to commit such a suicidal act, each of you has a right to protest in the manner deemed most appropriate, according to the circumstances.

You have a right to liberty in everything that is necessary to the moral and material sustenance of life: personal liberty; liberty of movement; liberty of religious faith; liberty of opinion; liberty of expressing that opinion through the Press or by any other peaceful means; liberty of association, in order to render that opinion fruitful through contacts and exchanges with others; liberty of labor; liberty of trade. All these things may not be taken from you (save in a few exceptional cases, which it is unnecessary here to enumerate), without your having a right to protest.

Nobody has a right to imprison you, or subject you to personal surveillance or restraint in the name of society, without telling you as soon as possible for what reason this is being done, and immediately giving you a hearing before the judicial power of the Country.

Nobody has any right to persecute you because of your religious opinions; no voice, save the great and peaceful voice of Humanity, has any right to interpose itself between God and your conscience.

God has given you the faculty of Thought: nobody has a right to suppress or restrain its expression, which is the act of communion between your soul and the souls of your fellow human beings and is our one sole means of progress.

The Press must be absolutely free. The right of intellectual expression is inviolable, and every *preventive* censorship is tyranny. Society may, however, punish the errors of the Press, or the teaching of crime or immorality, just as it may punish any other apparent mistake. This right of punishment is a consequence of our human responsibility; but every preventive intervention is a negation of liberty.

The right of peaceful association is as sacred as thought itself. God has endowed us with a tendency toward association as a perennial means of progress and as a pledge of that Unity which the human family is destined one day to attain. Hence no power has a right to limit or prevent Association.

Each of you has a duty to employ the life given to you by God to preserve and improve your existence. Therefore each of you ought to secure your material support exclusively by means of your own labor. Labor is sacred. Nobody has a right to impede it, forbid it, or render it impossible by arbitrary regulations. Nobody has a right to forbid free trade in the products of your labor. Your Country is your lawful market that nobody may limit or restrain.

But when these different forms of liberty shall all be held sacred, when the State shall have been constituted according to the popular will, and in such a way that each individual shall be able to freely develop his faculties—do not forget that high above each and every individual stands the *Goal* which it is your duty to achieve; your own moral perfectibility and that of others, through an ever more intimate and wide-ranging association between all the members of the human family, until the day may come when all shall recognize one sole Law. . . .

Liberty is but a *means*. Woe to you and your future, should you ever accustom yourselves to regard it as the *end!* Your own individuality results in specific rights and duties, which may not be yielded to anybody. But woe to you and your future, should the respect you owe to your individual life ever degenerate into the fatal crime of egoism. Liberty is not the negation of all authority; it is the negation of every authority that fails to represent the collective goal of the Nation, or that seeks to impose and maintain itself by other means than your free consent.

The sacred idea of Liberty has recently been perverted by some deeply flawed doctrines. Some have reduced it to a narrow and immoral egoism, making the *self* everything and declaring the aim of all social organization to be the satisfaction of personal desires. Others have declared that all government and all authority is a necessary evil, to be restricted and restrained as far as possible; that liberty has no limits; that the aim of society is to indefinitely promote liberty, which every man has a right to use or abuse, provided this does not result in any direct harm to others; and that government has no other mission than that of preventing one individual from harming another. Reject these false doctrines, my brothers! The first has generated the egoism of class; the second reduced society—which, well organized, would represent your collective life and goal—to nothing more than the soldier or policeman charged with maintaining an apparent peace. The tendency of all such doctrines is to convert liberty into anarchy, to cancel the idea of collective moral improvement. If you were to understand liberty according to these flawed doctrines, you would deserve to lose it, and sooner or later you would lose it.

Your liberty will be sacred so long as it is guided by an idea of duty, of faith in the common perfectibility. Your liberty will flourish, protected by God and man, so long as you perceive it, not as the right to use or abuse your faculties as you may please, but as the right to freely choose the means of doing good, according to your specific tendencies.

6. The Social Question

Many, too many of you, are poor. For at least three-fourths of the working class, whether laborers or mechanics, life is a daily struggle to gain the *indispensable* material means of existence. They are occupied in manual labor for ten, twelve, sometimes fourteen hours a day, and by this constant, monotonous, and painful industry, they scarcely gain the bare necessaries of physical life. Any attempt to teach such men the duty of progress, to speak to them of their intellectual and moral life, of their political rights, or of education, is sheer irony in the present state of things. They have neither the time nor the means to improve themselves. Fatigued and half-stupefied by a life consumed in petty and mechanical toil, all they do learn is a mute, impotent, and often unjust resentment against the class of men who employ them. They too often seek to forget the troubles of the day and the uncertainty of tomorrow in the stimulus of strong drink, and they sink to rest in places better described as dens than rooms, only to wake up the next morning to a repetition of the same dull exercise of their merely physical powers. It is a sad condition, and it must be changed.

You are *men*, and as such you possess not just physical, but also intellectual and moral faculties; and you ought to develop them. You should be *citizens*, and as such you should exercise for the common good certain rights, which require a degree of education and some free time. It is clear that you ought to labor less and earn more than you now do. As God's children, we are all called to constitute a single great Family. In this family there may be inequality resulting from differences in personal ability or disposition to labor, but it should be governed by a single principle: *whoever is willing to contribute that amount of work of which he is capable, for the benefit of society, ought to be rewarded in an adequate manner, so as to enable him to improve his individual life and develop the essential characteristics by which individual life is defined.* This is the ideal which all of us ought to pursue and seek to progressively realize. Every change, every revolution that fails to bring us one step closer to this ideal, that does not produce a moral and social progress corresponding to the political progress achieved, that does not improve the material condition of the poorer classes, violates God's Design and reduces itself to the rank of a mere war among factions, each seeking illegitimate power based on falsehood and evil. But up to what point can we realize this goal at present? How and by what means can we reach this ideal point?

Some of the more timid among your well-wishers have sought the remedy in the morality of the workman himself. They have founded Savings-banks, and similar institutions, telling the workers: *bring your wages here; economize and abstain from every excess, whether of drink or otherwise; emancipate yourselves from poverty by privation.* Now, such advice is excellent, insofar as it tends to the moral improvement of the workman, without which all reforms are useless. But it neither solves the question of poverty itself, nor takes any account of social duty. . . .

Under present circumstances, Capital is the tyrant of labor. This is the crux of the entire social question. Economically speaking, society is at present composed of three classes; that is to say: of *Capitalists,* who possess the means of labor, as well as the land, factories, available money, and raw materials; of *Middlemen,* managers of labor and dealers, who constitute, or rather ought to constitute, the intellectual elite of society; and of *Workers,* who carry out all material labor. The first of these three classes is the sole master of the field; it is in a position to promote, accelerate, or delay labor, and to direct it toward certain special goals as it desires. The ownership of this class is comparatively settled, and its members are masters of their own time, as they are removed from the pressure of immediate want. Compared to this, the ownership of the second class is more uncertain; it depends on their intellect, their activities, and above all on circumstances, such as the greater or lesser development of economic competition and capital flows, which are influenced by events beyond their control. Finally, the workman owns nothing but his wages, which are determined prior to the actual execution of his work, and therefore without regard to the greater or lesser profits of the undertaking.

The limits within which the workers' wages vary are determined by the relation between supply and demand, that is, between the number of workers and capitalists. Now, as the first tends to increase, however slightly, more than the second, the general tendency of wages is of course to decrease. The workers also have virtually no control over their own time. Financial and political crises, the introduction of new machinery, the irregularities of production, and the unequal distribution of the working classes in certain places or in certain branches of activity, as well as several possible reasons for the sudden interruption of labor, deprive the workers of any control over their own future. Their choice is between either absolute starvation or the need to accept whatever terms are offered to them. Such a state of things, I repeat, indicates the seed of a moral evil that must be eradicated. . . .

You have emancipated yourselves from slavery and from serfdom. Why should you not also emancipate yourselves from the yoke of *wage labor*, and become free producers, as well as owners of everything you create? Why should you not accomplish, through your own peaceful efforts and with the assistance of society, the most beautiful Revolution that can be conceived? That Revolution would gradually abolish all class distinctions and tyrannical domination of one element over another, by accepting labor as the commercial basis of human intercourse, and the fruits of labor as the basis of property; and it would harmonize and unite all the country's children, by proclaiming one sole law of just equilibrium between production and consumption.

Owing principally to the teachings of the republican party, an awareness of social duty toward the working classes has gradually arisen in Europe over the last thirty years. Especially in France, certain schools emerged that were for the most part composed of well-meaning and sincere friends of the people, but that were nonetheless led astray by an excessive love of system-making and by individual vanity. These schools introduced certain exclusive and exaggerated doctrines under the name of *socialism*, doctrines that frequently stood in opposition to the wealth already acquired by other classes and were wholly unfeasible economically. By terrifying the multitude of smaller shopkeepers, and creating a sense of distrust among the different classes of citizens, they made any solution to the social question recede, and they split up the republican party into two separate camps. I cannot now pause to examine these different schools one by one. They were called *Saint-Simonianism, Fourierism, communism*, and so forth. Nearly all of them were based on ideas good in themselves, and long accepted by all those who believe in Progress, but they spoiled or nullified these ideas by the wrong and tyrannical methods through which they sought to apply them in practice. . . .

Among the essential elements of human life, such as Religion, Association, Liberty, and many others to which I have alluded in the course of this work, there is also *Property*.

The first principle and the origin of property lie in human nature itself. Property sustains the individual's material life, which he has a duty to maintain. The individual needs to transform the moral and intellectual world, through the medium of religion, science, and liberty; likewise, he needs to transform, improve, and govern the physical world, through the medium of material labor. And property indicates the fulfillment of that task; it represents the amount of labor by which the individual has transformed, developed, and increased the productive forces of nature.

The *principle* of property is therefore eternal, and you will find it recognized and protected throughout Humanity's entire existence. But the *means* by which it is governed have changed, as they are indeed subject to the law of progress, like every other manifestation of life. Hence all those who, finding property constituted and established in a certain manner, declare that manner to be inviolable and struggle against any effort to transform it, actually deny progress itself. One only needs to pick up two volumes of history, dealing with two different epochs, to find evidence of change in the constitution of property. And those who declare that property must be abolished, because at a given epoch they happened to find it ill-constituted, deny one of the elements of human nature. If they were to succeed, they would inevitably delay progress by mutilating life. But property would inevitably reappear shortly thereafter, and probably in a shape very similar to that it held at the time of its abolition.

Property is ill-constituted at the present day, because the source and origin of its actual distribution generally lies in conquest. In other words, property originated from the violence through which, in distant times, certain invading peoples or classes took control either of land or of the fruits of labor they did not rightly own. Furthermore, property is ill-constituted today, because the fruits of labor are not distributed between owners and workman in a just and equal proportion to the work actually done. Property is ill-constituted, because, while it confers on its possessor political and legislative rights denied to the workman, it tends to become the monopoly of the few, inaccessible to the many. And finally, property is ill-constituted, because the system of taxation is ill-constituted: it tends to preserve the wealth of the owners, while it oppresses the poorer classes, and thus renders any saving virtually impossible for the latter. But if, instead of correcting these errors and slowly modifying the constitution of property, you should seek to abolish it, you would suppress a source of wealth, of inspiration, and of activity, and you would act like the savage who cuts down the tree in order to gather its fruit.

We should not seek to abolish property just because at present it is the possession of the few; rather we must make it easier for the many to acquire it. We need to think again about what *justifies* property, and we should make sure that in the future it will be labor alone. We must lead society toward a much fairer ratio of remuneration between the owners, or capitalists, and the workmen. We must transform the tax system so as to fully exempt the basic necessities of life from taxation, and thus move toward an economy that gradually makes property accumulation possible for the workers. But in order to make all this possible, we first need to eliminate all political privileges now attached to property, and everybody must be allowed to participate in the work of legislation. All these things are both just and feasible. By educating yourselves and seriously organizing yourselves, you may achieve them. On the other hand, by demanding the abolition of property, you would demand something impossible; you would do injustice to those who have already acquired it through their own labor, and you would diminish production instead of increasing it.

Nevertheless, the abolition of individual property is the remedy proposed by many of the socialist systems of which I have spoken to you, and above all by communism. . . . The following is the general formula of communism: the property of every element of production, such as land, movable or immovable assets, instruments of labor, and so forth, is to be concentrated in the state. The state is to assign to each man his part of labor and his share of wealth, some say in absolute terms, others say according to his wants. But such a life, if it were indeed possible, would be the life of a beaver, and not of a man. Liberty, dignity, and individual conscience would all disappear under this centralized organization of production. The satisfaction of basic physical needs may be possible by such means, but intellectual and moral life would be entirely cancelled, and with it all beneficial emulation and competition, all free choice of labor, all liberty of association, all the joys of property—in short, everything that stimulates and urges man to production. Under such a system, the human family would be reduced to a mere human flock or herd. . . .

The remedy to your sufferings is not to be found in any theory that seeks to eliminate individual liberty, since the latter provides a vital stimulus to labor. Nor is it to be found in anything that tends to diminish capital, which is the source and instrument of labor and production. The remedy is to be found in *the union of labor and capital in the same hands*. All the *permanent* causes of your poverty will be removed, when society shall recognize no other distinction but the distinction between *producers* and *consumers;* or rather when every man shall be producer and consumer alike; and when the profits of labor, instead of being parceled out among all those *intermediates* (along the way from the capitalist to the retailer, the price of a product now often increases by 50 percent), shall be enjoyed entirely by those who actually perform the labor. Your future depends on your emancipation from the present tyranny of capital. . . .

Association of labor, and division of the fruits of labor—or rather of the profits resulting from the sale of its products—among the producers, in proportion to the amount and value of the work done by each, this is the social future we aim for. You were once slaves, then serfs, then hirelings. You just have to *want* it, and you can shortly become free producers and brothers through Association. But your Association has to be free and voluntary; organized according to certain principles by yourselves, by men who know, respect, and love each other; it cannot be imposed by the force of governmental authority, without any regard to individual ties and affections, and conceiving of men not as free and spontaneous individuals, but as mere numbers and machines for production. Hence you need to associate, but your Association is to be led according to principles of true republican brotherhood by your own delegates; it should not be subject to any arbitrary Hierarchy, ignorant of your individual wants and position, and you should be free to withdraw from it anytime, at your own discretion. . . .

But what about the necessary Capital? The capital by which any association is to be launched in the first place—where should it be obtained? It is a serious question, and I cannot here treat it in as much depth as I would like to. But I would like to briefly point out your own duty in this regard and that of others. The first source of capital lies in yourselves, in your own savings and your own spirit of sacrifice. I know the daunting position of too many of you. But there are some of you who, either because of many years of work without interruptions or because of its better pay, are now in a position to put something apart for this aim. If some eighteen or twenty of you were capable for this effort, you could put together the small sum necessary to start your own cooperative enterprise. Now, the awareness that you would be fulfilling a solemn duty, and thus entirely *deserve* your emancipation, should give you the necessary strength to move ahead with this.

I could name for you many Industrial Associations, now all well established and flourishing, which were begun by a few workmen with their savings of a penny a day. I might relate to you many stories of sacrifices heroically endured in France and elsewhere, by the first few workers who began such enterprises, and who now own considerable capital. There is indeed hardly any difficulty that cannot be overcome by a strong will, when supported by the consciousness of doing good. Almost all of you may contribute something to the small initial fund, either in the form of money, raw material, or actual labor. Through your consistently upright behavior, you could gain the esteem of your companions and other fellow citizens; they may then offer you small loans and decide to become shareholders, earning interest on their investment based on the profits of the enterprise.

In many branches of industry, the price of tools and raw material is small, and so the capital required for commencing work on your own could be collected or saved among yourselves, if only you resolutely determined to do so. It will also be much better for you to rely *entirely* on your own capital, acquired with your own sweat and from the credit you have gained through conscientious work. As the Nations that have achieved their liberty by shedding their own blood know best how to preserve it, so your associations will derive a better and more durable profit from any capital acquired through your own labor, carefulness, and savings. This is in the nature of things. . . .

7. CONCLUSION

The State—the government—is an institution that is only legitimate when based on a mission of Education and Progress, which is still not properly understood. The State has a solemn duty toward you, a duty that will be easily fulfilled once we have a really National Government, the government of a free and united people. There are a variety of means by which the government might help the people to solve the social question, without violent seizures and other interference with the wealth *previously acquired* by any of its citizens, and without further stimulating that immoral antagonism between classes that is fatal to the national welfare and is visibly delaying the progress of France today.

In what follows I would like to mention some possibilities for the Government to effectively help the workers: first, the Government could exercise a moral influence in favor of workers' Associations, by expressing public approval of their activities, by frequently discussing their fundamental principles in the House of Representatives, and by legalizing all those voluntary associations that have been properly constituted as suggested above. Second, it could improve public roads and other means of transport and communication and abolish all the other obstacles that now impede the free exchange of goods. Third, it could establish public depots and warehouses, where the workers' Associations could directly deliver their merchandise and be paid according to the market value of their products; this would allow the workers to pursue their affairs without the ruinous need of relying on immediate sales with a lower return. Fourth, the Government could offer concessions for the execution of necessary public works to the new Associations of laborers, on terms equal to those granted to individual capitalist entrepreneurs. Fifth, all judicial procedures could be simplified, given that justice is at present exceedingly costly and often inaccessible to the poor. Sixth, the sale and transfer of landed property could be made much easier from a legal point of view. Seventh, the tax system could be radically transformed, by substituting a single income tax for the present complex and expensive system of direct and indirect taxation. Up to a given amount of income, deemed *necessary* for the maintenance of *life*, all earnings should be exempt from any taxation. This would publicly sanction the principle of the *sacredness of human life*, as neither labor, nor progress, nor the fulfillment of duty are possible without life.

But there are further means by which the Government could help those in need: the secularization or confiscation of church property by the State, which is at present unthinkable but will inevitably happen in the future, when the State shall take over all educational functions from the church, will place a vast sum of wealth in the hands of the Nation. To this may be added the value of any unclaimed land; the profits of railways and other public enterprises, which should be administered by the State; the value of property now inherited by *collateral succession* beyond the fourth degree of kinship, which should revert to the State; and many other sources of wealth which it is unnecessary here to enumerate.

Suppose that all this mass of wealth and resources were accumulated in a National Fund, devoted to the intellectual and economic progress of the entire country. Why shouldn't a considerable portion of such a fund be employed (proper provisions being made to guard against its wasteful use) to offer *Credit*, at an interest rate of 1.5 or 2 percent, to the Voluntary Workers' Associations that have been constituted according to the aforementioned principles and that can give evidence of *morality* and *capacity*? This sum of capital could help to promote labor not just among the present generation, but also in the future, since it would operate on so vast a scale that it could easily sustain any likely occasional losses. The management of the Credit Fund should not be in the hands of either the Government or a National Central Bank, but of *local* Banks, administered by elective Municipal Councils, under the supervision of the Central Government.

These measures would not subtract anything from the actual wealth of any existing class, and they would not unduly enrich any single class through public funds, which should indeed be employed for the advantage and benefit of all. Instead, the suggested measures would make credit more widely available; they would increase and improve production, lead to a diminution of the interest rate, and entrust the progress of labor to the commitment and interest of the producers. The limited and ill-directed sum of wealth at present concentrated in a few hands would thus be replaced by a wealthy nation, fully in control of its own production and consumption.

Such, Italian Workmen, is your future. You may bring this future about more quickly. Establish your own country, as well as a truly popular Government, the representative of our collective life and mission. Organize yourselves in a vast popular party, so that your voice will be the voice of millions, and not merely that of a few individuals. Truth and justice will be on your side, and the nation will listen to you. But be warned! Listen to the words of a man who has been seriously studying the course of events in Europe over the last thirty years, and who has seen the most sacred enterprises fail at the very last moment due to the errors and immorality of their supporters: *you will never succeed except through your own improvement.* . . .

I have pointed out to you, to the best of my abilities, what your duties are, the most important being those owed to your Country. The improvement of your present condition can only result from your participation in the political life of the nation. Until you obtain the franchise, your wants and aspirations will never be truly represented. On the day in which you should follow the example of too many French socialists, and separate the *social* from the *political* question, saying: "*We will work out our own emancipation, regardless of the form of Government by which our Country is ruled*"—on that day you will have decreed the perpetuity of your own social servitude.

And in bidding you farewell, I will remind you of another duty not less solemn than that which binds you to achieve and preserve the freedom and unity of your Country. Your complete emancipation can only be established and secured through the triumph of a Principle—the principle of the Unity of the Human Family. At present, all women, constituting one-half of the Human Family, are by a singular contradiction declared to be unequal from a civil, political, and social point of view, and thus excluded from the great Unity. You who are seeking your own enfranchisement and emancipation in the name of a Religious Truth, you need to protest on every occasion and by every means against this negation of Unity. The *Emancipation of Women*, then, must be regarded by you as necessarily linked with the emancipation of the workingman. This will give to your endeavors the consecration of a Universal Truth.

PART 2

National Insurrection and Democratic Revolution

CHAPTER SIX

Rules for the Conduct of Guerrilla Bands (1832)

Guerrilla warfare can be seen as the first stage of a national war. Guerrilla bands should therefore be so organized as to prepare the way for, and facilitate by their action, the formation of a national army.

The general method of organization, the authorization of leaders, and the moral and political precepts regulating the conduct of the bands with regard to the country and to individuals should be under the superintendence of a Center of Action, whose duty it will be to ensure the greatest possible amount of uniformity even in their apparently most unconnected movements. The political mission of the bands is to constitute the armed apostolate of the insurrection. Every band should thus fully incarnate the national party's moral outlook.

The most rigorous discipline is at once a duty and a necessity among them. It is a sacred duty toward their country and a necessity for the bands themselves, since they could not long exist if their conduct were such as to deprive them of the people's sympathy. Respect for women, for property, for the rights of individuals, and for the crops should be their motto. Guerrilla bands are the precursors of the nation and should thus attempt to rouse the nation into insurrection. But they have no right to substitute themselves for the nation. To the nation alone belongs the right to declare its intentions and belief.

Toleration, a consequence of liberty of conscience, is among the first virtues of a republican. Our guerrilla bands are therefore bound to show respect for the churches and symbols of Catholicism, and to the priests so long as they maintain their neutrality. The right of judging those guilty of past misdeeds belongs to the nation alone. The bands may not usurp this right. Any vengeance in the name of the country must not be entrusted to individuals, whoever they may be. A commission—elected by the soldiers and presided over by the captain—will be chosen to watch over the aforementioned rules and maintain their inviolability. The names of guerrilla soldiers who have been either punished or expelled for disobedience to any of those rules will be forwarded by the captain to the Center of Action for appropriate publication.

The captain of each band is responsible to the Center of Action for the conduct of his men. Any captain guilty of dishonorable conduct will be deprived of his commission by the Center of Action, and, if necessary, punished in public. When repeated complaints have been made of the collective misconduct of any band, proving it unworthy to represent the national cause, it will be immediately disbanded by the Center of Action. Should it disobey the command of the Center of Action, it will be regarded from that time onward as a mere horde of men without flag or mission.

Every band has the right to take measures for its own safety and preservation, as well as for promoting the national insurrection. All acts of aggression or resistance, all information given to the enemy by the inhabitants of the country, and all acts of hostility shown to individual Italians will be speedily and severely punished by the bands.

The bands have a right to sustain themselves, and it is their duty to increase the forces of the insurrection by adding to the means at the disposal of the national party. For their subsistence, the bands will generally rely on booty taken from the enemy, treasure seized from the government, forced contributions imposed on those of the wealthy notoriously adverse to the national cause, and supplies demanded from the provinces through which they pass. All seized booty is the collective property of the band. It will be distributed among the officers and soldiers as equally as circumstances permit, according to the regulations democratically agreed on by the bands themselves.

All seized governmental funds become the national party's property. The captain will be responsible for them. He will leave a document with the party official in custody of those funds, stating the amount. With regard to forced contributions, the captain will obey any orders given by the Center of Action. Demands and requisitions of food supplies should be made as rarely as possible, and they ought to be paid for whenever the band has the means to do so. When it has no such means, the captain or officer in command making the requisition will sign an acknowledgment of the amount of food received and will leave it with the civil authorities of the place. By this means the nation will be enabled, once the war is over, to note the contributions of each locality.

Whatever monies the captain can dispense with without injury to his band, he will forward to the Center of Action. The captain will keep an exact account of all the monetary transactions of his band. A copy of this account will be audited by a civil commissioner, to be employed in all possible cases by the Center of Action, whose duty it will be to watch over the observance of the aforementioned rules.

As a general principle, the bands will seek to foster insurrection in large towns and cities, while being cautious to prevent the enemy's vengeance on small localities. Hence, when passing through small and unarmed localities, the captain will rather seek to repress than promote any revolutionary activism among the inhabitants. Any patriots who are able and willing to join the bands will enroll as individuals and quit the locality.

Every band will aim to increase its numbers by admitting every possible element into its ranks. But as soon as the band shall have reached the maximum number indicated by the Center of Action as constituting a company in the future national army, all fresh recruits will be regarded as forming the nucleus of a new band.

The captains of the first guerrilla bands will be naturally either chosen or at least confirmed by the Center of Action. Any losses among the officer corps due to war will be replaced according to the principle of universal suffrage, exercised progressively from the ranks up to the captain. This same principle also means that the captain of any new band, formed out of the superabundance of recruits joining an already existing band, will be chosen by the captain and officers next in rank belonging to the existing band. The organization of each separate band—in view to the formation of a company within the future national army—shall in no way interfere with the practical character of their operations as guerrilla bands.

In order to increase their ability to sustain themselves without serious inconvenience to the country, and to enable them more rapidly to disband or conceal themselves, the bands will be divided into small bodies of twenty-five to fifty men. Those will act as detachments under the orders of a single commander, within the territory assigned to his operations.

The uniform of the bands will be a shirt or *blouse*. During the first period of the war they should perhaps better avoid all uniform and content themselves with the national cockade. The latter can be easily thrown away or hidden whenever it is necessary to abruptly disband or disappear. A ribbon—or another distinctive mark not visible at a distance—will be worn by the officers in action. If the blouse is going to be adopted, its color should be the same for the officers and the ranks.

The essential weapons are a musket or rifle with a bayonet, and a dagger. Each soldier will carry his cartouche box, a case containing bread and spirits, a thin but strong cord, a few nails, and if possible, a light axe. The clothes worn by the soldiers should be made so as to allow for rapidity of movement, and of a shape that won't betray them in case of dispersion.

Any signals and commands will be sounded by a horn or trumpet. The following are the most important movements, which the bands must first be taught to distinguish: (1) frontal assault; (2) assault on the right; (3) on the left; (4) combined; (5) riflemen's assault; (6) reassembling; (7) retreat. The noncommissioned officers will employ all leisure moments to drill their men in the few movements most necessary in guerrilla warfare, teaching them to acquire rapidity in loading and firing, and in dispersing and reassembling.

The bands' principal aim will be to constantly damage and molest the enemy troops with the least possible exposure or danger to themselves; destroy the enemy soldiers' ammunition and supplies; shake their confidence and discipline; and reduce them to such a condition as to secure their defeat, so soon as the regular revolutionary army or the united bands are able to give them battle. The means to attain this aim are the following: to attack the enemy as frequently as possible in the flank or rear; to surprise small detachments, escorts, outposts, and stragglers; to seize on their convoys of provisions, ammunition, or money; to interrupt their communications and correspondence, by lying in wait for their couriers, destroying the roads, bridges, fords, etc.; to continually break in on their hours of refreshment and sleep, and seize their generals and superior officers, and so on.

Guerrilla war is a war of judicious daring and audacity, movement, and *espionage*. The captain of a guerrilla band must be able to calculate and plan coolly, execute boldly, march unweariedly, retire rapidly, and keep himself thoroughly informed about the enemy's movements.

In guerrilla war, as in regular warfare, it is crucial to preserve the means of communication. The means of contact and communication among the various detachments of each band, and between the different bands acting in the same province, must be jealously maintained, so as to ensure simultaneous action at the decisive moment. The greatest merit in the commander of regular troops is to know when to fight and conquer; the greatest merit of the guerrilla chief is to contrive constantly to attack, do mischief, and retire. A band that is surrounded is lost. Therefore, the possibility of retreat must always be kept open. Also, no captain will ever command an assault without first establishing a point of reunion for his men in case of dispersion.

The best time for attacking the enemy is at night, during refreshment, or when he is tired after a long march. Unless circumstances compel the adoption of a different method, the best mode of attack is for the bands to spread their forces like sharpshooters. The greater the extension of the ground they occupy, the less dangerous will be the enemy's fire. Any terrain abounding in hedges, forests, or broken ground affords natural entrenchments for guerrilla bands. The mountains are their fortresses. Their movements must be rapid, constant, and unexpected. The enemy must always be kept in ignorance concerning them. From time to time the bands will hide in inaccessible positions, or temporarily disband, so that the enemy may lose their trace. . . . The band must be ready to assault when the enemy believes them to be retiring, and to retire when the enemy is prepared to resist their attack. The captain should constantly study three things in great detail: the nature of the territory where he will have to operate; the disposition and special abilities of each of his men; the organization, tactics, and numbers of the enemy's forces.

Absolute secrecy must be systematically observed in all things, unless it is essential that something be made public. Select as your zone of operations the neighborhood from which the majority of your men originate and do not abandon it unless compelled. Knowledge of the land, and friendly relationship between the soldiers and the inhabitants, are advantages of vital importance.

It is indispensable for each band to have a certain number of stationary members distributed over the various localities comprised in its zone of operations. These members, who should be unknown to all except the captain and his messengers, will function both as a reserve in case of a general operation and as a means of obtaining information. It will be their business to spy on the enemy's movements, its forces, plans, supplies, and scouts; and on the habits, places of resort, and lodgings of the more important officers. In addition, they will have to note the sympathies of the inhabitants in the various localities, the supplies they are able to furnish, etc.; and they should transmit minute details of such matters to the captain of the band. The captain will carefully organize these auxiliaries and be in charge of communications with them.

The captain ought to transmit his orders verbally. Written orders should always be avoided if possible. He should always try to obtain information from at least two different sources, so as to improve its reliability. He should distrust all information received from any spies not his own, or from deserters from the enemy. Such information is often deceptive.

Try to make the peasants your friends; it is at once your highest duty and your interest to do so.

Your bands will do the greatest damage to the enemy by directing their attacks against his officers, horses, and provisions. Spy on your enemy's convoys. Where you have determined to attack one, send some of your men ahead to interrupt the road at a given point with fallen trees or otherwise, so as to delay his advance and create disorder and confusion in the escort. Choose the hour of twilight if possible, or when the soldiers are fatigued by a long march, or passing a bridge, a gorge, or wood.

Let the first elements of the enemy troop walk past; then make a feigned attack on a given point with a small portion of your force. Strike the first blows at the first horses of the first wagon, always attacking on the side opposite to that from where assistance may arrive. Meanwhile, you will have concentrated the mass of your men on the center of the enemy contingent. Always keep back part of your band as a reserve.

The same rules must be observed in ambushes and surprise assaults while the enemy is engaged in passing a ford. Never attack until part of the enemy troops have passed the ambush, or entered the gorge, street, or ford. Fire a volley at the enemy's flank, and then throw yourselves on his ranks. Let your action be so rapid as to leave them no time for reflection. As soon as they recover and reorganize themselves, retreat.

Sometimes you may be compelled to retire fighting, in front of the enemy. This should be avoided whenever possible. But when it happens, you should divide your bands into smaller groups, to be kept at a distance of two musket shots from each other. They should be so disposed as to present a slanting front to the enemy. Let each group fire as soon as the enemy is within range. Then let it retire, running by the shortest path to an equal distance behind the next line, and so on from position to position, from obstacle to obstacle.

Avoid engaging in open country. Never pass a gorge or defile without being master or at least secure of the heights. Always remember that both for yourselves and for the enemy, every mountain has some practicable pass.

Attempt to deceive the enemy as to the position you have taken up and the direction in which you intend to advance. This can be done by lighting fires in an opposite direction, by bugle calls, and by false information given by men really your own but unsuspected by the enemy.

Teach your men not to be the first to fire when they find themselves facing the enemy's riflemen. Rather, they should threaten the enemy soldiers and compel them to fire, holding back their own fire until they see the flash. . . .

The numbers of the enemy may be calculated at a distance by the sound produced by their march. As a general rule, the more uniform the noise of their march, the greater the number of troops. The dust raised will be more or less according to the dryness of the ground and to the state of the wind. Much may be learned by listening with the ear close to the ground, and it does not require much practice. One fire at night generally represents twelve men, but the fires are sometimes multiplied for the purpose of deception.

Each of our bands should try to choose a zone of operations lying somewhere between the enemy's encampment and their own base.

CHAPTER SEVEN

Toward a Holy Alliance of the Peoples (1849)

I.

Napoleon had fallen. The tide set in motion by the French Revolution had been stopped for the time being.[1] Twenty-two years of war had worn out Europe, when the long-desired peace finally arrived. Those who brought it were praised, no matter who they were. Blessed by victory, the old dynasties resumed their interrupted domination. The Napoleonic rulers were dispersed into exile; and the echo of the rifle shots that killed Murat in Naples warned them against any attempt to regain the thrones they had once taken by force and which they had now lost forever.[2] Religion blessed the restoration: altar and throne supported each other, and the dualism of the Christian age seemed to fade into a pact of mutual love.

Yet the victorious kings were restless and tormented as if by a presentiment. They gathered together in council and devised new methods to protect themselves against a future storm, for which there were hardly any signs at the time. Usually, victory tends to weaken the bond between former allies in battle; yet in this case it suggested to them the necessity of a stronger bond. Hence they managed to stifle all competition and mistrust among themselves, in spite of their mutual jealousies and suspicions, and they set up a common force against an unknown enemy. This common force was established with the acts of June 9, September 25, and November 20, 1815.[3]

The Holy Alliance initiated a new policy in God's desecrated name. The masters of the world had united against the future. One hundred and seventy-seven years earlier, the Treaty of Westphalia had given the force of law to a system of equilibrium or, as the diplomats say, a *balance of power* that offered some hope of assistance in case of oppression. Now the strong were telling the strong: *let us join together to prevent any of*

---

[1] Original title: "La santa alleanza dei popoli."

[2] Joachim Murat (1767–1815), officer in the French revolutionary army, had been appointed king of Naples in 1808 after Napoleon's conquest. After Napoleon's fall in 1815, Murat was executed and the Neapolitan throne returned to its former Bourbon rulers.

[3] Those dates mark, respectively, the closure of the Congress of Vienna; the founding of the "Holy Alliance" among the rulers of Austria, Prussia, and Russia; and the signing of the second Paris treaty after Napoleon's ultimate defeat.

the weak from rebelling against the yoke that we impose on them. Should any nonetheless rebel, we will crush them. The Holy Alliance agreement itself had already foreshadowed a policy of intervention against the progressive principle. But this policy was further and more clearly developed at two subsequent congresses that were held in Verona and Ljubljana in 1821. Ever since, from the French intervention in Spain in 1823 to the intervention of three monarchies and one republic against Rome in 1849, wherever a people have risen up to improve their own conditions, or wherever an oppressed or dismembered nation has attempted to regain control over its own borders and to freely determine its own future, the *Holy Alliance* has descended to prevent progress and protect the oppressors.

The Vienna agreement of 1815 taught Europe a profound lesson, which those who fight for democracy have not yet understood. The powers that signed the Vienna agreement foresaw the future. They anticipated who would be the new adversary to rise up against their dominion once Europe had recovered from the exhaustion of war: the *people*, galvanized by the idea of *nationality*. Napoleon had in fact been brought down not so much by the brute force that the kings had marshaled against him, but by the strength of a popular idea; by an outburst of the idea of nationality, which he had offended with his arrogance. Paradoxically the kings thus understood very well what the common folk, terror-struck by the experience of almost a million bayonets commanded by the allied kings, failed to comprehend.

The monarchs knew that the first signs of the catastrophe that eventually unfolded at Waterloo had already emerged several years earlier, with the popular insurrection in Spain. They knew that the Spanish war of 1808, the attempts at rebellion in Calabria and elsewhere in Italy, and the German movements of 1813, had awakened to conscious existence and shaped a thought that told the different peoples: *you are the true masters of your native soil; you are the sole interpreters of your own law of life.* And the monarchs understood that this thought would have taken hold and developed further. They understood that once the peoples had dared to rise up against Napoleon, they would not pull back in the face of princes inferior to him in power and genius. The Treaty of 1815, unlike the leagues formed in 1793 against the French Revolution, was directed against all of Europe, and it was signed in the hour of victory. It acknowledged for the first time a powerful element previously unnoticed by most; it was a forced tribute paid to the notion of solidarity among nations and the unity of European life. It was a false and tyrannical application of a true *principle*, the principle of association, which is the soul of our belief and reveals that there is a collective dimension to the life of Humanity. Under those circumstances, we were called to protest vigorously and give that principle its true application, founded not on the arbitrary privilege of a few but on the duty and right of all. It was the European democrats' role to boldly raise a flag bearing the inscription *God and the Peoples* and hold it high against the flag on which the men of 1815 had written *God and the princes.*

II.

The presentiment of the princes turned out to be correct. The *people* rose up, and they rose up not only in France but almost everywhere in Europe, with a power and vigor proportional to the social and political progress to be made. At first the people rose up supporting the wealthier classes, which had promised to fight their same battle—everyone's battle. But then the people were disappointed by those wealthier men who, as soon as they had secured their *own* rights, suddenly became the enemies of the masses. Hence the people's action became more direct and their demands more explicit. But at the same time the people became divided, as they shifted back and forth between different programs and different schools of thought, some of which could have been outright dangerous but for their absurdity. In their inexperience, the people were guided more by instinct than by carefully developed plans. Sometimes, they were led astray by their excessive reliance on little-known leaders; on other occasions they had no trust whatsoever in some really good men. Hence they fell and they rose, only to fall again. The forces they wasted in the pursuit of illusions would have been sufficient to unmake and then remake again the entire world. The amount of pure and precious blood they shed would have sufficed to found a religion from scratch. But even repeated errors and defeats can only extinguish factions, not entire peoples. Nations do not die; instead they are transformed. This prophetic stirring of the multitudes has continued to gain ground like a rising tide. Urged by God himself, humanity is moving toward a new goal and is further developing its faculties by means of association. This movement becomes larger and deeper year after year. So today our victory is certain, regardless of how others are going to react. Princely alliances, Papal tricks and persecutions can henceforth only delay our victory and make it bloodier; but no human power can take it away from us.

Our victory is certain. I declare this with profound conviction, here from exile, and precisely when the monarchical reaction seems most insolently secure.[4] You, the monarchs, may be enjoying a short hour of triumph, but does it really matter? You are availing yourselves of every trick; you are turning to your advantage all the residual jealousies and

---

[4]After the fall of the Roman Republic in 1849, Mazzini had again fled into exile. He probably wrote this piece in Geneva, before returning to London in 1851.

prejudices that still remain among different peoples, and which are a source of selfishness, mistrust, and corruption; and by concentrating all your forces, you have temporarily repressed our movements and restored the old order of things. But you cannot restore anyone's faith in that order. Now, do you think you can maintain it for long with brute force alone, given that all faith in it has become extinguished? Just compare the Italian movements of the past two years with those of twenty-eight or even eighteen years ago; compare the recent, truly popular insurrections in Sicily and Lombardy with the movements of 1820 and 1821, which were led by the aristocracy and the military. Or compare the resistance put up in Venice, Bologna, and Rome with the flights and capitulations of 1831. Today our youth has learned to die honorably; therefore Italy will live. Through the cunning of Louis Philippe you overcame the constitutionalist insurrection of 1830; but we, the people, have answered you with the republican insurrection of 1848. You won in Galicia, availing yourselves of atrocious deceits; and we answered with insurrection in Hungary. Perhaps the Slavic peoples will answer shortly, too. And don't forget the popular uprisings in the German states and in Vienna. Millions of workers today are asking for bread and employment; meanwhile their governments are drained by the costs of espionage and corruption, by the burden of their standing armies, and by constant internecine strife. Listen, monarchs: your despotic leadership is threatened and undermined at every turn. So do you plan to hold Europe in a state of siege forever?

Europe's princes are blinded by their thirst for power and the desire to cling to it for even just a few additional days. But today no one except the princes themselves can believe that sixty years of stubborn fighting can be the work of only a sect or faction, or that the peoples won't actually win, when they have been willing to suffer so much without becoming discouraged. Only the princes themselves can believe that this war, which is currently going through a moment of calm, will not reignite itself and become more ferocious until the peoples finally achieve their goal. A grave responsibility weighs on those men who out of an inexplicable sense of fear either oppose the growing movement of the multitudes or remain passive and look on while their brothers fight. They ought to remember that Solon lambasted as shameful all those who refused to take sides in a quarrel. Moreover, this is not just a quarrel but a true revolution. Those who are openly hostile to our movement or give us at best lukewarm support should know that they will only prolong the crisis with all its attendant damage. It is apparent that a growing sense of anger and a desire for vengeance have been accumulating in the hearts of the multitude, and the consequences could be as terrible as their patience has been long.

The governments have tried everything from seducing the masses to scaring them—all in vain. God sides with the peoples; the march of ideas is moving forward. Formerly widespread beliefs in castes and human inequality have been shattered; the outcasts have raised their head and dared to stare their masters in the face without fear. From that moment onward the question had been decided. Now, if you, who have been skeptical or afraid so far, choose to join us and unite around the flag of brotherly love that the best among us have already raised, you can improve the social conditions of millions; you can also moderate their demands and actually lead them along the path suggested by history. But don't fool yourselves into believing that you can actually stop the people.

III.

Our victory is foreordained. Nevertheless, for the time being we have been vanquished and lie overthrown. Thousands of mothers weep for their sons lost on the battlefields, in the prisons, and on the scaffolds. Thousands of exiles roam through different lands, suffering from physical deprivation and discouraged in their souls. Now, if we rise up again without taking to heart the lessons of the past, quite inevitably thousands of new martyrs and new exiles will be added to their number. The lessons of the past can be summed up in a single word: *union*. What we need are, first, sincere and active unions at the domestic level in different countries that will bring together all the sons of a given land who share the same democratic faith; and second, a single union of all the European peoples who are striving toward the same goal.

The history of the popular uprisings that took place over the past two years proves one vital *fact*: we are stronger than our oppressors in every regard and in every European land. In Italy, Germany, and Hungary the monarchic governments were unable to stand up to the people on their own; so they relied on the help of others and were propped up by foreign Intervention. Two insights result from this fact: first, our work is truly the work and will of the people; and second, when we rise up simultaneously in *every* country where our movement is currently active, we will win. Foreign intervention will then become impossible.

IV.

We need to establish a Holy Alliance of the Peoples and oppose it to the existing league of princes. We need to set the *foundations* for democracy. Today we have various hints of such an alliance and some instinctive striving toward it; but we are still far from having actually established it. We have millions of individual democrats; we have several democratic schools of thought and small associations, but we still have no actual democracy. The reasons for our lack of success thus far are the following: all those popular aspirations are today without a common symbol; there are millions of dissatisfied individuals without a united center to inspire them; there is no organizing principle and no coordination among their efforts. Hence everyone rallies around their own different version of the same great banner. We are led astray by what appears to be an infinite number of possible solutions to the social problem, which are in fact all premature. And we remain intolerant and distrustful of one another, although we subscribe to a common program that exhorts us to mutual tolerance and love. In short, we are wasting our many efforts in a hundred different directions, while we could quite easily change the fortunes of Europe if only we joined our forces.

The peoples have been rising up one at a time, depending on their own specific circumstances and their suffering. They have been fighting alone and thus usually fell alone, often dishonored and at best strangely admired like doomed gladiators in a circus. Their brothers abroad have mourned them but always stopped short of actively coming to their aid. Sixty years have gone by since we first launched our struggle in 1789; and thirty-four years have passed since our enemies formed their own alliance in 1815. Yet today we are still missing a solid bond of brotherhood among the peoples, and worst of all we lack a common plan. Our faith requires that we establish a new type of *association* as the fundamental mark of our epoch and do away with the old and fatal *individualism*. But to be honest, we have not gone very far toward establishing such an association.

There is no doubt that the individual is sacred and constitutes a crucial element of all progress. Yet the individual is called on to enter into a harmonious social relationship with his fellow human beings. Our main problem today is that the individual continues to lack any meaningful social disposition, to such an extent that actually hinders our movement and undermines the coordination of our efforts toward the common goal. Let us not forget that we need to continue to fight; we are an army striving for victory and a church of believers who have to accomplish their Duty. So for the time being, we must develop the virtues of the soldier above anything else; the virtues of the free citizen will follow later.

There is a widespread opinion that to establish a strong association and unite our efforts, we first ought to develop a complete program with a detailed outline of our political goals for the future. Many use this argument merely as a pretext to vent their disagreements; but others sincerely believe that the absence of a common program is what actually causes all disagreements and the utter lack of discipline among ourselves. They swear by one or another of the abstract systems of social and political organization developed by the philosophers, and as a consequence they remain disconnected from the great popular movement toward democracy. There is another quite widespread opinion, which is again deployed as a pretext by some and sincerely held by others: it is the fear that any closely knit association may cancel out or at least reduce the free inspiration of individuals.

I want to remind those who share the latter opinion of two things: first, associations were indeed often tyrannical in the past, when their goals and their means were kept secret and their leaders operated underground. Back then those who had been formally initiated—under mysterious and often scary circumstances—were to swear allegiance not to a principled agreement but instead to individual leaders.[5] Today this has become impossible: any veil of secrecy has been abandoned; our goal is publicly known, and the same can be said for our doctrine and the names of our leaders. Everybody among our fellow associates is free to disagree with our internal hierarchy and its decisions; and everybody is free to withdraw, should any of those decisions become incompatible with the dictates of one's conscience. The second thing I would like to remind those who still remain skeptical of association is that by remaining isolated, men can never become entirely free. Left to their own devices, individuals can indeed hardly secure any amount of freedom at all. Hence to be blunt, the choice today is between either some very limited constraints on individual liberty that would result from freely accepted rules of association and participation in a popular movement, or the heavy chains of a forcibly imposed, foreign or domestic servitude.

So long as men remain isolated, our brothers will continue to be hanged and their women tortured, while our children are corrupted by a tyrannical, superstitious, and unequal education. Those who remain aloof and disconnected from the battles for their country sacrifice the very possibility of achieving any good, in the name of the putative independence of the individual; they deliberately condemn themselves to the impotence of egoism. One should not forget that while in the ancient world, several disconnected philosophers wrote books that are now largely lost, the first Christians bonded together by accepting a common religious hierarchy and thus were able to remake the world.

[5]Mazzini seems to have in mind the freemasonry, as well as the *Carbonari* clandestine association that organized political resistance in Italy in the early nineteenth century. He disliked both, due to their secrecy and their distance from the popular masses.

But let me briefly come back to the first group of critics I mentioned—those who believe that our lack of a full-fledged and detailed program is a cause of divisions and quarrels among ourselves. I believe that they are equally wrong in their analysis and actually quite narrow-minded. Our republican faith is very strong, and our beliefs regarding the future of our country, as well as of humanity as a whole, are deeply rooted in our studies and experience. Based on this, our goal is not simply to destroy but rather to build something entirely new. So of course, we believe that nobody has the right to call on a people to rise up without first explaining why this should be done and for what purpose. We have always been careful to lay out the moral principles from which we derive our right and our duty to act. We have explained at length the problem we aim to resolve, as well as the paths that ought to be followed to facilitate the pursuit of our goal. But beyond this, we believe that it is for the people themselves, with their collective wisdom and the force of their intuition that have been sharpened by the experience of great insurrections, to resolve the problem at hand. To put it differently: the people themselves ought to erect the specific institutional structure that will allow future generations to benefit from peace and development for many centuries to come. The principle itself has long been revealed; it is now high time to move toward its practical implementation. The "people" to which we so frequently refer is not just an empty concept, but rather the expression of a philosophical and religious idea; it is the *sacred word* of the future. Therefore, I believe that all those social and political doctrines that move beyond the sphere of the general *ideal* and pretend to clarify all the *practical* implications of the principle for a given society based on some absolute benchmark are inevitably incomplete and wanting in several regards.

I don't say all this out of a blind veneration for universal suffrage. Universal suffrage can indeed be an uncertain and sterile method if it does not serve to interpret an accepted Pact of Association and is not supported by a truly national education. If I have insisted on the need for the people to apply the principle themselves, it is because the secret of a given epoch can be revealed only through the progressive enlightenment of the human spirit, raised to its fullest development by a people of believers and by the perfect agreement among all human faculties. The various social systems that are being advocated today have been largely devised by single individuals, who in long and solitary studies have reflected on how human nature became servile, sluggish, and corrupt as a result of oppression. But nobody can fully understand human *life* and devise norms that ought to guide it without *living* a life of action as well as one of thought—through the heart as well as the mind, with love and not just meditation. Individuals who experience great events become themselves great. Hence any political philosopher will be able to learn more about the beliefs and abilities of a people from the embrace of a common man who has fearlessly confronted some great danger, or from the enthusiastic cry of a multitude gathered together in mutual affection, than from ten years of studies in the silence of an ivory tower.

We do not need a full-fledged program of the future in order to understand each other and come together as brothers, to join our forces in a large association: in short, to organize democracy into an army. What we ought to do instead is to rely on the foundations that are already laid and agreed on to establish a pact, to foster a more general awareness of our goals, and to join our forces with the goal of overthrowing all remaining obstacles to the free development of the peoples. In the meantime, every man and every league of scholars may well draw on their studies and the principles suggested by their intellect to work out an ultimate solution to our problems.

V.

The most important among these foundations that have already been laid for future progress is the concept of Nationality. In recent years there has been an increasingly clear tendency for the progressive movement in Europe to distance itself from the uncertain and dangerous *cosmopolitanism* that characterized the second half of the eighteenth century, and to rally instead around the flag of nationality. It could not have been otherwise. In our century the idea of a collective and progressive life of the entire human species, which was first affirmed by Dante, has finally become accepted by all the greatest minds after long historical and philosophical studies. It is now generally recognized that *humanity* ought to be the supreme beneficiary of every effort and of every advance; but the importance of the *nation* has been steadily growing as well—indeed it is now increasingly thought of as an intermediary between humanity and the *individual*.

The individual needs to be supported in his humanitarian efforts by the collective force of the millions who share his same customs, language, tendencies, and traditions. Left to himself, he would feel overwhelmed and quickly fall back into the egoistic pursuit of his *own* narrow good. The ultimate and disastrous result of cosmopolitanism as a philosophical doctrine has been exactly such a self-centered egoism. It is no accident that the primary axiom of its founders was the absurd and immoral "ubi bene ibi patria" [where you find your own good there is your country]. The idea of nationality emerged at the right time: it multiplied the forces of the individual and crucially illustrated how each man's efforts and sacrifice can benefit humanity as a whole.

Just as without the organization and separation of labor there can be no efficient production, so without independent Countries there can be no progress of Humanity as a whole. Just as citizens are the individual components of the nation, so nations are the individual components of humanity. Just as every person lives a twofold life, one inward bound and one outward oriented and relational, so does every nation. The citizens of a nation ought to make it prosperous and strong through the exercise of their various faculties. Likewise, every nation ought to pursue a special mission according to its abilities, thus carrying out its share of the work needed for the development and progressive growth of humanity. Country and Humanity are therefore equally sacred. If we were to forget about humanity, we would be left without an ultimate goal; if we were to erase the nation, as some appear to desire, we would suppress the instrument by which to achieve that goal. In other words, the country is a necessary pivot for the lever that needs to work for the benefit of humanity.

A new epoch has begun: there is an undeniable trend toward the restructuring of Europe into a certain number of States, approximately equal in size and population, according to the different national vocations that are present today. These states, which have remained divided, hostile, and jealous of one another so long as their national banner merely represented the narrow interests of a dynasty or caste, will gradually become more and more intimately associated through the medium of democracy. The nations will be sisters. Free and independent in the choice of the means by which to contribute to the common goal and in the organization of their domestic affairs, they will gradually unite around a common faith, and they will enter a common pact to regulate all matters related to their international life. The future Europe of peoples will be united through a new type of federation, which will avoid both the anarchy of absolute independence and the tyrannical centralization that results from conquest.

VI.

Everyone who believes in progress and in the collective life of humanity will agree with what I wrote above. But our agreement goes much beyond that. Indeed, we all share the following articles of faith: first, there is a providential law of progress, which God has given to humanity together with the necessary forces for its fulfillment; second, association is the means of this fulfillment; and third, the harmonic development of all the moral, intellectual, and physical faculties of mankind is the law's ultimate goal. We all believe in the people as the sole and continuous interpreter of this law. And we all declare the old monarchical authority to be dead forever. For these reasons, we do not allow that one or several individuals be entrusted with the government of humanity or of single nations on the basis of chance, privilege, or hereditary succession. Instead we want the best of us, that is, the most magnanimous and the most intelligent, to guide us in our journey. We want our leaders to be recognized and accepted as such by a popular vote. That will make it possible to replace today's struggle with a relationship of harmony and trust among the governors and the governed. Hence the republic is the logical form of democracy.

We seek to improve human beings morally, so that they can increasingly raise themselves toward the *ideal* pointed out by universal reason and by God himself. We want people to love each other and to develop the internal drive needed to translate love into action. To facilitate this process we want to educate people, and our goal is to ensure that each person can be educated locally. In addition, given that education is impossible under conditions of abject misery and more generally of social inequality, we want to fight both misery and inequality. All inequality is morally reprehensible, except for inequality of talent, which is God-given, and inequality in the performance of good and praiseworthy deeds. As for outright misery, it can never be justified except when it is the result of personal guilt, in which case it is usually deserved. The individual has a duty to work for society. But in exchange society ought to sustain both the individual's body and soul, and it ought to provide him with education and the necessary tools for his labor.

We believe that both the individual and society are sacred. We do not intend to cancel out the former for the presumed benefit of the latter, which would result in a collective tyranny. Nor do we want to suggest that the individual can fulfill his rights outside of society, which would be a recipe for perpetual anarchy. Instead, we seek to harmoniously balance the achievements of individual liberty and those of association. We believe that life is a mission: our goal is to improve both the nation and humanity; by improving the nation we hope to contribute to the improvement of humanity. But each individual should be free to choose how he wants to contribute to this mission, according to his own particular abilities.

Family, country, property, and religion: we believe that they are all sacred and inviolable in their essence; they are the harbingers of true democracy. They are the perpetual elements of human activity and life.

But above anything else we believe in the sacredness of *progress*, which constitutes the primary element and timeless law of life. None of the elements I have just mentioned can or indeed should be abolished. Instead, they all need to be gradually improved to better serve our purpose. History should be our teacher in this regard, and historical experience suggests that human progress is indeed inevitable. . . .

VII.

There is hardly anybody among the supporters of democracy in Europe today who does not agree with the aforementioned beliefs. There is hardly any leading school of thought today that would openly refuse to submit the adoption of its own system and program to a free popular vote. So given this widespread belief in democracy, why shouldn't the inhabitants of different towns and districts come together in a brotherly bond? Meanwhile we could leave it to time and individual efforts to work out how general democratic principles shall be applied to particular contexts and circumstances. Each people should be left free to develop the specific details of its social edifice.

We need to join together and *actually establish* a fraternal bond with other supporters of democracy across the European continent. We cannot just rely on random popular aspirations, or on occasional manifestations of sympathy and support by other peoples in the face of unforeseen events. It is time to establish regular and constant relations, which ought to be directed from a single center by men known for their virtue, energy, and firmness. We need to coordinate the activities of all Europeans, but also Americans, who fight and suffer for the sacred cause of liberty and who pursue our same *ideal*. We need to ally ourselves with all those who subscribe to the following formula: *one sole master, God; one sole law, progress; one sole interpreter of that law on earth, the people, with virtue and reason as their guides.*

So far we have merely fought a guerrilla war; it is now time to organize a regular army and start a war of the masses. Democracy will not take hold in Europe and transform the continent unless it first becomes organized at the level of States and national governments. Democratically organized states will constitute the basic core of a Europe of the peoples; a concrete and collective manifestation of the general idea that will rule the future. We cannot at this time fully erect the Temple of our faith; the peoples will erect it when the time is ripe. But we can and indeed we ought to found a Church of pioneers.

I hope that we will one day establish a large international democratic association. It would be divided into different sections, with its members representing all the different human activities and professions. All those who believe in our new Era and share the widely held principles mentioned above would thus become part of a common political structure. The association would marshal its members' different inclinations and individual abilities, so as to direct their efforts according to a general plan. The association would be led by a supreme international Council, composed of a few European and American men highly respected for their knowledge, virtue, and reason, as well as for the sacrifices bravely endured for the sake of our common cause. This Council would be able to make short, collective statements to the world. At the same time there would be a series of national Councils, composed of men more closely united by a bond of brotherhood and common origin. In order to secure the coherence of our project, each national Council would be presided over by that nation's leading representative on the supreme international Council. The supreme Council would clarify and express the peoples' general mission. Meanwhile the national Councils would coherently express the special mission of each nation. To put it differently: the first—the supreme Council—would represent the *principle* in virtue of which humanity is now so restless and seeks a new synthesis; it would also work out some guidelines for humanity's future development. The second—the national Councils— would represent the application of that principle among the various peoples; they would also identify the various means through which each nation could contribute to achieving the common goal. Under the impulse and guidance of such a twofold organization, the efforts of all associated members would begin to fall into a coordinated pattern, both in terms of their *theoretical underpinnings* and their *practical implementation*.

The national Councils would prepare each people for their future membership in the great federation of Nations; they would also be responsible for spreading the European idea among each people. Meanwhile the supreme international Council would design the new map of Europe; it would promote a Holy Alliance of the oppressed against the oppressors. It would point out the path to progress, unconstrained by the limits of any existing system; and it would harmonize the movements and efforts of different peoples, as if they were the different divisions of a single army. Then, as soon as the peoples had gained new hope, the supreme Council would introduce a Democratic Tax. A first portion of this tax would be used to set up a credit institution for the common folk: this would make it possible for the common people to come together and invest in agricultural and industrial enterprises, thus practically illustrating in different places how associations can be established and their moral and material rewards apportioned. Another section of the tax would be used to support the press and popular education. Our goal would be to make sure that opportunities for education would not be limited to just a few large population centers, as is currently the case, but rather would become available in each village and town as needed. Finally, a third portion of the tax would be set aside and held as a sacred fund, which would serve to offer brotherly support to those peoples who have risen up to vindicate their rights.

Thought and Action, those two essential components of human progress, are too often disjoined today, resulting in serious dangers for the future. What is needed to bring them together with new vigor is a sincere process of human Association. In all previous great historical epochs that resulted in significant progress, thought and action were united. Today the multitude is more suspicious of abstract thought than is commonly believed. But it could easily develop faith and confidence in a new authority that was neither despotic nor arbitrary but rather founded on love and concrete deeds.

I do not know for certain how much of this plan may ever be realized. But I do know that the supporters of democracy need to put into practice as much of it as possible. Otherwise we will continue to drag ourselves indefinitely along a path of isolated uprisings, which may be glorious no doubt and beneficial to humanity, but which crucially will not lead us to victory. All our brothers should think about this. To pretend that a majority must agree on virtually every future step before moving to action is to condemn oneself, not so much to long delays—after all, time matters little in an undertaking such as ours—but rather to the impossibility of transforming the crowds that are currently forced to live in an atmosphere of selfishness and corruption. We must remove the crowds from this mortal influence and lead them out into the fresh pure air under God's eye. We must awake them from their torpor by a violent shock; rouse their hearts by the enthusiasm of battle. The excitement of all their faculties will then result in a strong and determined spout of life. And the spirit of Truth will descend more rapidly on a people once its members have actively joined together to enrich this new life.

In other words, we must act, for action is like a divine revelation to the multitudes. But it would be a grave error to rise up at this point without a reasonable hope of success. We must therefore first unite, for unity is the only means to success. Let us unite! The times are very serious. Today's evil and despotic governments weigh like a nightmare on our abilities and on the soul of our nations. They have made known their program in Germany, Hungary, and Rome; they have formed an *alliance in order to oppress*. Let ours be an *alliance aimed at emancipation*.

Let us join together, organize ourselves, and prepare again, publicly or secretly, depending on the circumstances. When like the early Christians we will be able to say: *in the name of God and the People, we are united*, then the new pagans will be powerless; the old order will have been defeated. God will then let us know how we shall proceed from there.

From a Revolutionary Alliance to the United States of Europe (1850)

WE HAVE MADE important progress.[1] The idea expressed in one of our previous writings—*The Alliance of the Peoples*—has been translated into action. A *European Central Committee*, composed of men from all the European nations, and who are influential in the field of Democracy, is now actively promoting the development of such an alliance.[2] . . .

The *individual* and the *collectivity*, the *I* and the *we*, are both sacred and eternal elements of Life, the manifestation of God on earth. They are the two sides of the problem that since its inception has preoccupied Humanity. To achieve harmony between these two elements is the true intent of Democracy.

Freedom without *association* inevitably leads to anarchy. *Association* without *liberty* is despotism and tyranny. Humanity abhors both anarchy and tyranny alike. It seeks a balance between the two inseparable conditions of life; so inseparable are they that one cannot be achieved and maintained without the other. Every association sooner or later provokes men to rebellion, unless they have freely consented to it; all personal liberties are precarious, if the association itself is not designed to preserve them. This is true for every country and for all peoples. No political system can become established within a State if it does not respect these two elements, *liberty* and *association*. At the same time, no conquest of liberty in a nation can function for long unless an analogous process is achieved in the nations that surround it.

---

[1] Original title: "Organizzazione della democrazia."

[2] Following the Europewide failure of the democratic revolutionary movements of 1848–49, Mazzini founded the "European Central Democratic Committee" in June 1850, together with a few other revolutionary exiles in London. The organization remained politically weak, partially because of the broader ideological opposition between Mazzini and Marx within the European democratic movement. In this short essay, Mazzini effectively reiterates his argument that human freedom and emancipation can only thrive through the progressive association of individuals in self-determining nationalities. Mazzini suggests that these free nationalities will form an ever closer union among themselves, leading one day to the establishment of a United States of Europe (an idea that had already been theorized in Italy by Carlo Cattaneo, a liberal federalist and the leader of Milan's revolution of 1848).

The leaders of the socialist movement almost always eliminate from their systems either the vital concept of association, looking only to the *individual* like Fourier and Proudhon, or they eliminate the concept of liberty, looking only to a formula of *association* like the followers of Saint-Simon and communism. As a result all those leaders are utterly ineffective. For a brief moment their doctrines may shine like a beacon amongst the ruins; but they inevitably are swept into oblivion by the tide of other systems, which are themselves transient and will ultimately be rejected by Democracy and the common sense of the multitudes.

In 1848 Italy was misled by courtiers and dynastic intermediaries into believing that a Nation could be constructed in the name of local interests, without establishing a brotherly bond with militant Democracy throughout Europe in the name of the popular principle. Therefore the various insurrections failed, crushed by foreigners and betrayed by their own. Germany disowned the principle of national freedom with the foolish demands put forward at [the 1848 Constituent Assembly in] Frankfurt.[3] Hence, to this day it wavers between the dissonant ambitions of Prussia and Austria; two governments that are equally pathetic and usurping. Hungary wanted to substitute its own idea [of regional hegemony] for the free federation of the Slavic, Moldavian-Wallachian, and Magyar races. As a consequence, those who should have fought at its side became its enemies, or offered at best only lukewarm support. France deluded itself that it could establish republican liberty within its own boundaries, seduced by pride and the narrow-minded views of its leaders, and thus abandoned the European cause. In consequence, today it founders and suffers in the mire of anarchy under a government that betrays its mission and dishonors its intellect.

Every revolution derives legitimacy and strength from the purpose that guides its efforts. If you rise up only for yourself and for your narrow *interests*, then you will inevitably also have to fight alone. But things will look very different if you rise up for everyone in the name of a *principle*, for the good of your brothers in Humanity: then there will be comrades willing to support your cause wherever there are men who believe in the same faith.

You can fight alone, but you cannot win alone. The enemies of Liberty and Progress are allied and have joined their forces; and their united forces are more powerful than your valor. Russian troops descend on Hungary

[3] The assembly lacked the necessary power to impose its authority on the German sovereigns and on the Prussian monarch in particular. In April 1849 a delegation of representatives from the assembly offered the Prussian king the German imperial crown, which he scathingly rejected. Mazzini wants to suggest that the German democrats were naïve in assuming that they could unite Germany by attempting an alliance with the Prussian monarch rather than by opposing him.

alongside with Austrian ones; meanwhile France supports Austria against Italy; and Austria and Prussia together support every small principality that is threatened by popular movements in Germany.

Europe is thus divided into two camps with their own flags. The first flag reads: *People, Right, and National liberty*. The second flag reads: *monarchy, power, privilege, servitude*. But the latter also reads: *alliance of the princes*. Our faith, logic, and the need for a common defense demand that we add to the first flag: *alliance of the peoples*. This need and this faith are accepted by the majority, at least *in theory*. Unfortunately various reasons have so far prevented us from moving beyond the realm of theory to the realm of *facts*. Chief among these reasons have been the machinations of our masters, the tenacity of our national prejudices, and the guilty mistakes of the men who were leading the national movements. In every state, the members of the democratic party kept talking of Association, while they actually remained divided within the enclosures of their own little backyards. Likewise, the National Democracies [of 1848–49] spoke and wrote about Alliance, but they never came even close to putting it into practice. That disjuncture between theory and practice, between *thought* and *action*, has today become a mortal wound to our party in France and elsewhere. We have the formula, but we lack any faith in sacrifice. Hence the supreme concept of alliance, which alone could vindicate our efforts, has so far been condemned to sterility or to the feebleness of individual attempts.

The mission of the *European Central Committee* is precisely to translate ideas into *facts*. The two essential components of our project are, first, to direct the entirety of the movement into our camp so that not a single people will have to rise and then succumb in isolation; second, to establish the foundations of that Alliance of Peoples, which a future Congress of free Nations will one day transform into the law of Europe. Ours is not a national project but an international one. We hope that the active part we claim within this project constitutes a sufficient guarantee to our fellow Italians that any suspicion of subjection to foreign influences is unfounded. . . . Indeed, the establishment of a European Committee, within which every nation is represented by an individual with an equal vote, constitutes a new defense against any attempts at usurpation. The sole required basis of our alliance is the acceptance of the popular principle, the spirit and life of Democracy.

The life of each nation is twofold: it is both internal and external, self-regarding and outward oriented. The task of the people who comprise each Nation is to organize their own life. Similarly, the task of the Congress of Nations is to organize the life of international relations. *God and the People* should be the motto of each single Nation; *God and Humanity* that of all of them together. We do not simply strive to create Europe; our goal is to create the United States of Europe.

We have also formally constituted an *Italian National Committee*, which is allied with the central, European organization, in order to improve the condition of Italy and set an example from which other subject nationalities can take comfort. The *individual* and the *State* need to live and progress in harmony within every national Democracy. Likewise, *Country* [*patria*] and *Humanity* need to thrive and evolve fraternally within the context of European Democracy. . . . Oh fellow Italians, be steadfast and faithful! From a moral point of view, we are already stronger than we were before 1848, and soon this will be reflected in our actions.

CHAPTER NINE

Against the Foreign Imposition of Domestic Institutions (1851)

OUR IDEA IS STEADILY ADVANCING.[1] The active forces of revolution are growing; they are bonding together and getting organized. The European thought that led us to form the Central Democratic Committee is spreading day after day amidst the most diverse peoples.[2] Unfortunately, so far, from the mouth of the Danube in the East to the Iberian Peninsula in the West, the popular movements, enfeebled by their isolation in the face of united enemy forces, have succumbed one after the other. Yet those defeats have accomplished the precious work of unifying the movements internally and creating international sympathies among them. A unity of convictions has thus been established. A common aspiration toward the formation of a *United States* of Europe has been gradually brought to life. Thus when the hour of your awakening will have arrived, a *Holy Alliance of Nations* shall emerge from all these unfulfilled aspirations and all the preparatory works. It will be the fulfillment of your efforts and the supreme synthesis of an epoch whose meaning can be summarized in the following three words: *Liberty, Association, Labor.*

There and there alone lies the guarantee of our success, and one should not get tired of repeating it to the peoples. You are stronger than your enemies. Whenever you have taken them on in a direct fight, one by one, you have knocked them down and they ended up defeated. But since 1815 your enemies have been united [in the monarchical Holy Alliance], while you have continued to fight one by one. They have marched together, they have overcome their disagreements and centralized their action under a single flag—the flag of interests, which they have nearly elevated to the level of a principle. Meanwhile you the peoples, who had been entrusted with the true principle by the common law of humanity, have weakened that principle and shrunk it until it disappeared under your pursuit of purely local interests!

Germany forgot the mission that the great voice of Luther had outlined for her in the world. She declared: "The self is sacred," and thus she proclaimed her own right to liberty, while allowing that the indi-

---

[1] Original title: "Le Comité Central Démocratique Européen."

[2] Mazzini founded the "European Central Democratic Committee" in London together with other revolutionary exiles in June 1850. See chapter 8 above.

viduality of other peoples be suppressed by the [Austrian] Empire. *Italy* let her national thought be wiped out under the dynastic interest of a monarchy, and thus she broke all solidarity with the European Democratic movement. *Hungary* forgot that she could achieve a genuine and deserving victory only by promoting the emancipation of the Slavic and Romanian peoples on the basis of a broad conception of equality. *Poland* remains stuck in between an extinct idea [aristocracy] and a new idea [democracy], and although she has increasingly rallied her convictions around the latter, she has not yet felt the urgency of harmonizing thought and action and of centralizing her forces in a universal and unified organization. Hence she missed the peoples' call. And then there is *France*! France thought she could solve the social question on her own by maintaining a peace that actually delivered Europe to the despots.

For all these reasons, you, the peoples, had to fatally fall again under the yoke of oppression and pay for your error with new sorrows. But raise yourselves up again now, under a unity of faith and action! Wherever there is going to be a revolutionary initiative, let it be for the good of all. Throw down the gauntlet to the conspiring monarchies, in the name of all those who suffer; and may all those who suffer rise up and follow the initiative! Fight for everyone and you will win for everyone. Each soldier of liberty must be the armed apostle of a principle. Every people must be ready to function as a pivot for the lever that will move and push all of Europe forward. From now on you can hardly achieve any rights except by first accomplishing your duties.

Unity is our watchword today. It is urgent; because it is the only thing that really worries the enemy camp. We learn this every day, from the persecution of our followers and the calumnies spread on our behalf, beginning with the dispatches that several European diplomats regularly address to England concerning some of our exiles, and which sometimes draw on falsified documents to which our counterfeit signature has been attached.[3] Our oppressors feel that the beliefs we stand for and seek to advance must ultimately be fatal to them. They feel that those beliefs will strengthen our organization and thus lead us steadily closer to victory, and they hope that by misrepresenting those beliefs their forward march can at least be delayed. We can only have contempt for anybody who spreads similar calumnies, and as a result our activism is redoubled. But some men have indeed been misled by the lies of

---

[3] The conservative European chancelleries, led by Austria, regularly insisted that the British government expel liberal or republican exiles like Mazzini and his followers. The conservative governments also intercepted the revolutionary exiles' correspondence and sometimes produced fake documents to accuse them of criminal intent, thus seeking to undermine their reputation, a practice that was publicly denounced by leading British intellectuals such as John Stuart Mill and Thomas Carlyle.

certain reactionary writers, and those men now believe in good faith that our only goal is to spread terror and disorder, so as to bring about some savage anarchy that would eventually swallow all social guarantees. It is to those men that our word is addressed. May they be reassured: we have no ulterior motives. All our goals are proclaimed openly and with a proud spirit.

We do not want anarchy. We clearly reject it, and we will fight it with all our means, in whatever form it presents itself. We seek order and peace. But we know that no genuine order is possible without liberty and justice. The result today is a round-the-clock struggle: just think of the martial laws that govern roughly two-thirds of Europe; of the armies that spread oppression and support those laws everywhere; of the thousands of men banished from all the continental European countries and who are pushed into exile in England and America; of all the prison dungeons and the rising scaffolds. The struggle can only end with the victory of right, or rather with the victory of popular sovereignty that embodies this right. The final result will be a free association of all the elements that make up the state, a fraternal alliance of all nationalities. Poverty will be abolished, and every rule that rests only on force, ignorance, or lies will be overthrown. That is what we seek and that is what we will obtain, nothing more and nothing less.

We do not want terror. We reject terror as both cowardly and immoral. Wherever we have triumphed, we have abolished the scaffold. But energy and commitment are the Peoples' only guarantee against the fatal necessity of terror. Weakness only nurtures martyrdom; and while martyrdom is often sacred for the individual who pursues the good, it is absurd for nations who actually have the power and courage to realize the good. The People's desires must be fulfilled, nobly and logically, without excesses and without relying on questionable dealings. We will be steady and strong, we will be neither executioners nor victims.

We absolutely do not want to abolish anything that forms the essence of social order. But we know that as the association of human beings becomes stronger, more closely knit, and broader in scope, everything will be transformed and everything will be improved. Each serious and permanent expression of human life is sacred to us, but that is only because by progressively refining itself, it moves steadily forward on the path of progress toward the ideal whose realization is our goal. Family, country, personal convictions, individual liberty, work, and property are all different components of the association in which we believe; we could not destroy even a single one of them without mutilating human nature itself. But they all change and evolve in their mutual relationships and in their organization, depending on a people's education and on the epoch.

We do not want either immobility or arbitrary will. Our project is far from being purely negative; we just want every powerful and rational project to be discussed in broad daylight, under the eyes of the People, who must then judge and decide. We are not promoting a specific and exclusive, fully thought-out system of political organization; we are merely suggesting a method, although of course we are well aware of all the problems that seethe in the heart of contemporary societies. Anyone who affirms the contrary probably confuses our ideas with those put forward in works of a wholly different character and understands nothing of our mission.

The *Central Committee* has a European mission; all its activities have an international character. As already anticipated, the goals of our collective endeavor are the following: to provide a common source of inspiration and give a sense of direction to the efforts of different Peoples; to give proof through our actions of the solidarity that exists between the emancipation of each single People and the emancipation of them all; to bring all those who fight for the sacred cause of right closer together, wherever they may be; to prepare the terrain for a genuine alliance of peoples that will be able to defeat the existing alliance of kings; to promote a congress of nations that will replace the congress of Vienna, whose spirit is unfortunately still alive and always in action; and finally to remake the map of Europe according to the popular will, beginning with the elimination of various obstacles such as racial prejudice, the memories of monarchical wars, and the artifices of reactionary governments.

This goal can obviously only be attained if we all start from a common ground; that is, the pursuit of national sovereignty for every people and of an alliance based on equality among all the emancipated nations. Sovereignty cannot be truly national unless it aims at progressively embracing all the elements that form the nation and the universality of citizens who make up the state. Hence, the democratic principle is for us inseparable from our conception of the nation!

Democracy can have but one logical form: the republican form. And the republican principle cannot be said to have been truly applied to the nation unless it encompasses and links up all branches of human activity and all different aspects of individual and associational life. Our work is thus essentially republican, democratic, and social; it is for the sake of all the peoples that we call for an alliance of all those who are devoted to our cause.

All the rest should be dealt with by the different national committees. Every national committee has the right and the duty to study and work out, as a preparatory task for its own country, the special solution that the moral, economic, and social conditions of that country demand. Likewise, within each state, every citizen has the right and the duty to work out and suggest the solution that seems best suited to him to the problems at hand. The People, like a supreme judge, will then ultimately decide. The *European Central Committee* can see to it that those specific national solutions do not diverge too much from our common ground, outside of which there can be neither justice nor any enjoyment of rights. In other words, the Central Committee will seek to make sure that no agents of inequality, discord, and internecine struggles shall be instilled in the midst of our alliance of peoples. But it has no powers beyond that.

We are against the kingship of men as we are against the kingship of peoples. If a people were to impose their own solution to the specific social problems of another country, they would thereby commit an act of usurpation. It is the same as if an individual or a school of thought were to impose their own model on their brothers, by making its acceptance a sine qua non condition of their cooperation. They would thereby commit an act of tyranny and violate the central belief of Democracy, the dogma of collective sovereignty. All of them would have understood absolutely nothing of the life of humanity, which is at once united and manifold.

One first needs to exist in order to be able to discover, judge, and apply any political formula. One needs to fully live the life that ferments inside oneself, in freedom and love. Now, are the peoples really alive today? Are they free to look inside themselves and then express their wishes, their inclinations, and their collective desires? Can they fraternally love each other and multiply their faculties and their forces in this atmosphere of corruption, suspicion, oppression, and espionage that surrounds them?

Above and before anything else, the peoples need to be called back to life and action. We must open to them the great paths of liberty. We must erase the shameful marks of servitude from their front, so that great and noble thoughts may surge within their hearts. Their intelligence must be renewed by the enthusiasm of an immense affirmation of collective life, solidarity, and sovereign freedom. That is the first step we must take; it is the first rung we must climb on the ladder of a progressive education that will be both national and European.

The Central Committee is concerned with all these things, all the more so as others seem to be oblivious to them. We, the Committee's members, and all those who work with us, are not just planning to contemplate the solitary product of our own intelligence; instead we want to inspire and stimulate everyone's intelligence. In other words, we do not content ourselves with just thinking; we are oriented toward *action*. This should be the watchword for every patriot today.

CHAPTER TEN

To the Patriots of Serbia and Hungary (1863)

YOU ARE OUR BROTHERS.[1] Like us, you are seeking to establish your own Country; and as with us, the watchword that rouses your spirits is Nationality. You have suffered and fought for it, with your own heroes and martyrs. Now we must reach our hands across the Adriatic Sea to support each other. Italian populations are intermixed with yours along the eastern coast of that sea, to which both of us retain a right, and which must be open to the free exchange of our goods. It is in your interest that there be a united Italy, just as it is in our interest that there be a great Illyria, as well as a free Hungary as the center of a Danubian Federation. In the name of the memories shared by our fathers; in the name of the future Alliance of free Peoples; in the name of the present, which points to an easy emancipation through the union of our forces, let us come together and actively cooperate. Like us, you have been patient for as long as the circumstances required: now you must be as audacious as we are. The circumstances have changed, and patience would today be equal to abdication.

Will you rise up, oh brothers, when we rise? Will ours have to be a confined and exclusively Italian battle, opposed by all and hostile to all? Or shall it instead be a battle of everyone for everyone, fought in the name of a common Principle, for our Liberty and for yours? Will our blood sow the seeds of rancor and future disagreements, thereby being advantageous only to our masters, or will it instead seal a real pact among the family of Peoples, which can alone establish the foundations of a new Europe of Nations? Will you seize the opportunity that we shall offer you? Our enemy is your enemy. Oh Hungarian brothers, is not your entire people kept under the yoke of occupation by Austria? Oh Serbian brothers, is not half of your people scattered and cut off from its common Mother under Austria's Dominion? Can you even *exist* without freeing yourselves from this rule?

---

[1] It was one of Mazzini's life-long projects to promote and coordinate a European alliance among subject or recently liberated peoples. In particular, he believed that if only all the various oppressed nationalities within the Austrian Empire were to coordinate their revolutionary activities and rise up at once, the multinational Habsburg Empire would almost certainly collapse under the pressure of combined centrifugal tendencies. His prophecy would not be fully realized until the end of World War I. (Original title of this essay: "Ai patrioti della Serbia e dell'Ungheria").

We share the same goal. God and the conditions of Europe have entrusted us with the same great mission. Two different Empires, the Turkish and the Austrian, are weighing heavily on the heart of Europe and deny any right, any conscience and life to the peoples. They are two different incarnations of the Spirit of Evil and represent nothing but the Tyranny of conquest. We must undo them. You, Serbs, need to take up the lead in fighting the Turkish Empire. Meanwhile we, Hungarians, Serbs, and Italians, will fight the Austrian Empire all together. But these two fights are inseparable. The Turkish and Austrian Tyrannies are entwined like a serpent with two heads around the tree of national life; it is thus necessary to lop off both heads at once.

Let us find an agreement among each other and get ready. May our Parties be blended into one, the Party of Action. You, Hungarians, ought to hold out a fraternal hand to the Romanians and the Slavs. You, Serbs, ought to extend it to the Romanians and the Greeks. Delay any domestic issue until victory over the common enemy has been achieved. Liberty will then suggest to all of us the most appropriate solutions to our domestic problems and the means of reconciliation with our former enemies, which we cannot even conceive of as long as we remain slaves.

And listen well. Don't you hear a sacred and powerful voice coming from the North, from beyond the Carpathians, imploring you to rise up, just as we implore you to do, and telling you: *Arise, follow the example that I have given you for almost a year*? It is the voice of a people [the Poles] that have fought for long years against your enemy the Turk, oh Hungarians, and of which a part is now enslaved by Austria; a people that have common origins with you, oh Serbs.[2]

So let us find an agreement and get ready. A brotherly League under a common flag of Action, stretching from Poland to Hungary, Serbia, and Italy, will be a European fact. And at that point, no other force shall be able to deny us victory.

[2] Mazzini is referring to the January 1863 insurrection in eastern Poland against Russia's oppressive rule. The Polish-Lithuanian kingdom had been attacked by the Ottoman army in 1672; hence Mazzini's claim that like the Hungarians, the Poles also have a history of past conflict with "the Turk."

CHAPTER ELEVEN

Letter to a Polish Patriot (1863)

Dear Friend,

I am harboring a feeling, perhaps slightly exaggerated, of shame.[1] Because we, the other peoples and especially all of revolutionary Europe, should have risen to the call of Poland.[2]

Your insurrection taught us a duty, it plotted for us the way, and furnished us with an opportunity. Hungary should have risen up as one. There were no reasons for it to fear any foreign intervention similar to that which put down its revolt in 1848. Greece, Serbia, Bulgaria, Romania, and all those populations whose nationality remains contested by the Turks and the Austrian Government should have seized the opportunity provided by your insurrection. You held and still hold the Tsar in check, whose ambition it is to monopolize the future life of several subject peoples. Italy should have been the first to answer your call. By attacking Austria through the Venetian lands, she would have given the signal for a crusade of nationalities. Then we would have been able to speak to you and you would have listened to us.

The gust of a European Revolution would have driven you along the only possible path to victory. And on that path you would have met numerous brothers in action. But instead of fulfilling our own duty, and thus in turn gaining the right to point out your duty to you, we limited ourselves to expressions of support for those among you who were dying bravely.

The Greeks are presently begging foreigners to provide them with a king, when you have just shown what a people can actually achieve without a king. The Hungarians follow the advice that Imperial France is sending them through Kossuth.[3] Serbia has sacrificed the hopes of her

---

[1] Mazzini wrote this letter in French. The recipient's name is unknown.

[2] Mazzini is referring to the January 1863 uprising in eastern Poland against Russia's oppressive rule. The Polish insurgents, severely outnumbered and lacking meaningful outside support, relied on guerrilla warfare and were finally put down by Russian forces in late 1864. In this essay, Mazzini regrets the lack of coordination and active solidarity among Europe's revolutionaries.

[3] Lajos "Louis" Kossuth (1802–94), Hungarian lawyer and freedom fighter. He met Mazzini in London in the 1850s and joined the latter's revolutionary committee. Yet as this passage suggests, relations between Mazzini and Kossuth were not devoid of tensions.

national party to the cowardly tactics of a prince without genius and without a mission. And Italy, my Italy, on behalf of which I had almost been able to promise our cooperation, waited until the drive to action that was seething within her bosom got dampened, relying on some dismal calculation that a better opportunity would be offered later by the *moderate* party that threatens today to forsake you. Hence perhaps we just ought to keep silent.

But as for yourselves, you are on the slope that leads right into the abyss. After the Langiewicz dictatorship your revolution has become distorted.[4] It deeply hurts our heart to see how the people do not seem to remember any lessons from the past; it hurts to think of all those brave young men who die and their mothers who weep. It hurts to see how all those heroic sacrifices are being accomplished, only so that a party that already lost Poland twice, that did absolutely nothing to stir up the Polish people, and that contributed neither its blood nor its gold at the beginning of this battle, will eventually come to monopolize the entire movement. That party is now placing its faith in some deceptive foreign promises, and thus it will slowly replace your revolutionary energy with a tactic that is doomed to slay you.

It is not a question of Republic or Monarchy. Had you been victorious, you could have chosen as you liked, based on God's will and your national traditions. The question today is about succeeding, winning, and acquiring for your soil the liberty of choosing to be or not to be. But you can only succeed by enlarging the base of your Insurrection. If you want to erase from your movement all the intrigues and the hostility of the enemies who surround you, you must clearly distance yourselves from them, and you must seek to attack them on their own terrain. If you want to get the assistance of revolutionary Europe and of all the other subject nationalities, you must raise the revolutionary flag and shout out loudly: "For your liberty and for ours." You need to prove to all those other peoples that you are not simply seeking to revive an aristocratic and Jesuitic Poland, as your enemies suggest, but that you want to establish instead a new Poland of the people, based on liberty of conscience, a Poland oriented toward progress and not toward past centuries that are forever dead.

And you will not obtain (yes, in speaking of Poland, I must lower myself to speaking about tactics) the foreign interventions against the Tsar that several of you desire, except by making it clear to the Western governments that your movement is becoming increasingly general-

---

[4] Marian Langiewicz (1827–87), Polish patriot who played an important role as military leader during the January uprising in 1863. After beating the Russians twice, in March 1863 he proclaimed himself dictator, but soon had to flee into exile following a series of military defeats.

ized. If they believe that you are turning against each other and thus will most likely succumb, they will not intervene.

By launching a movement in Galicia, you would have shaken Hungary and thereby opened the great path to international assistance. By giving the signal for a general uprising in Eastern Europe, you could have brought about a European war. By showing through your acts and the choice of your leaders that your cause is indeed that of the people, you could have stirred up the peoples.

Yet so long as your insurrection remains isolated, it is condemned to perish. You have deferred to Prussia when it attacked you, and to Austria when it tricked you. You have carried the *flank* to all your enemies' accusations, and you alarmed the peoples by choosing aristocratic men as your representatives abroad, who are best known for their submissiveness to foreign monarchical corruption and who entirely lack the necessary energy to succeed in an Insurrection. And you may not know this, but you, to whom I am writing, you have discouraged the Italian party of action that was about to come to your aid with your dishonorable proposals: you were in fact willing to offer us the necessary funds to mobilize our elements only on the condition that *one may not touch Austria*. . . .

Let me tell you that you will perish if you do not quickly appeal to all your revolutionary energies, if you don't reassure the Europe of peoples about the ultimate goals of your insurrection, if you don't expand your base, and if you don't call for a war of nationalities. I beg you to repeat these things to your compatriots and make of my letter whatever use may please you.

Farewell.
Your brother,
Giuseppe Mazzini

CHAPTER TWELVE

For a Truly National War (1866)

I WOULD LIKE TO publicly respond to several requests that I express my opinion concerning the present political situation.[1] First of all, *the country* [Italy] *must demand that there be war* [against Austria]. The Government's intentions today may seem clear. But the Government does not have any moral initiative of its own; it does not believe in National Duty; and throughout these past years it has openly displayed its lack of trust in the Italian patriotic forces and judged them unequal to the fight. In recent years, believing it had no allies, the Government let the opportunities of the Polish insurrection and the German-Danish war pass by. Today it believes that the moment to challenge Austria has finally arrived, because it feels confident about its alliances. Yet tomorrow it might again retreat, should those who now secretly spur it on choose to retreat due to unexpected events or different calculations.

Our country must make sure that the war becomes inevitable, with or without allies. The war for the emancipation of the Veneto has long been a matter of moral *duty*, but today it has become an absolute *necessity*. If after all the movements, preparations, and current declarations Italy were to abandon its goal, it would prove to all of Europe that it is unworthy of a true national life and is a mere instrument of foreign interests and designs. Its reputation among the Nations would be badly damaged for many years. It would find itself facing a new deficit in addition to the old; it would undermine the army's sense of dignity and confidence; it would place a potent weapon in the hands of the most retrograde domestic factions; it would open the floodgates to moral anarchy, or to a feeling of skepticism and discomfort worse than anarchy. Hence, the country must make its voice clearly heard, and it must cry

[1] Original title: "La Guerra." Mazzini wrote this essay in May 1866, when most of Italy had already been unified. About a month earlier, a secret alliance treaty had been signed between Prussia and Italy, according to which Italy would support Prussia in a likely war against Austria. In exchange, Italy would obtain the Veneto region and other Italian territories still controlled by Austria. Mazzini's main argument in this essay is that Italy should declare war on Austria as soon as the circumstances allowed, in order to free those Italian territories still under the latter's imperial control. However, the war should be a truly national war, fought by Italian patriotic forces out of their own strength, and not relying on short-sighted alliances with one or the other of Europe's great powers. As to the actual course of events, when the war against Austria was launched during the following month of June 1866, Italy suffered a humiliating defeat. Nonetheless, Italy ultimately acquired the Veneto region thanks to Prussia's victory over Austria at the Battle of Sadowa.

for war. I do not know why the Venetians [still under Austrian occupation] do not understand that today they are the arbiters of the question and that the smallest act of insurrection on their part would open the way to the torrent. But even if they do not want to rise up, or cannot do so, the country should act. Today all of Italy is Venice; our nation's life, its future, and its honor await vindication through the liberation of the region that lies between the Alps and the lagoons [i.e. the Veneto].

The war must be exclusively Italian, fought with our own forces and without any foreign intervention on our own soil. Everybody knows what it means to accept the aid of Imperial France and how one must pay for that aid. But even if for once France were truly willing to fight for an *idea*, the arrogant language of supremacy that the French have used toward us since 1859 should be sufficient for us to refuse their aid as a dishonor and an outrage, provided that there is any proper national pride left in Italy. Today Italy presents herself as a free nation to the rest of Europe, but now she must fight her *own* war, to acquire a genuine liberty that will not be bound to any fate other than her own. Otherwise she will be considered as a satellite of France. May Italy shine from her own light as one of the brightest stars in the sky of Humanity.

There must be no alliance with Prussia. If such an alliance is made, it will be kept secret like a sin. Italy must not taint the sacredness of its flag any further; it cannot announce to Europe that it seeks allies only among the forces of despotism. Three years ago, the Prussian government was the only supporter of the Russian Czar in suppressing the Polish insurrection. Soon thereafter, it violated every principle of justice and right by attacking Denmark. In that nefarious effort, Prussia broke all faith in treaties and lied unashamedly to the European powers, as well as to the conquered populations and the German Confederation. The Prussian government has continually repressed both Parliament and Liberty on its own soil. In short, Prussia represents the worst element under present circumstances. An alliance with Prussia would therefore be manifestly immoral, and immorality prepares one poorly for victory. Such an alliance would also be a mistake, because the Prussian government is currently hated by three-quarters of the German populations, and the loathing of it would soon turn on ourselves. The alliance would be more dangerous than is generally assumed, because to mollify the German Confederation and to avoid being seen as a traitor, the Prussian government would probably force us to abandon any operations in the Trentino and the Tyrol.[2] And finally, what purpose would this alliance serve?

[2] The German Confederation, created by the Congress of Vienna in 1815 to serve as the successor to the defunct Holy Roman Empire, collapsed with the Austro-Prussian war of 1866. The Trentino and the majority German-speaking South Tyrol, two Alpine regions claimed by Italian nationalists, were eventually ceded to Italy only after Austria's defeat in World War I.

Any advantages that one can expect from it would more likely be gained by keeping ourselves pure and independent. . . .

May Italy ally itself with the peoples who are forcibly kept under Austria's yoke; with the peoples who also want to vindicate their liberty and independence. May our war be a war of Nations. Let us raise up high our flag, not in the name of local interests but rather in the name of a principle; the principle that for more than half a century has inspired and led every European popular movement. Let us write on our flag these sacred words: *"For our own sake and for yours."* Then let us protect that flag with all the swords that can be unsheathed in Italy, and let us wave it before the eyes of the Hungarians, Bohemians, Serbs, Romanians, the southern Slavs, and all the other populations ruled either by the Austrian or the Turkish Empire. Europe's fortunes and our own depend on the formation of such an alliance with Europe's subject peoples. Such a principled alliance harbors the secret of an epoch that we can make our own, if only we can marshal the necessary political will. We ought to bless God, who is offering us such an opportunity to emancipate ourselves while we help to emancipate others, and thus to make ourselves powerful as well as internationally admired.

May this be a truly national war, jointly fought by the regular army and by voluntary militias. This appears desirable for several reasons: first, the noble emulation of strong deeds that will be stimulated between the two brotherly elements will double the likelihood of victory. Second, the terrain on which our victory will be achieved, provided that the war is conducted wisely, is admirably suited to the free and independent, swift and unforeseeable action of the volunteers. Third, we need to take advantage of the strength and the courage of all those who are ready to sacrifice their own lives in our struggle and yet appear reluctant to forsake their individuality for the rigid and blind discipline of the army. Fourth and most important, the Volunteers represent our country's spontaneity; they can provide our war with a popular sanction and thus assure the army that the entire, omnipotent Nation actually stands behind it. The volunteers will imprint the beloved and esteemed name of Garibaldi on our undertaking; they will provide a living pledge to the peoples that we are fighting not just in execution of some superior order, or perhaps for the sake of a dynastic interest, but rather by virtue of an *idea.* We shall be fighting by virtue of a feeling, of a principle incarnated in a people that is ready to rise up for itself and for others; that is not tied to previous agreements, nor susceptible to conquering ambition or unconsciously lured by evil designs.

May there be no limits to the number of Volunteers to be recruited. Nobody has the right to impose constraints on the enthusiasm of a country that arises for its own well-being and its own honor. *May the Volunteers be free*

*from any formal bond with the existing monarchic regime, except insofar as is
required by the necessary unity of our war plan.* Or does anybody have the
right to tell the country in the midst of a national war, "I am suspicious
of you," without provoking or deserving in turn suspicion? The volunteer in arms represents the unity of our Country before the armed foreigner. Who would dare tell that volunteer: "You cannot protect that
Unity against the foreigner unless you disgrace yourself, renouncing
your conscience with oaths or pacts concerning matters extraneous to
the war?"[3] Faith inspires faith. Today, our *only* plan is the emancipation
of the Veneto for the cause of National Unity. Any government that
sought to impose a different plan on anyone who shows up to fight
would thereby allow all other plans to come to the fore, and it would
trigger the division that must be avoided.

There must be no ill-considered and dishonest restrictions of liberty. Rulers
of Italy, let me speak to you as follows:

Look around yourselves: can you really be suspicious of the country?
Can you truly fear any regressive factions? The cry of "War for the
Veneto" is the most powerful weapon you have against any enemy.
Once the spirit of patriotic enthusiasm is revived among the people,
every attempt against our national Unity would be inexorably
crushed. Do not weaken that enthusiasm with any acts that may re-
kindle feelings of mistrust and suggest hidden purposes. Do not in-
sult the true Representatives of our country [the Volunteers], whoever they may be, by telling them: "You are an obstacle and you must
retreat." Don't you perhaps believe that you could get from them everything you may need for your patriotic objectives, without delay or
hesitation? Do not limit the Press, for it is called on to express all those
things that you need to know today—the opinions, the trends, and
desires of the nation. Do not obstruct public demonstrations and the
gathering of Associations, for each of those will encourage our combatants while instilling doubts and terror in the enemy. You cannot
demand that a people fight while being left in the dark. You cannot
require that those who must give their blood and everything they had
put aside for their children should suddenly place unlimited faith in
a few men who have been made the arbiters of everything, and whose
smallest error could lead the entire nation into ruin. Leave it to the

---

[3]Beginning in 1859, the Savoy monarchy of Piedmont had begun to gradually unify
Italy, relying on an international alliance policy, and exploiting the domestic popular element while openly despising it. In the face of these developments, Mazzini argued that
the Italian popular militias should continue to support the process of national unification,
for the sake of their patriotic convictions. However, nobody could force the militias to
swear allegiance to a monarchy whose instrumentalism they utterly condemned.

country as a whole to look out and advise you. Only thus can you have all its strength at your disposal.

These are the requirements for victory. Italy needs to win. Hence the country has a right to demand that the Government step up to the challenge in its declarations and its actions, as well as in the choice of the individuals appointed to guide us during the period of war. This is a matter of life or death for our Nation. Today, unreasonable mistrust and blind, servile enthusiasm are both equally dangerous: the first breeds inertia, while the second can lead to tremendous disappointments. If we want to be successful in the future, we should not be forgetful about the past.

As a republican, I also want to tell all those republicans who think that the hard experiences of the past justify an attitude of passive inertia today:

> My brothers, you have until now preached like myself that in order to acquire republican liberties one must first earn them. Well, so earn them! Seize every opportunity that presents itself to liberate those of your countrymen who groan under the yoke of foreign oppression. And once your mission has taken root within your soul, you will move forward united toward the conquest of our ideal. But in the pursuit of this ideal, you should provide only that kind of help that is required as a matter of sacred duty. Would you perhaps have told Jeanne d'Arc not to drive the English out of France, or would you have told the Spanish in 1808 not to push back the French invader, if there had been a corrupt and inept monarchy in France, or if a majority of the Spanish had not been mature enough for republican government? Keep in mind that if the domestic political question remains unresolved, that certainly constitutes a *mistake*; but meanwhile if you do not attempt to resolve the national question, you are outright *guilty*. You will not be able to cancel out the mistake if you do not first cleanse yourselves of your guilt.[4]
>
> By fighting against the foreigner under our present domestic political circumstances, you neither renounce nor undermine your right to subsequently seek to transform those political circumstances and to erect a grander edifice above the one that presently exists. Quite the opposite: you will remain pure and indeed you will be morally improved by your sacrifice, and you will be more certain of being heard one day when you launch your regenerating effort.

[4] Mazzini's underlying claim here is that in a moment of danger, the *national* cause should have priority over the republican cause. Hence even those Italian patriots who deeply dislike the monarchy ought to fight against the foreign enemy and put aside for the time being their domestic political demands.

If you do not fight today you will betray an urgent duty, out of anger for not being able to fulfill another duty. You will thus leave the field free for others to commit all the likely mistakes and misdeeds that you could perhaps prevent. You will abandon the sacred flag that says: "I help all my brothers who suffer," because that flag does not reflect all the preferences that you have in your head. In short, you will condemn the Country to a prolonged dishonor, just because you have not been able so far to remake it to your liking. Should you end up betrayed, your protest will be more welcome to God and more likely to be listened to by other men, after you have fought and are thus already known to your brothers, instead of suddenly stepping out of a corner where you had remained hidden out of fear of unknown risks.

But what should I tell those men who are almost drunk with the thought of war; who do not care about the means; who do not try to assess the likely dangers, not so much for themselves but rather for the entire country, and who say: "We will follow any ruling power who gives the signal for battle"? I feel the duty, and thinking about past events, I could almost say, the right, to tell those men who are trying to persuade the country to give itself blindly, without any agreements or precautions that look toward the future:

Remember Villafranca, remember Nizza [Nice], remember how the dishonor of five years of subjugation to the French Empire weighs on Italy. And remember the disaster and dishonor that derived exactly from plunging into battle blindly, when others who were informed and foreseeing warned you to negotiate instead and called on you to be vigilant. Will you constantly repeat the same errors? Do you forget that while one may well be able to overcome an illness and any related weakening of the organism, a subsequent relapse is almost always irreparably fatal? It is not so much a question of fighting; it is rather a question of winning. We need to insure ourselves against the consequences of a victory attained through foreign armies; we need to get Venice without Plombières.[5] And only the conditions to which I have referred here can successfully lead us toward that *goal*.

[5] In 1858 Piedmont had entered into a secret alliance with France, known as the Plombières agreement after the town where it was signed. Napoleon III, who had imperial ambitions over Italy, promised that in case of a successful war against Austria, Piedmont would gain control over all of northern Italy, while central and southern Italy would fall into France's sphere of influence. In late April 1859, Piedmont succeeded in provoking a war against Austria, but after only two months of fighting Napoleon negotiated a cease-fire with Austria at Villafranca. Piedmont acquired only the region of Lombardy and some central Italian territories; in exchange it had to cede the town of Nizza and the Savoy region to France. Hence Mazzini's reference to the "dishonour" of Villafranca and Nizza.

Can our country succeed? I am deeply convinced that we can succeed, if only we truly want to. The expression of a country's will is almost always conducive to its objective, but that will needs to be universal, insistent, explicit, and validated by deeds that show awareness of both rights and duties. May our Associations take upon themselves the task of expressing such a national will. May all the patriotic groupings that exist in Italy today, regardless of whether they are independent or joined in brotherhood, whether they are united in the same faith or divided over details, adopt the aforementioned principles and say so aloud. May every locality have its own assembly and speak with one voice, peacefully, yet solemnly and severely. May the country's program of action reach up to the government.

May the nation arm itself, to prove that Italy can, and indeed wants to, stand alone in this effort. May every locality summon its Volunteers and send them forth. Our Associations shall assemble the necessary funds to arm and sustain our volunteers, and to aid a popular insurrection within the Veneto itself. In order to gather those funds, we shall rely on patriotic subscriptions, as well as on the Municipalities' financial support. And may every volunteer about to depart swear to himself and his companions that he will not lay down his arms until the Unity of our Country has been achieved. This advice of mine derives not just from my faith in Italy, which is indeed ever present in my soul, but also from everything I know about the intentions guiding the foreigner's attitude toward war.

May 9, 1866
Gius. Mazzini

Neither Pacifism nor Terror: Considerations on the Paris Commune and the French National Assembly (1871)

I.

If what has motivated me over the years was just the result of an *opinion* and not of a deeply held *belief,* then the orgy of anger, vendetta, and bloodshed that Paris has for many days now displayed to the world would fill my soul with desperation.[1] This spectacle reminds me of the most horrible visions of Dante's *Inferno*. Here a people, an entire nation, is turning its teeth on itself in a drunken fury and lacerating its own flesh while howling for victory. They dance an infernal reel around a grave dug with their own hands; they kill, torture, burn, and commit crimes without any plans, objectives, or hope. And with a crazed cry, they are setting fire to their own funeral pyre, under the eyes of a foreign invader [i.e. the Prussians] against whom they did not know how to fight. . . .

The Commune sprang forth not from a superior *principle* of Country or Humanity, but from a narrow Parisian *interest*. It deliberately butchered hostages even though their deaths did not in any way aid its cause. Then, as its members gradually abandoned their posts, it deliberately condemned the City's buildings and historic glories to flames.

Meanwhile the National Assembly, elected to choose between war and peace, has no legal title to its existence today. It calls for the atrocious slaughter of prisoners, not combatants, and dishonorably cheers an unleashed soldiery to bloodshed. The soldiers willingly murder their brothers, thus seeking to suppress their sense of shame for the defeats

[1] Original title: "Il Comune e l'Assemblea." In this essay Mazzini presents a scathing critique of the revolutionary Paris Commune, proclaimed after France's humiliating defeat against Prussia in 1870 and the subsequent fall of Napoleon III. Mazzini sees the revolutionary turmoil in Paris as an instance of violent class warfare, which he opposed throughout his life. He thought that any violent class struggle would be incompatible with a genuine republican spirit, since it would unnecessarily undermine the patriotic bond among citizens. Mazzini appeals to the middle classes, who should support the workers' desire for social improvement as a matter of moral duty and for the sake of social stability. This essay also clearly illustrates Mazzini's wholehearted opposition to wanton violence and acts of terrorism against civilians.

suffered in the war against the German armies. And all this in spite of the fact that even the shadow of revolutionary danger has now disappeared and the men of the Commune are either exhausted, imprisoned, or have fled. The blood that has been shed and continues to be shed serves no purpose other than that of vengeance against the winners on one side and the vanquished on the other. It has been shed out of hatred or cruel fear, out of base passions that are always guilty and unworthy of any good cause. Such passions become outright horrific when they recall the crime of Cain and are viciously committed amongst the sons of the same soil.[2] . . .

But what about us; what about Europe and Italy? Don't we have duties? And what are we doing to fulfill them? Faced with the convulsive agonies of a suicidal people, should we abandon ourselves to the cowardice of skeptical distress? Or should we rather, depending on our personal disposition, react with anger or crazy fear to all this death—at the risk of bringing on ourselves those same horrors that have occurred elsewhere?

Our first duty is to openly and definitively distance ourselves from both sides in that struggle and make sure that the *moral* sense that unfortunately has been lost in France is not lost in Italy. Woe to us if we don't recognize deep in our souls that the entirety of our future progress is at stake here! Woe if the sacred battle between Good and Evil, Justice and Arbitrary Power, Truth and Mendacity, which has thus far been fought in full daylight and under God's eye all over Europe, is converted into a war conducted in the shadows without a defining standard, without a beacon to guide the combatants, and with no other inspiration than the impulses of the moment and the miserable passions of each individual!

Without alluding to anyone in particular, I deplore the fact that our own public opinion is undeniably divided into two opposing camps at present: one camp more or less openly sides with the Commune; the other more or less supports the Assembly. Both tend to either downplay or magnify the importance of certain facts, while they say nothing about others, and both tend to exaggerate or distort the characteristics

[2] In the chaos that followed military defeat, the population of Paris, and especially its working-class elements, had rallied around the Commune and its radical experiment in direct democracy. At the same time, France's conservative rural majority, together with the aristocracy and the rich bourgeoisie that had largely fled Paris, elected a new conservative National Assembly in February 1871, which provisionally met in Bordeaux. By late May, the new French government led by Adolphe Thiers had reassembled a sufficiently strong army to move against the radical insurgents in Paris. The ensuing, extremely bloody fighting between the French national army and the revolutionary militias in Paris is what Mazzini refers to. Almost 20,000 captive revolutionaries were summarily executed in little more than a week.

and consequences of specific events, depending on what side they have chosen to support. . . . Let me repeat that we must once and for all distance ourselves from both sides. Neither of them possesses Justice and eternal Right, and these should be the only standards guiding our judgments. We are republicans. We are convinced that if there is a way that France can slowly rise again, relearn the value of Truth and of the Moral Law, and rescue herself from the sad need for periodic and frequently violent revolutions, it lies in the institution of a Republic built on just foundations. French corruption is the product of two Bourbon monarchies and two empires, and it would continue to grow into a cancer if the monarchy should last. There are no examples in history of any peoples that have been regenerated by the return of twice-fallen dynasties.

It is frequently claimed that to found a republic one needs first of all republicans and republican virtues. This comes down to saying that even before tearing down the existing monarchies, we should begin to impart a republican education to the people; in other words, faith in the republican principle should be taught starting from its opposite—the monarchic principle. But as a matter of fact, republics need to be founded first, so that republicans can then be created through republican education. In France the source of all internal disagreements lies in the profound imbalance between the cities, which are republican, and the rural areas, which are not. The latter remain uneducated and are still frightened by memories of the *terror* and slaughters of 1793. Only a uniform National Education can overcome this imbalance, and that education cannot be imparted without first establishing a Republic. Threatened monarchies, knowing that their days are numbered, cannot give that which they anticipate will sooner or later be converted into a weapon in the hands of their enemies. But we are republicans. And since we are plainly seeking to convert those who are not yet republicans, we must know and openly declare to friends and enemies what kind of Republic it is that we are calling for. We must do so without regard for tactical considerations. . . .

Now more than ever it is time for republicans to show themselves to be a *party* and not a *faction*: that is, a collectivity of men gathered around a *principle* and not just a group of individuals who momentarily come together to pursue the *interest* of one or several among them. This *principle* is for us the sole source of *authority*, the sole standard by which to judge the plans and activities that are gradually unfolding during this period of transition. This principle embodies an idea of Life, and it is founded on the Law of moral, intellectual, and economic Progress. It is to be developed through the brotherly Association of all the elements that make up the nation and of different Peoples with each other. The republican form of government is nothing but a means—and a quite unique one in our view—to quickly translate the aforementioned *association* into reality. Our belief in this *principle* determines our solidarity with all those who call themselves republican. We reject every attempt at political and social renewal that is not inspired by this *principle* or that violates it by insisting on the supremacy of the *self*. We likewise reject every attempt that closes the pathway to *association* by dismembering the unity of the highest form of association—the *Country*, or that contaminates the flag with unjust and unnecessary acts of violence that are damaging to the moral progress of a people. Any victory of such attempts—if it were possible—would not be our victory, nor would it fill us with strength or hope. Their defeat is not our defeat; it does not weaken us like a sudden setback and does not diminish the likelihood that our beliefs may succeed.

II.

How could a civilized city such as Paris in the nineteenth century witness the excesses that we mentioned above? Why is it that such a generally happy, refined, and warm-hearted people as the French have lost all sense of morality? How could it be that in a Nation whose citizens appeared to incarnate more than elsewhere a sense of Unity and pride of Country, aggressors and aggressed suddenly forgot both? One side [the Commune] set itself a project of dismemberment, which has been recently put into practice through the senseless destruction of men and property. Meanwhile, once the foreigner's victory had been quietly and dishonorably accepted, the other side [represented by the Assembly] fought other native Frenchmen with a baseless ferocity and a rage of drunken savagery. Now, shouldn't we Italians seriously meditate on the reasons for these sad events and do everything possible to avoid them being repeated among ourselves? Instead we divide ourselves into two camps: one composed of angry children who loudly clamor for vengeance on the basis of opinions and facts that are not theirs; the other made up of heartless Machiavellians who see in the ruin of a people nothing but a weapon with which to unjustly wound their own adversaries. . . .

Some of our friends advise us to keep quiet with regard to some of these questions and to modify our language concerning others: "You run the risk," they say, "of alienating from your cause the young and most enraged enemies of the system that you are fighting, who might be the first to act if needed." But we cannot accept this advice. As republicans we cannot disregard the question of means and accept the absurd, backward, politically immoral notion of the republic recently witnessed in Paris. . . .

We believe in the sacredness of ideas. We can thus not disguise our own ideas, nor can we administer them in small doses to please others, hoping that at least some tiny part will eventually be absorbed. We do not like parliamentary tactics. Besides, they are not really able to change states and place them under a new principle. We love Italy above anything else, but we want it to be connected with the life and progress of Humanity. We want it to be a beacon of morality and virtue among other peoples. In other words: we want a republic, but one that is free from mistakes, lies, and faults. What purpose would a republic serve, if it had to feed itself on the very passions, anger, and selfishness that we are fighting?

We disagree with those dreamers who preach peace at any cost, even that of dishonor, and who do not strive to make Justice the sole basis of any lasting peace. We believe war to be sacred under certain circumstances. But war must always be fought within the limits of necessity, when there is no other way to achieve the good. It has to be governed by a religious principle of Duty and needs to be fought loyally and solemnly, with the altar of Mercy erected face to face with the altar of Courage. No war must ever be contaminated by a spirit of vengeance, or by the brutal ferocity of a boundless egoism. If our war resembled that of the African-trained soldiery that carried out the massacres of December 2 and that recently fought in Paris, we would not deserve to win. I do not know for certain whether we will be up to the challenge of the present situation. However, I know that the Republic has an inherent obligation to the world to be better than its opposite institution, Monarchy. It would be disastrous to our cause if our fellow republicans were to forget this. . . .

France's materialism became fully apparent toward the end of the eighteenth century. It had first been announced by certain sad examples of corruption among its princes and monarchical Courts. Then it was further developed by the cold, uncertain, and insincere Deism of Voltaire and others amongst the so-called philosophers, who in the name of who-knows-what intellectual aristocracy wanted absolute liberty for themselves and some trivial religious bond for the people.[3] . . . The seed

---

[3] Deism as a religious philosophy became prominent in Great Britain, France, and the United States in the seventeenth and eighteenth centuries. Deism accepted the existence of a creator on the basis of reason, but rejected belief in a supernatural deity who interacts with humankind. The most famous of the French Deists was Voltaire, whose teachings Mazzini rejected as one of the main rationalizations for of the amoral *materialism* that had led France into ruin.

of France's ruin lies precisely in the conscious or unconscious acceptance of those foolish, odious doctrines, both as a theoretical guidance and in practical life. Those same doctrines might well spell our own ruin if they were to prevail among us—propagated by inconsiderate youth who might want to impress the people with their rhetoric.

The *goal* assigned to our earthly existence is that of achieving a collective life for Humanity. It is our commanded Duty to help bring it about. But the very possibility of worshipping this superior, shared *idea*—which also acknowledges the supremacy of a preordained Moral Law—was erased in France. What has been left is the bare notion of *right* and the belief in the supremacy of the *individual*. This latter belief in particular lacks any solid foundations; it has also been quite incapable of solving the great problems that have now been stirring our souls for some time. Only the great idea mentioned above can lead to a genuine *liberty*. Now, to make this idea effective and to solve all related problems, it would first have been necessary to tackle the problem of *association*. This has not been done in France, and so the consequences that can be observed there today appear to have been almost inevitable. And they are indeed fatal. . . .

The false theory of the supremacy of the *self* fully expressed itself during the French Revolution. The resultant, equally false doctrine was that every people and every individual ought to be concerned only with themselves and not with the prescribed *goal*, which instead ought to be pursued at all costs since it alone gives value and meaning to life. These beliefs culminated in the negation of all National Sovereignty, in the dominion of the smallest localities over the whole. The notion of federalism was thus taken to its logical extreme, with each tiny village claiming to be sovereign. . . .

Over the following decades, the times had become ripe in France for the so-called *social* question to arise. This was mainly due to a faulty distribution of economic wealth but also to the gradual emergence of intellectually more advanced, skilled workers with their specific needs. For anyone who truly understands it, the social question is a sacred and religious question that stands above all others. It aims to ground the Economy on a sense of Duty and mutual love and thus seeks to promote human *unity*, which is our ultimate *goal*. But in France the social question too was impoverished and misdirected by the materialism of its leaders. It became focused on the sole question of material satisfaction, and thus it put forward as an *end* what should only have been a *means* to intellectual and moral progress. In addition, it divided the republican camp into two, by increasingly alienating a multitude of workers from the great ideas and duties that alone can make and improve a people. Thus in France the social question weakened the workers' love and worship of Country, fomenting hatred between those who were already enjoying the fruits of their labors and those who hoped they could soon enjoy them.[4] . . .

For these reasons, France witnessed several insurrections without a clear plan, which eventually culminated in civil war. The Republic of 1848 was thus destroyed. That Republic had admittedly lacked a strong faith and always remained inferior to its mandate, but popular unity could have improved it over time. In subsequent years, we saw the workingmen of Paris remain surprisingly passive when faced with the many usurpations of the Second Empire, out of an uncertain and sad hope that this corrupt regime might implement the desired social change. All this suggests that the moral sense of the French people had been perverted by their single-minded focus on material satisfaction, to be gained by any means necessary. In the meantime the French Army rallied behind the materialism of the *flag*, thus substituting a mere symbol for the idea. It fought several wars in this spirit, namely against the Roman Republic, the Russian Tsar, Mexico, and even against its fellow Frenchmen.[5] We believe that human *life* is always and forever sacred, given by God and destined to immortality. But unfortunately, life has lost all its sacred character among the French Army and the French people. Thus France has fallen. Similarly, every people will fall that accepts the materialist teaching according to which the objective of life is to *enjoy* oneself and overcome all obstacles to pleasure. May the newborn Italian nation not fall in this way! . . .

III.

We have spoken frankly to our fellow republicans. It was a duty that we had to fulfill, even at the risk of displeasing many of the militants who worship our own banner. But we cannot stop at this point and just be silent. We would regret it later if we did not also discuss more generally the guilty errors of the class of men who are represented in France by the Assembly, but who exist elsewhere as well. We do not want to mention again the inclination to fierce vengeance exhibited by this

---

[4] To the end of his life, Mazzini remained resolutely opposed to the idea of class consciousness and class struggle, which he thought would undermine the unity of the nation. He stubbornly refused to acknowledge that by mobilizing the workers, class consciousness might usefully contribute to advancing the republican cause.

[5] In 1849 France had led a military expedition against the revolutionary Roman Republic; thereafter it joined Great Britain in the Crimean War against Russia (1853–56); finally it went to war against Mexico in 1861 and installed Maximilian of Habsburg as the new Mexican emperor (1863–67).

class. Such acts of vengeance and ferocity appear particularly wicked, taking into account that they have been committed by the stronger party, which so far has been victorious. Members of the other party [i.e. the Commune] have also committed similar ferocious acts, but those were largely reactive. Hence their actions can at least be understood, if never justified.

The question we are grappling with goes far beyond the sad circumstances of our present. Let us therefore seek some remedy for the future. What could be done to ensure that the shameful events of the recent past will not repeat themselves tomorrow? I would like us to think of Italy in particular: in view of the present situation, it appears that our followers' healthy instincts and their apostolate have thus far been crucial in preventing major turmoil amongst ourselves. But the danger continues to loom on the horizon, and it might become much more real if the rulers were to persist in their present carelessness or stubborn resistance to the people's actual needs and sacred aspirations.

How did the spirit of materialism generally descend on the people and the craftsmen? What is the origin of this exclusive worship of earthly goods; of the idolatry of *interests* that has replaced the veneration of *principles* and sacred ideas? The roots of this materialism lie in the miscreant attitudes and the vices of monarchical Courts; the corruption and conduct of the high Clergy; and the ostentatious habits of the wealthy. But perhaps its origins can be traced back most clearly to the *goal* which that group of men who collectively call themselves the *bourgeoisie*, but whom we shall here call the *middle class*, have visibly chosen for themselves. This class is not just composed of the capital holders and those who possess the means of production. It also includes those who have been able to benefit from favorable circumstances, by educating their intellect for the performance of various tasks. This latter group of educated middle-class citizens has come to dominate in different professions, such as public offices, teaching jobs, the press, industrial enterprises, and in everything that more or less officially represents the country.

The middle class as a whole was thus called on to embark on the most beautiful, grandest, and holiest mission that one could imagine: to extend a friendly hand to the immediately inferior class and raise it to one's own level. It could thus have employed the vast means at its disposal to educate the uneducated. It could have disclosed the pathway to free labor and a more humane life for all those who until then had spent their existence in poverty and uncertainty. In short, it could have promised to the millions of disadvantaged people on this earth that which Christianity had promised them in heaven, namely a native Land of free and equal human beings.

Did not religion abolish the perpetuity of classes eighteen centuries ago, by condemning the dogma of the two natures [human and divine] and teaching that *all men are God's children*? Didn't History prophesize to the descendants of those who were emancipated from serfdom seven centuries ago that, like *slaves* had first become *servants* and then free inhabitants of Municipalities, so there would be a time when *wage laborers* would become *associated workers*? And does not every political tradition teach the following harsh and enduring lesson: namely, that Humanity advances either by the slow and peaceful initiative of those who are at the top, or through the turbulent violence of those who are at the bottom?

The middle classes forgot both their Duty and the most basic standards of prudence. They were misled by a false philosophy and the ensuing politics, which could not go beyond the *rights of the self*. Hence they forgot that all their advances were achieved with the help of the multitudes, which had been motivated and inflamed by promises of betterment and liberty. The middle classes had become secure in *their* rights: freedom of the Press and of Association, access to various offices, election rights and rights of eligibility. Meanwhile the large masses of uneducated people did not enjoy those same rights, and they had to work constantly just in order to survive. But why should the middle classes have cared? Why should they have fought for others? The members of the middle class lacked any notion of Duty, which can only be derived from a Supreme Law. They similarly lacked any belief in a common *goal*, which can only result from a prearranged and intelligent plan. They did not even believe in the existence of an afterlife, except insofar as it was implicit in their sterile and cold Deism. What remained was the worship of ease, of comforts, interests, and more generally of all material things. And thus they were overcome.

All the sad consequences of Egoism thus became evident among the middle classes: jealousy of all those who showed the intention to rise up to their level; suspicion of every progress of freedom among the multitudes that could have realized that intention; a tactical allegiance to the privileges of the monarchy, which they hoped would strengthen their own privilege; opposition to any extension of the franchise; preference for standing armies and resistance to arming the Nation; finally monopoly of legislative power. In short, they took care of their own interests while those of the larger population were neglected and betrayed. . . .

With regard to our own situation, the official or semiofficial policies of the powers that be point toward the following lessons for Italy: first, international politics is guided by the materialism of short-term *interests* without any form of *moral* principle to guide it. Second, policy more generally reflects the government's momentary interests, without any attempt to unite the people and the leaders under a common *goal*. Third, materialism dominates in religious matters as well. The religious bond is invoked when it can buttress political authority, while it is denigrated and violated whenever it attempts to limit or direct that same authority. In the current dispute with the pope, this materialism culminates in the sheer hypocrisy of those who conspire against him even while they display a needless servility.[6] Fourth, there is a general mistrust of thoughts and ideas considered to be dangerous; of all innovative proposals, which are dismissed as "utopian"; of every increase in liberty and of every Association that seeks to bring it about; and finally of every idea that opens up or heralds a new horizon to the spirit. Attendant *practices*, which unfortunately confirm these lessons, are well known to Italy. We do not want to soil our pages by discussing them.

Time and materialism have worn out the age-old religious faith, which at least promised the blessings of heaven to those condemned to suffering on earth. No Education is offered today which could replace that old faith and give hope to the disadvantaged, by guiding them toward a higher and more unifying belief in *duty*. Gone are those great ideas that can instill the virtue of sacrifice in the heart of the multitudes, and which go by the names of Country, Honor, Glory, Liberty, Independence, and Mission. Given all this, why should the aspirations of the feared working classes not focus exactly on obtaining all those material goods that have thus far been denied to them? Why should they not have acquired the desire for material pleasure, after having observed for all too long how the socially superior classes indulged in those pleasures? Worst of all, the more moderate demands put forward by these classes have been rejected, thus condemning them to the immobility of their current condition. And this has happened in a world in which the hand of God has imprinted the word *Progress* everywhere. So why should the disadvantaged classes not rally behind the first person who revealed their force to them and urged them to achieve with violence and at others' expense that which in principle they should have obtained by other means, without ruining those who had already made gains from past labors? No doubt, the workers themselves have made many mistakes. But why has the class that holds Power not educated those millions of disadvantaged men to the Truth, having the intellec-

---

[6] Between 1859 and 1861, all of the papal territories in central Italy, except for the Vatican itself, were annexed to the new Italian state. This led to a strained relationship between the pope and Italy's new civilian leadership for several decades after national unification. The conflict between the Vatican and the new Italian state would reach its high point in 1874, when Pope Pius IX pronounced his famous *non expedit* formula, which explicitly called on Italian Catholics to refrain from taking part in national elections.

tual and material means to do so? And why has it not subsequently led those same men, step by step, to actually *practice* this Truth?

Today the souls of all those disadvantaged men appear wary and annoyed. The working classes display a guilty tendency to vent their anger at the prosperous and seek vengeance against those who offended them and laughed at their requests. Now of course *we* can reproach them for their behavior, and indeed we do so. But how can the wealthy classes, who were at first uncaring and now react ferociously against the workers, demand that the latter behave according to virtues which they simply do not possess? For more than forty years now, the question to which Paris has in these past few months made a sad example has been explicitly tossed about all over Europe, among the working classes of France, England, and Germany. But has anybody seriously thought about resolving the problem? Has anybody been working toward peaceful progress on this matter? The governing classes inside and outside of parliament, the owners of public offices and capital, sneered at the demands of the working classes and bloodily repressed their *acts*. Far from cooperating with the workers to solve the social question, the governing classes chose to engage in a duel. They said: "*We will hinder your path toward progress with Force.*" The likely consequences should have been foreseen. But it is useless to curse the situation in which we find ourselves. The very premises need to be changed, and this needs to happen quickly. For the sake of what we hold dearest; we need to hurry. . . .

We believe in God, the sacredness of the Family, individual Property, and the Nation. We reject those foolish theories that underpin the Paris Commune and the leanings of the [communist] *International* as we know them.[7] What Italy's working classes want, we [the republicans] want as well. And that is the following:

1. Within a People that rise to the Unity of a Nation, the workers want to rise as well. After all, they have spilled a lot of their own blood in the struggle for national unification. They want to be part of that Unity as citizens and as free inhabitants of a free land. They want to improve their moral and intellectual conditions. But given that intellectual progress requires time and resources that they lack today, they want to improve their economic conditions, too.

2. The workers want a truly National Education. They want a state willing to share with *everyone* the traditions, the universally accepted

[7] Mazzini is referring to Karl Marx's Communist International. Mazzini considered Marxist communism to be among the most pernicious enemies of the republic, because its theory of class struggle implied a conflicting conception of politics, and as mentioned above, Mazzini feared that this would disrupt the principle of national unity.

principles, and the *goal* of the country in which they live and act, as a guarantee of moral equality and future progress. They also want a state capable of facilitating the special education necessary for the type of work they choose.

3. The workers want the right to *vote*. They want a political order where they can express their needs, habits, and desires by means of *their* elected representatives. So far, the workers have been represented by men from other classes, who have different interests.

4. They want the organization of a National Militia. When necessary, this Militia should be able to call on them to fight for the integrity, independence, honor, and the mission of their land. The Militia should train them to exercise this sacred duty. But all this should happen without endangering the liberty of the country and with the least amount of time taken away from family life and production.

5. They want a structure of local self-government that allows them to actively exercise their freedom. Without minimally hurting the moral and political Unity of the Nation, local representatives (elected through universal suffrage at the municipal level) should thus be entrusted with the management of local economic interests and other municipal affairs, including local public security. Finally, the municipality's elected representatives should appoint most of the officials who will execute national laws.

6. They want a fiscal system that leaves the bare necessities of life unaffected by any direct or indirect taxation, and weighs equally on anything that oversteps that limit.

7. They want to peacefully and gradually substitute *associated* labor for the current system of *wage* labor, where workers are paid by the holders of capital. In other words, they want to unite *capital* and *labor* in the hands of free and voluntary Associations, be it in the industrial or agricultural sectors.

This is what the working classes want, and they will achieve it. Their wishes and demands are based on justice; they are the natural result of historical progress in Humanity's collective life. They can be realized without any plunders or brutal violations of legitimately acquired rights. Indeed, the realization of their wishes could be useful to every class of citizens, since it would lead to an increase in production and a less anarchical organization of economic life. For half a century these wishes and demands have been despised, neglected, and strongly opposed; yet they have become stronger year after year. Today not thousands, but millions of men are brotherly united in their pursuit, and this suggests that the times are ripe for their triumph in the not-too-distant future.

We speak not to the professors, senators, and noblemen who would probably turn a deaf ear to our advice anyway, but to the numerous middle-class men. For they are not bound to privileged structures or interests but own what they do because of their labor. They want the good in principle, but they are overwhelmingly mistrustful of all change and fear troubles at every turn. It is hence to the middle classes that we speak: if this popular element that will inevitably attempt to climb the social ladder finds in those above itself nothing but blind resistance—fierce repression and outrage from some, and disdain, scorn, diffidence, and dislike from others—then you will bring much closer all the dangers that you fear. The popular element will then advance not like a quiet river that fertilizes the surrounding land, but like a turbulent mountain stream that breeches the levees, inundates, and drowns. Abandoned and rejected, the popular element will easily become aroused by all those words of anger and vendetta, those purely *negative* and subversive ideas that today abound in Europe. You will then have an imitation of the Paris Commune, the *International,* and the periodic scourge of civil war.

The part you need to play today is the following: you ought to love, to make concessions when faced with the aforementioned demands and actively support at least some of them, and finally to become associated with the workers' movement so as to keep it moderate. But will you be *able* to rise to this challenge, given your present situation? Will you be able to place yourselves as effective pacifiers between, on the one hand, the feared popular element and, on the other hand, those governing classes who out of necessity seek to suppress it and who don't actually care if you also succumb along the way? This is the first question that each of you should try to answer in their own mind. As for ourselves, we already answered this question a long time ago.

PART 3

International Politics, Military Intervention, and a New World Order

CHAPTER FOURTEEN

On Publicity in Foreign Affairs (1835)

I.

I know of only one decisive means to foil all diplomatic tricks—that is, to never rely on those questionable means in the first place.[1] There are some individuals who are so feeble-minded and so prone to misunderstand the true meaning of words, that they confuse the *Law of Peoples*[2] with diplomacy, although the two are of course utterly distinct. This confusion is indeed a very serious mistake. The Law of Peoples is as old as the world itself: it is an expression of the necessary relations that exist between different populations and different nations; it is the inevitable consequence of different peoples' external mission, which is itself a crucial and timeless component of their very nationality. The Law of Peoples follows the peoples' own development, it changes with the evolution of ideas and adapts to the gradual expansion of international society. It will go through a radical process of renewal once we have established a Holy Alliance of the Peoples; once all hate and international jealousies have been overcome and even the very memory of the Vienna settlement of 1815 along with its reactionary politics have been erased.[3]

Diplomacy stands to the *Law of Peoples* like hypocrisy stands to virtue. The former undermines and often blatantly violates the latter. The contemporary practice of diplomacy was born in the seventeenth century, when Europe's freedom had already begun to die and corruption was

[1] Original title: "De la publicité dans les affaires extérieures." Mazzini's central argument is that publicity in foreign affairs is desirable both as a matter of principle and in view of its likely consequences. Popular support can greatly increase a small nation's bargaining power internationally. More specifically, public support for a given course of action will generally advantage democracies when they are negotiating internationally with authoritarian states. Mazzini addressed this essay to his Swiss republican friends, but his arguments are of more general theoretical and practical relevance.

[2] Mazzini uses the French term *droit des gens*, after the Latin "jus gentium." Literally translated it means "law of peoples," but it could also be translated as "international law." Mazzini clearly emphasizes the customary and even the moral components of international law.

[3] In several of his essays on international relations, Mazzini called for the establishment of a "Holy" alliance among Europe's democratic and nationalist movements, in opposition to the existing and deeply reactionary Holy Alliance among the despotic governments of Austria, Russia, and Prussia.

gaining ground.[4] The new practice quickly acquired a central position in the mutual relations of the European monarchies. And in little more than a hundred years, it has done more damage to the world than all the bloody wars that ravaged Europe from the times of ancient Greece until Napoleon's recent fall at Waterloo. The effects of diplomacy have been corrupting, discouraging, and dividing. Diplomacy has erased entire nations and entire peoples—just think of how it dismembered Poland and killed the Venetian republic. It has built an organized structure of deception, and treason has become all but institutionalized. The diplomats know very well how much money or how much flattery is typically necessary to buy off a people's honor, and they know how to rely on treason to subsequently seal that same people's death.

However, faced with the first stirrings of solidarity among the European peoples, today the practice of diplomacy is about to be overcome. Insofar as diplomacy is still working at all, it is mainly due to two factors: first, the forced passivity of several peoples that are being kept down largely by foreign armies; and second, the guilty inertia and unforgivable feebleness of several representative governments—like the Swiss government, for instance—which would just need to open up foreign affairs to popular scrutiny in order to do away with the corrupt practice of diplomacy once and forever.

If you want to defeat an enemy, you should never accept to fight on his own terrain. You should instead disorient him and force him to descend onto a terrain unknown to him. You should develop a tactic radically opposed to your enemy's—to anything he has ever known and understood. You should lead him astray, surprise him. You will thus enjoy the twofold advantage of fighting on familiar ground while also holding the initiative. Meanwhile your enemy's strategy will out of necessity change from offensive to primarily defensive. A small change in your methods will be sufficient to render a large chunk of your enemy's capabilities useless, while your own capabilities will remain undiminished. You will force your enemy to retreat before your own advance, and you might even crush him entirely.

Thus, should you ever need to defend your country against a powerful, bold, and energetic aggressor, such as the French, for instance, you ought to disperse and launch a genuine guerrilla war. You should give your struggle a national character, as the Spanish did in 1808.[5] You should

---

[4] Mazzini bemoans the breakdown of the res publica Christiana, which he links to an idealized notion of European brotherhood and freedom, and the concomitant emergence of sovereign states in the seventeenth century.

[5] The Napoleonic invasion of Spain in 1808 was met by a determined popular resistance movement. Even after the French had gained control of nearly all the important towns, small guerrilla bands continued to attack French occupation forces with near impunity, inflicting a heavy toll on Napoleon's army. The Spanish popular resistance inspired several Italian patriots during the first half of the nineteenth century.

never let the outcome of an entire campaign be decided on a single day and never place your bets on a single battle. You should instead tire out your enemy; harass him through a series of small engagements with no apparent effect. You would need to attack, then withdraw, and then advance again. You should let your enemy anticipate victories that would never materialize and prepare for battles that would never happen. He would advance surrounded by dangers, and amidst dangers he would retreat. Ideally, every acre of land would cost him some of his blood, every step forward some of his confidence. The most important thing is to demoralize one's enemy. If you followed this advice, you would no doubt defend your country successfully.

But what if instead you had to regain or conquer a piece of territory from a slow, obstinate, and patient enemy who lacks any vigor but is very disciplined? In short, what if you had to fight the Austrians? If you were ever to find yourself in that situation, you shouldn't waste any time trying to anticipate every possible battlefield success and seeking to explore the terrain beyond what is strictly necessary. Audacity and rapidity would be your means to victory, after the model of Napoleon's early Italian campaigns. You would have to concentrate your forces, advance at the speed of lightning, and attack the enemy head on. More than anything you would have to believe in victory, and by following the aforementioned advice you would be likely to achieve it.

In yet another scenario, imagine you are a subject people. You want to break your chains and establish yourself as an independent nation. Thus far, your liberty has been denied by some tough and reactionary opponent. Imagine, for instance, that you are facing Prince Metternich, that preeminent genius of conservatism who has resisted every popular demand. You should oppose him boldly, with a fervor and desperate courage that he could never have expected. You should conspire only as much as strictly necessary to launch a coordinated action; then you should openly throw yourself at the enemy, with all your physical and mental strength. You should organize a generalized resistance movement. You should not waste any time in complex advance planning; and certainly you shouldn't work out several different scenarios on paper. You would just have to act! Act! Act! Only by rising up would you be able to overcome that evil man and his politics.

But let me come back to my initial topic of discussion: What are the constitutive elements of *diplomacy*? Secrecy and cunning. What are the forces we need to marshal in order to oppose it? Publicity and frankness. Mr. Bignon, himself a diplomat,[6] once put it rather eloquently: "The arms that are most rarely used, namely rectitude and faithfulness,

---

[6] Louis Pierre Édouard Bignon (1771–1841), French diplomat and historian. He held diplomatic posts under Napoleon and signed the surrender of Paris after Waterloo. In 1830 he served a spell as foreign minister under Louis Philippe.

are those that would most certainly and infallibly lead to success." You should thus refrain from following any muddled and intricate pathways. Don't flatter yourselves into believing that you can successfully stand up to your opponent [i.e., European monarchical diplomacy], that master of intrigue, by adopting its very same means. Any such attempt would fail quite miserably. On top of that you would have to carry the burden of dishonor, which would pull you down much more than that canny, old devil you are opposing.

My Swiss friends! Never seek to play by the rules of diplomacy; never even suggest that you might want to do so. Anyway, nobody would trust you, and rightly so. You can actually do much better: you ought to *negate* diplomacy, try to make it utterly ineffective. Imagine that some ambassador comes to see you in the name of a foreign king, his master, and asks you to lower the republican flag, which you are holding high in the name of the people, your own master. Or imagine him telling you that the hospitality you are granting to some exiles is an outrage to the king, and that you should arrest them at once. He may also insist that the freedom of the press enshrined in your constitution conflicts with his own country's laws, practices, and decrees. You should answer the ambassador as follows:

> What you request may be entirely sensible from your own point of view. In fact, your own safety depends on the lack of any free discussion and on the forced passivity of your subjects. But those requests seem entirely unreasonable to us: our own safety and well-being depend entirely on the calm and peaceful activity of our people, on the progressive development of their faculties, and on the existence of a generalized spirit of brotherly solidarity that cannot be sustained unless everyone's freedom is guaranteed. We [the Swiss] have been a republican, freedom-loving people for five centuries now; we are a frank and honest mountain folk. Each of us has acquired a taste for independence early on, while being fed from our mothers' bosoms and while breathing the fresh and pure mountain air that God sends down on us from the peaks of his eternal Alps. We do not know anything about your diplomacy; the People are our only master. That same master has placed us in the position of responsibility we presently occupy, so that we may carefully watch over his freedoms. We look after his interests and administer them in his name. We will accordingly convey to him your demands and shall forward you his response.

This is what you ought to say, and you should say so aloud.

Disclose everything to the people. Not even a single negotiation should be kept secret; not a single demand should remain hidden from the public eye. Everything that concerns the foreign life of your nation should be made public as quickly as possible, and the information should be widely distributed. This would only be a logical consequence of the principle to which you subscribe. But today, your safety and your very existence as a republican people crucially depend on the implementation of this advice. Your Great Councils accordingly ought to transmit a request to the executive power to introduce full publicity in foreign affairs. It may well be that secrecy is inherent to the despotic monarchies that surround you—for them, any negotiation is ultimately dependent on an individual will. But here, in this republican and popular nation, even the smallest diplomatic transaction becomes a matter of public policy. In this land, only the people can say: *l'état, c'est moi;*[7] and properly understood, only the people as such have interests. Now, it is quite evident that what concerns everyone ought to be known by everyone. The people want nobody else to guard their honor but themselves.

You should insist that everything be made public and act accordingly. Because it is right. It is urgent, too. Your very existence as a free people is at stake. Every secret agreement may contain the seeds of treason. You have not yet been betrayed, but nobody can say for certain that it won't happen tomorrow. We do not place our faith in human beings, but rather in God and the principles that originate from him. The *people* are one such principle. We have an unlimited faith in the people, their good sense, and their patriotic spirit. It is quite impossible for us to have that same faith in diplomacy and its various ploys.

II.

It seems to me that publicity in all matters that so far have fallen into the domain of diplomacy is vital for Switzerland. I would thus like to add a few words to what I already wrote on this question. There are many Swiss citizens who harbor a strong patriotic spirit in their hearts and have a right conception of their duties, derived from honor and the vital principle of their country. Nonetheless, those same citizens often pull back when called on to fulfill their duty, out of an exaggerated fear of the consequences that might follow. They see foreign intervention—armed intervention—as the outcome of any principled national stance in opposition to what the great powers demand. They believe in the words of any ambassador as if they were taken right out the Gospel. They dream of war and disasters every time the diplomats show signs of some bad temper.

[7] The phrase "L'état, c'est moi" ("I am the State") is generally attributed to the absolutist French king Louis XIV (1638–1715).

Exceedingly fearful, those Swiss patriots have so far mainly reasoned as follows: "What shall we do? We are weak and they are strong; we are standing alone and they are united. A heavy responsibility weighs on our shoulders. Shall we trigger a foreign invasion of our lands? Shall we challenge the great powers out of a principled stubbornness, when we know that we won't be able to sustain a serious fight against them? In view of the circumstances, we need to lower our heads under the heavy yoke of necessity. We need to make concessions, so that we can save our future." And thus they make concessions. They get down on their knees and accept the requests of foreign diplomats in the most submissive manner. When they get up again, their faces are stained with mud. But they find solace in telling themselves that they have saved their country. They have soiled the republican flag with a mark of dishonor, claiming that they have at least secured its survival.

Yet all those who act in this way forget one important thing; namely, that under current European circumstances it is *impossible for the kings to launch any war at all*. Among all the foreign powers that are menacing Switzerland today, not a single one would actually be able to carry through on its threats. Imagine that one morning the following news spreads around Europe: "The [Swiss] republicans have become tired of their suffering and their constant victimization. About one- or two-hundred thousand of them have raised the flag of rebellion. They are standing at the heart of Europe, in strong and impregnable positions, waiting at the bottom of mountain gorges that remind one of the Thermopiles. They are well armed, equipped, and organized. There they are, calling on the God of battles, the flag of European freedom raised in front of them and the European peoples supporting them from behind. They are united in a sacred oath, ready to push back any attack with their own counterattack and defeat any hostile initiative with their own counterinitiative. They have spoken words that make any oppressed nation bounce: Awakening! Humanity! Crusade! They have further announced: the hour has come, rise up!"

Imagine all this happening. Then tell me, hand on your heart, if you don't think that this could indeed resolve most of the Peoples' ills. The monarchy's final hour would have arrived; we would be heading toward the final showdown. Our victory would be certain and absolutism would soon be a thing of the past. You must indeed think so. Because you will remember how only a few years ago, about two hundred exiles were able to scare the European monarchs for several months; how a handful of workers—now we know for certain that they were not more than a handful—held up for five days an enemy force four times its size. The despotic governments turned pale at the time, and every patriot was trembling with excitement. What was lacking in those days to carry through the revolution in France, and to subsequently spread it all over Europe, was simply a known leader up to the challenge who would have been able to understand the mission and carry it out successfully.[8] . . .

The flag that is flying above our heads is the republican flag. It is the symbol of every insurrection today; it represents the goal of every effort undertaken by the progressive people of Europe. It could quickly change our current purely defensive and reactive war into a genuine war of principles. To make that happen, it would suffice for the Swiss people to wave the republican flag along their borders. Probably nothing else would be needed except a few words of brotherhood, forcefully spoken and addressed to all neighboring peoples. The kings actually know this; they know very well that even the smallest people in Europe—such as the Swiss—could seal their destiny forever, if provoked. All that would be necessary is for that people to combine their struggle with some active international propaganda effort. The kings are fully aware that the first cannon ball fired to mark the peoples' uprising will seal the end of monarchical Europe. As I have already explained, for this reason it is now practically impossible for the monarchs to launch any successful war. I believe that foreign governments will never actually carry out their threats. Any time the monarchical despots attempt to encroach on your liberties, to silence their claims it will be sufficient to speak up to them and let them understand that you are quite aware of your strengths.

By speaking out aloud, as suggested above, Switzerland could safeguard its liberty without any need to actually fight. But will it ever speak this language? Of course it won't. Where is the Swiss statesman who in the silence of his cabinet would dare to speak in such a way to the ambassador of a so-called great power? There aren't any. There can't be any, as long as negotiations are pursued in secret; as long as all foreign matters are discussed exclusively between governments, with the government of a powerful state on one side, and that of a small state on the other. Of course, any diplomatic negotiations today are deeply affected by the apparent inequality of power at the international stage. Hence, secrecy remains entrenched. . . .

But you ought to tear up the veil of secrecy. Everything should happen in full daylight and, so to speak, on the public square. Make sure that the foreign ambassador has to face not just the timid and weak representative of a tiny government, but rather an entire People. Make

---

[8] Mazzini is referring to the popular uprisings against the oppressive rule of King Charles X, which shook Paris in July 1830 and led Louis Philippe of Orléans to be installed as the new French ruler. When popular insurrections spread to other parts of Europe, such as central Italy and Poland, they were quickly repressed.

sure that he will be forced to tell an entire People: dishonor yourself. In other words, your representatives in foreign affairs should be backed up by the entire country, itself grumbling and menacing. Your negotiators' honor should be shielded by the honor of an entire nation. No longer should such crushing responsibilities weigh on your negotiators alone. The people ought to shoulder their own part. Your governmental representatives will then be able to say: "This is what the people want." And you will see—their attitude will become much more proud and courageous as a consequence. The envoys of the great powers will quickly change their tone if faced with such an energetic expression of the national will and the government's full adherence to it.

In all matters, but in political affairs more than anywhere else, publicity is life. It is a source of energy, force, independence, and honor; it leads to a shared conscience, emulation, and glory. . . . It is for these reasons that we urge publicity in all matters that so far have been shrouded in the mystery of diplomatic practices. The people ought to be peacefully, but nonetheless explicitly, involved in all matters that concern them directly. Their involvement could manifest itself in several ways, but essentially it would come down to expressing the national will through the press, through public meetings, speeches, and motions presented to the Grand Council members. I have no doubt that this would be sufficient to put a break on all diplomatic intrigues.

Complete publicity in foreign affairs is also the most powerful available means to rapidly sharpen the citizens' political skills. It is an effective tool of national education; it develops and invigorates a people's spirit of independence, and it more clearly defines the mission that a country is called on to pursue. Furthermore, it crucially nourishes the citizens' love of liberty; and finally it undermines those habits of egoism and indifference that typically divide the nation in all despotic states, with a class of rulers on one side and a class of subjects on the other. Every republican state should elevate the requirement of total publicity in foreign affairs into a defining characteristic of its existence.

It is quite striking to observe how even in those countries where the dogma of popular sovereignty is proclaimed, in foreign affairs the republican principle has so far been constantly made to defer to a vital element of its opposing, despotic principle—namely *secrecy*—which has also made it necessary to adopt most of the tactics associated with the latter principle. Thus the people have been denied any knowledge of those matters that are actually of greatest concern to them. In the United States there has been a growing awareness of this paradox. Major efforts are being undertaken throughout that country to introduce publicity in diplomatic relations, and sooner or later it will be achieved. Unlike the United States, Switzerland is today surrounded by active and powerful enemies, several of which are constantly plotting against it. My Swiss friends, shouldn't that give you a thousand good reasons to demand a strict and wholehearted application of our own governing principle—*publicity*—to foreign policy? Perhaps for the United States this is just a matter of logic and genuine moral commitment. For you, however, it may well be a matter of survival.

CHAPTER FIFTEEN

Foreign Despotism to Civilize a People?
Italy, Austria, and the Pope (1845)

A letter to Sir James Graham Bart [British home secretary]

Sir,

I thank you much for having afforded me the long desired opportunity to lay before a free nation, full of generous instincts, the sorrows of a brave, unhappy, misunderstood people.[1] I would like to submit to your judgment the complaints of 20 or 22 million men, whose ancestors headed the march of civilization in Europe, and who now demand for themselves the right to participate in the free, active, and continually progressive life that God has ordained for his creatures. Domestic and foreign oppressors have deprived the Italian people of all liberty of thought, speech, and action.

Your nation, Sir, has further aggravated our unhappy position. When you opened my correspondence at the request of one or several of our governments, you sowed seeds of mistrust in the hearts of our Italian youth.[2] You proved to them that the Union of the Governments against us is complete, and you destroyed the *prestige* that in their eyes was attached to the respected name of England.

---

[1] The original title of this essay, written by Mazzini in English, is "Italy, Austria, and the Pope." It was originally published as a separate pamphlet in London and addressed to Sir James Graham Bart (1792–1861), an influential Whig politician and British home secretary at the time. The essay offers a vivid and passionate description of the oppressive rule endured by the Italian people under Austria's colonial rule in the North and the Papal theocracy in central Italy. Mazzini's goal is to arouse sympathy for the Italian cause among English politicians and liberal public opinion. He insists that the Italian people are clearly ready for democratic self-determination, contrary to the argument put forward by some English conservatives at the time that the Italians required a despotic government to promote economic development and secure public order. Language and sentence structure have been updated for improved readability.

[2] During Mazzini's exile in London, for some time his correspondence was being systematically inspected by the British authorities, on Austria's explicit request. Mazzini found out about it by addressing several letters to himself and putting some rice grains inside the envelope, which fell out during the inspections. Once the issue became public, it was debated at length in the British parliament and the press, greatly increasing Mazzini's personal standing in liberal and progressive circles.

But at the same time, you also revealed to me, an Italian, exiled for the national cause, a duty that in part I am able to accomplish. That mistrust that you have caused to grow must be destroyed, for the good of *my* country and the honor of *yours*. I must demonstrate to my fellow countrymen that they would err in confounding the English Government with the English Nation. While seeking to elicit (so far as it may be done by a solitary individual) an expression of public opinion in favor of our sacred cause, I must also convince my native Italy that on the day when her national Flag shall float in the wind carried by strong and pure hands, here as everywhere else it will be greeted with active sympathy. I clearly reject—not just for ourselves but also for the cause we represent in a foreign land—all those odious accusations of *Conspiracy;* all the suspicion, Sir, that your calculated silence casts on our actions. The struggle in which the noblest amongst us have for so long been engaged is for us an affair of Duty, and the means through which we strive to pursue our end are the only ones left available for us. God willing, we shall continue to pursue our struggle: calumniated, yet proud, steadfast, and firm before God and our own consciences, the only judges we can recognize, in the exceptional position into which we have been thrown.

It is all the more necessary that this should be made clear, because throughout the whole of the controversy arising out of the shameful matter of the letter opening, the cause of the Italian People has not obtained a single, decisive demonstration of sympathy. The cause has been admirably pleaded by the Press as well as within the House of Parliament, so far as the individuals whom it so nearly touched were concerned, and so far as concerned the Country whose character for honor and loyal good faith was implicated. However, the question as it concerned Italy has not even been touched upon.

The *means* have been condemned, but nobody has taken the trouble to enquire into the *end* for which they were used. Everybody proclaimed the practice to be immoral, but nobody turned his attention to the theory involved, and of which the act in question was only an application. From every side, people have cried out to you, Sir: "You have no right to open the letters of this man any more than those of other men; you don't have the right to interfere in the affairs of other people. Restrict yourself to watching that the safety of the kingdom be not directly menaced, and do not, by overstepping these limits, violate the rights of individuals." But I don't know of anybody who has risen up to say: "You have rendered yourself doubly guilty in opening the private correspondence of this man. You have by so doing not only violated the rights of an individual whose conduct toward us Englishmen is irreproachable, you have also violated the law of Nations, the law of the entire world, and of God who governs it. Placed between right and wrong, you have chosen the wrong. Between a flagrant injustice sustained by brute force, and the efforts of those who were attempting to overcome it, you have declared yourself for *brute force*. You have ranged England on the side of the oppressors against the oppressed, on the side of the executioner against the victim. You have raised her flag in the service of European despotism. You have replaced the national motto: *Religious and Political Liberty for everyone, everywhere,* with the motto: *Liberty for us, and Tyranny for everyone else.* As if egoism could ever be made the basis of freedom; as if the true interest of England could ever be contrary to God's Law: *Love of all, for all; amelioration and development of all, supported by all.*"

It is here, however, as it seems to me, that the whole point of the question lies, for you and for your countrymen. Now that we are once warned, it matters little to us whether you open our letters or not: either we shall write nothing that could compromise our poor friends, or else we shall not transmit them by the Post. What concerns us more is whether in her efforts and in the struggle which she is preparing, Italy should count one additional enemy. It matters little to the country that you represent—or rather that I trust you do *not* represent—whether you have committed another particular abuse of your prerogative or not; unless there is uprightness in your heart and in your political tendencies, you will always possess sufficient power to do ill. This country needs to know where it is being led. It must be precisely informed on the principles of your international policy. The country should take care that the Government does not prostitute its name to diplomatic *chancelleries,* nor consign it to the curses of the mothers of Italy or the contempt of brave men who are being punished for their good actions. Whether you open twenty of our letters or merely *eight* (the actual yearly number according to the Lords' Committee), it will not retard the progress of the cause of Italian liberty. However, even one single betrayal authorized by the Government of a people professing to be free and Christian, aimed at protecting an unjust cause, leaves a lasting stain on the honor of the country. It tempts others to immorality; it augments everywhere that want of faith in virtue and in political honesty, which is the principal feature of our epoch.

One man only amongst you, Members of the Cabinet, has felt this. While you, Sir James, attempted to justify yourself by referring to the dead letter of an Act that had been passed under entirely different circumstances, he saw at once that your cause was irredeemably lost, unless you could ground it on some general *principle.* Hence, *he* sought a justification of the *espionage* exercised against me in a definition of England's mission in Europe. "It is," said the Duke of Wellington on the fourth of July 1844, "the proud distinction of the policy of this country that our object and our interest is not only to remain at peace ourselves with the whole world, but to maintain peace throughout the world and to promote the independence, the security and the prosperity of every country in the world."[3] I accept, for my part, this definition as it stands, and I find it very superior to all those theories of nonintervention under which all questions of international order and European progress are effaced. The absolute nonintervention doctrine in politics appears to me to be what indifference is in matters of Religion, namely: a disguised atheism. It represents the negation of all belief, of all general principles, of every mission of nations on behalf of Humanity. We are all, thank God, bound to each other in the world. Let us not forget that intervention has often resulted in good, great, and eminently progressive consequences. I am only astonished that in the midst of Parliament no one arose amongst all those who have recently traveled to Italy, or who are even superficially acquainted with her history, to tell him: "Security! peace! independence! My Lord, that is precisely what the man whose correspondence your colleagues have violated is seeking for his country. It is what was sought by those men who were shot several months ago in the Italian region of Calabria, possibly as a consequence of this violation.

There is no *Security* except under Laws, under wise laws voted by the best men and sanctioned by the love of the people. But there are no laws in Italy; there is instead the caprice of eight detested masters and of a handful of men chosen by these masters to support their arbitrary rule.[4] There can be no *peace*, except where there is harmony between the Governors and the Governed, where the Government represents the country's Intelligence called to direct its affairs, and the people are the country's executing arm. Our struggle, my Lord, has continued without interruption for fifty years, amidst the tears of the good and the blood of the brave.

As to *Independence,* you know well, my Lord, that this word as applied to Italy is bitter irony. You well know that nearly one-fourth of the entire peninsula is governed by an army of eighty thousand Austrians, and that the Princes who govern the remainder are little more than Austria's Viceroys. Whenever a cry for Liberty, progress, or amelioration arises from the bosom of any of these Viceroyalties, the Austrian army, in spite of the principles that England and France have proclaimed

[3] Arthur Wellesley, first Duke of Wellington (1769–1852); most famous for defeating Napoleon at Waterloo. In 1844 he was the influential leader of the British House of Lords.

[4] The Italian territory was carved up among eight different rulers at the time: there were the Austrian colonies in the North; the kingdom of Piedmont-Sardinia; the Papal state in central Italy; and the kingdom of Naples in the South; in addition to several city-states.

ten times within the last twenty years, comes forward to silence it with its *veto*. The mission that you believe ought to guide England toward our country is very beautiful, my Lord—a mission of protection, of fraternal benevolence, a generalization so far as is possible of the benefits you enjoy; such in truth is the mission a Christian nation would do well to exercise. But how can you make this compatible with your sanction of the current system of espionage, with your acceptance of torture and the scaffold? Have you ever asked yourselves whether they desire good or evil, justice or injustice, those men whom you are branding as Revolutionists in order to justify your policy of spying on them? Therein lies the whole question, and have you taken the trouble to examine it? They desire to obtain the same liberty which *You* Englishmen—let it not be forgotten, thanks to a revolution—are now enjoying: liberty of conscience and true religious freedom; liberty of speech, so that they may preach righteousness; liberty of action, so that they may put it into practice; the liberty, my Lord, which *you* promised us along with independence when you were commander-in-chief of the Allied Armies, and when you needed our aid to overthrow Napoleon.

The Italian revolutionaries desire to substitute the current state of affairs, characterized by hatred, mistrust, and fear, with a new situation under which they would be able to know each other, love each other, and help each other in the pursuit of their common goal. They desire to extinguish falsehood, to bury all those lifeless corpses of despotism, in order to replace them with a new *Reality:* something *true*, acting, living, with a power that shall be strong enough to guide them, and to which they may without shame yield allegiance. They desire to *Live*, my Lord, to live with all the faculties of their being, to live as God commands; to advance with the rest of the world; to be surrounded by brothers and not spies; to have instructors and not masters; to have a *home* and not a prison. Can you imagine that England is properly exercising her mission when she tells them: "*No! The World may well advance, but you shall be stationary. There is no God for you; you have the emperor of Austria and the pope. You are of the race of Cain, of the cursed race; you are the Pariahs of Europe. Resign yourselves in silence and suffer, but stir not, seek no relief, because Europe slumbers and you might disturb her repose?*" Christ—my Lord—also fulfilled a revolutionary Mission. He came to destroy the idols of the old world; he destroyed the illusory *peace* of paganism. In the face of a false religion that sanctioned the separation of races, castes, and human natures, he announced a new religion, the fundamental doctrine of which was the unity of the human family as God's offspring, so that we might arrive at universal brotherhood. Would you, my Lord, if you had been living in those times, have declared yourself on the side of Herod against Jesus, in the name of *Peace* and of the established Governments?

The Italian question is very little understood in England. The English people know in general terms that the country is suffering, but few are aware of the level that suffering has reached. The English know that some efforts are being made there to change the form of Government, but they believe that those efforts are merely the result of a handful of conspirators, who don't have much influence and lack any sympathies among the masses. In short, the Italian insurgents are thought to be exclusively moved by the blind and dangerous promptings of their own hearts.

In Italy nobody speaks: silence is the common law. But the people are silent out of terror; the masters are silent as a matter of policy. Conspiracies, civil strife, political persecution, and vengeance all exist, but they make no noise. They excite neither applause nor complaint. One might fancy the very steps of the scaffold were spread with velvet, so little noise do heads make when they fall. The stranger in search of health, or the pleasures of arts, passes through this fairy land on which God has lavished without measure all the gifts he has divided amongst the other lands of Europe; he comes on a spot where the soil has been recently stirred, and he does not suspect that he is treading on the grave of a martyr. The earth is covered with flowers, the Heaven above smiles divinely. Two great epochs of the human race—two worlds, the world of ancient paganism and the Christian world of the Middle Ages—lie before him to study; so why should he care about the *Present?* He tells himself: there is abundance of food here; there is sunshine; there is music in the air. What more can this indolent people desire?

Other men, men of numbers and statistics, *utilitarians*, are judging Italy according to their usual standards, as they would judge any other normal country. But they neglect on the one hand the current situation of political slavery and the trampling down of all indigenous elements; and on the other hand the vitality, the desire to *live*, which in spite of all obstacles is becoming apparent. Observing Italian affairs, those men find some fragments of superficial reform here and there, but they give credit to our governments and not to our own efforts or to the spirit that sustains us in the strife. They exhort us to be patient, to confine ourselves to peaceful efforts that will at best achieve small-scale improvements. Thus they somehow reconcile their lukewarm support of progress with what they are pleased to term the slumber of Europe. Once they cross their own frontiers, they leave behind their Faith, their historical memory, and more generally all heroic and social views. The idea of a *Nation* is too abstract for them. They see in Italy nothing but a country, a territory of so many thousand square miles, inhabited by so many million *bodies* (the souls do not enter into their calculation), who cannot reasonably expect from their political rulers anything more than a certain amount of food, clothing, and material comforts—*panem et circenses*. They would willingly efface the name of Italy from the map of Europe, in order to substitute it with a number. And above all this, influencing both the thoughtless traveler and those self-styled practical men, hovers the *Vae Victis!*[5]—the worship of actually existing circumstances, the incessant confusion of Might with Right. "You have risen up twice, thrice; and equally often have you fallen. Hence you are destined to suffer. We side only with the strong—we admire Victory." The conclusion is brutal. Such cynical statements also have a greatly negative impact on our situation: they engender indifference among foreign populations and embolden our despotic Governments. While we, exiled patriots, have our letters opened, it is highly probable, Sir James, that you would respect the missives of the Italian monarchy or republic.

Besides the aforementioned two classes of observers, another party exists. It may be called *your* party—the governmental party—that which sustains Austria as the civilizing power in Italy. This latter party says: "Peace, peace; we must have peace at any price. Italy is restless and her princes are weak, while Austria is strong. Hence, Austria cannot help extending her influence in one way or another over the entire country." . . . But it is *not true* that the Italian provinces under Austrian rule are well governed. The habits and local customs of those provinces are *not* taken into account. It is *not true* that existing central, provincial, municipal assemblies are free to speak, let alone sure of being listened to. It is *not true* that owing to the care of a paternal government, the material comforts are so great as to let the people forget that our government is a foreign yoke. That government actually deprives us of what is most precious to a man in this world: Independence, Spontaneity, Liberty.

There is no doubt that the region of Lombardy, which is controlled by the Austrians, has recently made some progress. In spite of our exhaustion as the result of foreign occupation, the heart of the country still beats: no doubt, elementary instruction is becoming more widespread; our industry is growing; and the population is increasing. But all this is primarily the result of our own vitality, of the general European progress that surrounds us, and of twenty-nine years of peace. To prove the disadvantage of a foreign and despotic government, must all of Lombardy become a wreck like Venice? It seems that we *can* live and *will* indeed do so, to take advantage of the Future and fulfill the destinies that are in store for us. But should this change our judgment with re-

[5] *Vae victis* is Latin for "Woe to the vanquished." The phrase is thought to have been pronounced by Brennus, leader of the Gauls, who captured Rome in 387 BC. It is commonly used to suggest that the vanquished have no rights.

gard to Austria? You like to compare the year 1839 with 1829 or with any other year of the period beginning in 1815. But why don't you instead compare the situation of Lombardy during all of this period with that of a previous period, say, the stormy period of the Cisalpine Republic or that of the kingdom of Italy (which, incidentally, we are far from regarding favorably)?[6] Why don't you study the strength of our vitality as it revealed itself at the slightest hint—nothing but a hint—of liberty from 1706 to 1799? Why don't you contrast that period with the thirteen months of Austrian possession that immediately followed? Or rather, if you would like to know what a Lombardy free from foreign control is capable of, why not go back to the thirteenth and fourteenth centuries? Why not compare the paltry advances so pompously advertised today with the 200,000 inhabitants of Milan at that time; with its seventy clothing factories; its sixty thousand workers in wool; and its 40-million-francs worth of wool exports, which five cities alone—Milan, Como, Pavia, Cremona, and Monza—traded every year through the port of Venice? We advance, you say; yes, undoubtedly we advance, thank God. All the reactionary genius of Mr. Metternich cannot dry up the energy of our old Italian race. But are you aware what tears and sweat every step of progress costs in those lands? Are you aware that most of the industrial enterprises seen in action now originated as far back as 1818, and that most of those who first developed them have actually been imprisoned? Are you aware how many of those schools the diffusion of which you admire owe their existence only to individual generosity and unheard-of determination? . . .

In the Italian territories controlled by Austria there is a censorship of the press and of all books, overseen by two ad hoc offices situated in Milan and in Venice. There is another system of censorship at the district level, exercised by the Austrian Delegate or any one he may employ, which carefully checks even writings that may not exceed a printed sheet. Yet another system of censorship applies to paintings and theatrical representations. Then there are special censors for all church-related matters, as well as for works on medicine, mathematics, and other subjects. Their straightforward goal is to prevent the development of new opinions. There are no political newspapers except the privileged *Gazette* in Milan and Venice, which actually belongs to the Government. The Police choose what news is printed there. No foreign newspapers are allowed, except those that represent royal power, and even those are suppressed whenever they contain anything disagreeable to the rulers.

[6] The Cisalpine republic (Repubblica Cisalpina) was formed by Napoleon Bonaparte in June 1797, in conquered territories centered in the Po River valley of northern Italy. Napoleon subsequently united a large chunk of northern and central Italy in the Kingdom of Italy (1805–14).

The high taxes imposed on all foreign papers are anyway sufficient to render their circulation next to nothing. A special application to the authorities in Vienna needs to be made before a literary journal can be launched, and those same authorities determine the content of any such journal. . . . And when you have complied with all these demands, when you have satisfied the rabid censors by erasing the best passages you had written, you are still constantly threatened. The Police, more powerful than the censors, may turn on you and seize and destroy your work, confiscating any volumes you may have already published.

I confess, Sir, that I am running out of patience. I am tempted to believe, not necessarily in the widespread existence of bad faith, but certainly of some bitter irony, whenever I hear murmured the word *intellectual progress* in regard to the measures pursued by a government whose real intention was so frankly declared by the Austrian emperor Francis I at Ljubljana in 1820: "We have no need for knowledge; it is enough for me if my subjects know how to read and write." You point to certain elementary works issued by the royal printing press. But have you actually read these books? Do you know that their aim is to denationalize us as much as possible? You mention a few incontestable signs of intellectual development, a few illustrious names: Is there then nothing short of death, degradation, absolute helplessness, which will prove the evil influence of Austria's leaden yoke on our faculties? Do you not perceive that it is precisely from our struggle that these developments result? We are forbidden to print in Lombardy: we print in Lugano, behind the Swiss border. We are forbidden to read good foreign books, but we at least partially overcome this absurd prohibition by smuggling in books from abroad. Is there any reason why you should attribute the steps of progress taken amongst us to the working of the Austrian system? After all, do you not find the same intellectual progress in those parts of Italy (the Papal States, the kingdom of Naples, for example), which you have no scruple in declaring horribly governed?

Ah! if your actions—I do not speak to you, Sir James, but to your countrymen—if only your actions were more influenced by that principle of Christian brotherhood that you so often mention; if, instead of following I don't know what scraps of the treaty of Vienna, you were to respect the eternal covenant of God with his children; if you could only convince yourselves that all injustice sanctioned against one of Humanity's members is an injury to Humanity as a whole! you would then recollect that under this Government, ostensibly so *favorable to Intellectual progress*, not a single literary man of note (Manzoni alone perhaps excepted) has gone through life without meeting with persecution. . . .

Education, intellectual development, administration, justice, public finances: all are corrupted and ill-organized in the provinces governed by the Austrian regime. And any little progress there is made not *through* the government, but *in spite* of it, thanks to our own strength and our own struggle.

In the foregoing pages I have highlighted the fundamental disease of our age. There are some men today who believe they can replace a people's heart and their head with some sort of technical mechanism, exclaiming: "Behold, man! the great problem of statesmanship consists in oiling the wheels, in order that the *circular motion* may go on forever." But that is not the position I take: it is not a *circular motion* that we require, but rather a *progressive* one, which can only be accomplished through liberty and love. It is not some modest economic growth or a little tax reduction that can determine the character of a people's life. We are not, thank God, of a nature to content ourselves with *panem et circenses* [bread and entertainment], in whatever abundance.

It is the *Soul* of the Italian Nation—its thought, mission, and conscience—that is at stake. It is *that* Soul they are attempting to destroy; it is *that* same endangered Soul which raises its voice through its martyrs and exiles, appealing to God. Have you become materialists to such an extent that you can only appreciate what can be weighed in gold or valued in commodities? There are between 4 and 5 million human creatures in the Italian provinces occupied by Austria, endowed with an immortal soul, powerful faculties, and energetic thoughts, with ardent and generous passions. They have aspirations toward free agency, and to achieve it they aim at a national union with other millions of brothers. Between 4 to 5 millions of men want to live and advance, under the eye of God, the only Master, toward the accomplishment of a social task they have in common with 16 or 17 million other men who speak the same language and tread the same earth. All of them were cradled in their infancy with the same maternal songs, strengthened in their youth by the same sun, inspired by the same historical memories and the same sources of literary genius. Country, liberty, brotherhood, vocation: everything is denied to them. Their faculties are curbed; they can move only inside a narrow circle traced for them by men who are strangers to their customs, their wants, and their wishes. Their tradition is broken by the cane of an Austrian corporal; their immortal soul is subject to the stupid caprices of a man seated on a throne in Vienna. And you go on indifferent, coolly inquiring whether these men are subject to this or that *tariff*, whether the bread that they eat cost them a halfpenny more or less! That tariff is always too high: because *they* have not decided on it themselves. That bread is always moistened with tears, for it is the bread of slaves.

Do you have an arithmetical figure in your statistics that accurately represents the costs of slavery? Slavery, I say: not just national slavery— which is death to us as a country, which inscribes a foreign name on the old flag of our fathers and dissolves the brotherhood of millions—but *moral* slavery, which enervates and corrupts; the yoke of the mind, the leprosy of the soul. What does it matter to us that they allow us to open schools for our children, if it is to teach these ignoble phrases: "*Subjects ought to conduct themselves as faithful slaves toward their masters . . . whose power extends over their goods as well as over their persons*"? What does it matter to us that two Universities are tolerated, if their Professors must have their lectures approved by Vienna? And what does it matter to us that there is some economic development, some progress in material well-being, if in the absence of all social aim and public life, this material progress—precious for a free people—will only serve to stir up egoism and drown the aspirations of our Italian soul in a gross sensuality? It would be a hundred times better to remain stuck in honest, dull ignorance and poverty rather than experience this phantom of science and prosperity in the service of a Lie.

Let me repeat it once again: if we go forward, if some signs of progress manifest themselves among us, it is not *thanks to them;* it is actually *in spite of them* and consequently *against them. . . .*

But why mention all these detached facts to prove the iniquity of the Austrian government in Italy? How could it be otherwise? In Lombardy there are occupying *Austrians* and native *Italians:* two peoples, having nothing in common, neither origin, nor language, manners, literature, beliefs, or vocation. The former are a people of conquerors, of usurpers more properly speaking—for Austria has never conquered except by treaties and marriages—and the latter a people of subjects. In other words, two distinct and hostile elements, which nothing, as both sides readily admit, has been able to fuse together. Their antagonism is manifested through periodical crises; their unending conflict is a constant source of agony that racks every member of the nation. As a consequence, whatever material progress may result from the activity of the subjects or the policy of the masters becomes useless and often outright dangerous. Is there any other country where such circumstances can exist without resulting in criminal charges against the government that upholds them? How can that government maintain itself amidst an unfriendly population, except by spreading terror and relying on brute force, sowing division and mistrust through a system of espionage! Indeed, the Austrian government is obliged to rely on treacherous spies and maintain in Lombardy, at our expense, an army of sixty thousand Germans. Meanwhile it sends our Italian conscripts to ruin their health for eight or nine years in Hungary, Bohemia, and Galicia. . .

Yet the greatest immorality (save for the first step—the unlawful possession of foreign lands) is actually *not* on Austria's side today. It is, I am bound to say, on the side of Europe, which looks at this crying injustice as if it were a normal fact; it is on the side of those who try to avert any possible international tension by misleadingly insisting on the material prosperity that the victims of this injustice may enjoy. The greatest immorality was on your side, Sir James, when you broke the seal of my letters for Austria's protection; it was on the side of England's Parliamentary majority, when, no doubt due to a lack of information on these points, it sanctioned such a proceeding by its vote.

So far I have sketched a few traits of the *best* government existing in Italy. I shall now outline, more briefly, the characteristic traits of the *worst*; the Papal State. I cannot here analyze each of the seven governments that rule over different parts of the Italian soil and which, like the seven heads of the Hydra, are insulting Italy's mission today. But I may state that they all lie somewhere between the two of which I am writing, as far as the political question is concerned. At one extreme we find the Austrian government, which is characterized by central despotism. At the other extreme there is the Papal State, which is characterized by organized anarchy—to the extent that such a thing is actually possible. This anarchy-like situation is an inevitable consequence of the government's constitutional structure. It can thus not be modified by written laws or any attempt at partial reform, come from what quarter they may.

The Papal government is elective and despotic: it rests on a man who is pope and king at the same time, and who proclaims himself to be infallible. No rule is prescribed, nor can any be prescribed, to the Sovereign. His electors, each of whom is also eligible, believe themselves to possess a divine character, and together they direct all governmental affairs. The chief offices in the different administrative departments are all filled by priests. Very many of them are entirely unaccountable, not merely in fact, but of right.

The pope, generally a member of the faction opposed to that which elected his predecessor, overturns the system in operation prior to his accession. His electors, the cardinals, each in turn eligible after him and feeling themselves his equals, govern according to their own whimsical interests, everyone in his sphere. The bishops, also partaking in this ostensibly divine form of government, exercise a wide and almost entirely independent power. The same, too, can be said about the chiefs of the Holy Inquisition. In general, the high clergymen who formally hold the principal offices are entirely incompetent to carry out their administration, given both their habits and their past studies. Hence, they discharge their duties with the aid of inferior employees. But those employees feel their position to be uncertain, dependent as it is on a necessarily short-lived patronage, and thus they are guilty of every possible embezzlement, aiming solely at personal enrichment. At the very bottom, the weary people, subject to constant mismanagement and exploitation, have themselves adopted the culture of corruption initiated by their superiors. They react by revolt or committing petty crimes. Such is, in short, the current situation in Papal Italy.

In such a system there is not, and there cannot be, any room for general social interests; the only interests being actively pursued are those of the self. The priests who govern have nothing in common with the governed: they may have mistresses—they cannot have wives; their children, if they have any, are illegitimate and have nothing to look forward to, except for intrigue and favoritism. Even love of glory and the ambition to do good—the last stimulants left to individuals when everything else is wanting—are entirely nonexistent in the Papal state. Their development is made impossible by the absence of any coherent political system and the instability of every principle of Government, which become evident in Rome with the election of each new pope and in the provinces with the appointment of each new Legate. How should people commit themselves to achieving even the smallest incremental change, when it can be in force for at best only a few years and will disappear before it can bear fruit?

As I have already mentioned, the ecclesiastics are driven, by their want of political abilities, to govern by Assessors or Secretaries. Why should these be at all concerned with the common good, when all the glory would go to their chiefs? Why should they not rather pursue their own narrow interests, when the resulting dishonor will likewise fall on their superiors? Fear has no hold on the subordinates: since they are not acting in their own name, they have nothing to be apprehensive about, save their patron's unlikely reaction. Fear has no hold on the chiefs themselves: for either due to their power and the part they take in the election of the pope, or more generally due to the Apostolic Constitutions and traditions of the church, they are entirely irresponsible and immune from prosecution both in fact and by law. In the Papal States, *the Minister of Finance (Treasurer-General) is entirely unaccountable. He may rob the Government with impunity; and he can be removed from his office only by promotion to the Cardinalate.* From this example you may judge of the rest. In consequence of this generalized irresponsibility, combined with the absence of any specific limitations on official authority, no irregularity is too extravagant for the popedom. . . .

Hence, we have on the one hand, misgovernment and foreign despotism in Lombardy; and on the other hand, misgovernment and the worship of Fraud in the popedom. Sir, you only have to apply these things to Italy in its entirety, and you will have a quite accurate picture of our current situation. The pope is the cross, or the pommel of a sword, of which Austria is the point; and this sword hangs over all of Italy. The pope clutches the soul of the Italian nation; Austria the body, whenever it shows signs of life. And on every part of that body sits a petty, absolute prince; essentially a viceroy under either of these powers. Three despotisms in place of one! But without any of the advantages that sometimes accompany despotism, when it is national and when it operates on a grand scale. . . .

We are a people of 21 or 22 million, known from time immemorial by the same name, as the people of Italy. We are enclosed by clear natural limits—the sea and the highest mountains in Europe. We also speak the same language, with a variety of dialects that differ from each other less than the Scotch and the English. More generally, we have the same creeds, manners, and habits, with differences not greater than those which in France, the most homogeneous country on earth, distinguish the Basques from the Bretons. We are the proud guardians of the noblest European tradition in politics, science, and the arts. We have twice unified Humanity: first through the Rome of the emperors; then again through the Rome of the popes, although the latter betrayed their mission. Not even our calumniators deny that we are gifted with active and brilliant faculties. Finally, we richly possess every source of material well-being, which, if we became free to cooperate fraternally, could make us happy and offer great prospects to our sister nations.

Yet we have no flag, no political name, and no rank among European nations. We have no common center; no common pact of association; no common market. We are dismembered into eight states—Lombardy, Parma, Tuscany, Modena, Lucca, the popedom, Piedmont, and the Kingdom of Naples—all independent, without any alliance, with no unity of aim and no organized connection between them. The resulting eight lines of custom houses, without even counting the impediments stemming from the different internal administration of each state, keep our material interests divided; they oppose our advancement and make it impossible for us to develop any large industry and commercial activity. Prohibitions and extremely high duties hinder the import and export of almost any article, including primary goods, to and from every state of Italy. Agricultural and industrial products that abound in one province are deficient in another; we cannot freely sell any excess production or exchange among ourselves according to our needs. There are eight different systems of currency; of weights and measures; of civil, commercial, and penal legislation; of administrative organization; and of police restrictions. They all divide us and make us foreign to each other as much as possible. And *every single one* of these states among which we are partitioned is ruled by a *despotic* government, with no agency whatsoever for the people. In all of these states there is no liberty of the press, of association, of speech, education, collective petition, or of anything else for that matter. The introduction of foreign books is equally forbidden. One of these territories, comprising nearly a fourth of the Italian population, actually belongs to a foreigner—to Austria. Meanwhile the others, some as a result of family ties, others due to their feebleness, tamely submit to Austria's influence.

This contrast between the actual condition of our Country and its aspirations resulted in the establishment of the National party, to which, Sir, I have the honor of belonging. . . . I share with many of my countrymen the opinion that by following a different and better coordinated course of action, in the future our Italian insurrection might successfully resist any Austrian intervention. I think that serious faults of management were committed by our leaders in the past, and that none of them has so far been able to fully exploit our potential. But this opinion, right or wrong, has nothing to do with my present argument. My *present* argument, which you, Sir, cannot refute, based as it is on unassailable historical facts, is simply this: *that the National party in Italy includes a large majority of my fellow citizens; that it has been, and would now more than ever be, master at home, were it not for the repeated armed intervention of a Foreign Power.*

Sir, ours is the *only country in Europe* that is deprived, thanks to the Diplomacy you personally so well represent, of the right of managing its own business in its own way. We are also the *only country in Europe* that cannot ask to lead its own common life—based on a common bond, or even just a partial amelioration of its laws—without a *foreign army* pouring in and contesting by brutal force its right to progression. We are the *only country in Europe* where a confirmed unanimity of opinion does not constitute acknowledged right.

Sir, I believe that this is a great injustice—a great crime for which Europe's major states are responsible. I also believe that it is the duty of every Italian to protest against this great injustice by word and deed, by risking his life if necessary. . . .

CHAPTER SIXTEEN

The European Question:

FOREIGN INTERVENTION AND NATIONAL
SELF-DETERMINATION (1847)

I AM NOT AWARE that many Englishmen in the present day occupy themselves with the condition of the peoples of Europe and their probable future.[1] What I see of the opinions on foreign affairs uttered by the press inclines me to rather think the contrary. But one thing I know, and all serious men on the Continent know it too: it is that *Europe rapidly approaches a tremendous crisis, a decisive struggle between the peoples and their despots, which no human power can henceforth hinder, but which the active cooperation of all the brave and good could render shorter and less severe. The final result of this struggle will be a new map of Europe.* This violent crisis might have been avoided, if only at the time when the Vienna settlement was concocted [in 1815], there had been in Europe an assembly of statesmen, wise, foresighted, and above all convinced that there is a Humanity here on earth living its own life through God, that every statesman should serve. But instead at Vienna there were none but shortsighted politicians, knowing nothing of Right, believing only in actual (de facto) governments. Coming out of a long war, and almost frightened at their own victory, they only dared to organize a balance among the then existing powers and to mutually compensate each other for the services rendered during the previous war. They changed the map of Europe accordingly, without consideration for the European peoples and their tendencies. It was a partition of *matter,* without any regard to *spirit.* And ever since, the struggle has been ongoing. Dull at first, the thunder has growled menacingly for the last seventeen years;

---

[1] Mazzini wrote this essay in English and primarily for a British liberal audience, as the revolutionary uprisings of 1848–49 were already in the air. It contains several key elements of his international thought: (1) every well-defined people deserves to determine their own future and ought to be politically independent; (2) when peaceful change is impossible, popular insurrection and violent revolt become legitimate means to topple despotic regimes and seek national self-determination; (3) existing liberal nations, such as Great Britain, ought to morally and diplomatically support the emancipation of subject nationalities and the fight against despotism, but without engaging, as Mazzini puts it, in a military "crusade, which no one dreams of invoking." Language and sentence structure have been partially updated.

and tomorrow or soon thereafter there will be an explosion. Every attempt at reconciliation will then be useless, and between the two champions, Force alone will judge.

The struggle of which I speak is invested on the Continent with a special character, to which sufficient attention is not paid in England. On the Continent, as everywhere, the end is doubtless the same: Liberty, the development of all the faculties that constitute the human being; the progressive perfection of society and the individual. But the form that the question takes and the means by which it manifests itself on the Continent are different. We are fighting today under the flag of nationality. Several races are struggling: millions of men placed by God's hand within fixed territorial boundaries, having a language of their own, as well as specific manners, tendencies, traditions, and national songs. They are leashed and governed by other men whose manners, tendencies, and language are altogether foreign to them. These subject peoples have no name and no flag; no outward sign of life in the congress of nations. But they feel a spontaneity stirring at the bottom of their hearts and the conscience of a mission to fulfill in the world. These peoples feel that they are called to represent an epoch in the progress of humanity, characterized by the individuality [self-determination] of the nation.

There is Poland, a nation thrown into the grave alive, violently partitioned at the very moment when the work of national transformation was beginning in her bosom that would have made of an aristocratic republic a people of equals. There is Italy, made ready for national unification by three hundred years of a general and uniform oppression. She raises her head, blessed by her Genius, by the Good she has done to Europe, and by her Martyrdom. She is now determined to emancipate her lively, eager, and artistic nature from the Austrian nightmare that weighs on her.

There are the Slavic peoples of the Austrian Empire: the Czechs, Slovaks, Rusniaks, Wendic, etc. They form more than half the population of the Empire, groaning, like the Lombard-Venetian Italians, like the Walachs of Bukovina and Transylvania, under the yoke that 6 million Austrians impose on them. Over the last twenty years these peoples have expressed their nationality through a series of literary and political works entirely unknown in England.

Then there is Switzerland: her ill-understood internecine quarrels suggest a lively need for national centralization, which could free her from too powerful foreign influences. There is Greece: she suffocates within the limits that diplomacy has imposed on her and aspires, far more actively than is suspected, to rally under the national flag her children of Thessaly, of Candia, of Macedonia, of Roumelia. If Greece were to succeed in her aspiration, she would raise against Russian projects a barrier more natural and much stronger than that carcass which is known as the Ottoman Empire. There is Germany, peopled by a slow and patient, but tenacious race, which after being intoxicated with pure thought, is now willing to become practical and advances through intellectual and commercial unity toward political unity.

There, among these peoples who have acquired consciousness of themselves and wish to become Nations, a new Europe is being conceived: a new Europe that shall rise in full vigor like Minerva from the head of Jupiter, as soon as a single one of these peoples shall raise itself, inspired either by the feeling of their right, or by despair, in the name of all those who suffer. . . .

If there was an established, powerful government willing to understand this and move beyond the factious world of Courts and Embassies, toward this Europe that is still subterranean but ready to reveal itself; a government that correctly understood where life and death are; that managed to raise itself above the petty political combinations of the day and regard itself engaged to the future of its nation—that government could by a single step arouse the sympathies and gratitude of all those peoples who desire to rise. In so doing, that government could obtain for itself the finest possible result: thanks to its moral supremacy, it could achieve the highest position in Europe. In addition, it could assure a series of new channels to its industry, since the newborn nations would quickly open their economies to the government that alone had protected and lovingly saluted their advent.

It would not be necessary for that government to plunge itself into a revolutionary crusade, which no one dreams of invoking. No, it would only be necessary, as I said above, to remember that sovereignty belongs to God alone, and that governments are established here below to aid in the development of his law of life. It would only be necessary to tell the European despots in a firm and calm voice, so as to be heard by all: "You entered into treaties which should have bound us, yet you have torn them. You have destroyed the charter of international law and thereby lost all claim to legitimate intervention. Stay at home now, and let not your action overpass your frontiers! Leave God's life to manifest itself freely, and once manifested in the heart of a people, let it be sacred for all of us. We cannot tolerate that the law of the world be brute force; that any limits to your power may be simply abolished by the violation of agreements. If you interfere for evil, we will interfere for good. Then God will judge." It might be worth remembering that this would only be the faithful application of a principle laid down by England and France in 1830, nothing more.

There are no apparent reasons to hope that this will happen. The governments of today have evidently abandoned all feeling of European unity and consolidation. In their actions they are not moved, and they do not believe that they ought to be moved, by any great religious belief or by the conscience of a high moral mission to accomplish changes for the better on the earth. Instead they deal as they can with the necessities of the day; they are dragged along by public opinion, instead of actually leading it. They seem to have become incapable of any great initiative. . . .

But I believe that a moral conscience exists, as ever, in the heart of all nations, indifferent and asleep as they may appear. Just think of that general unrest which, if only for an instant, stirs the masses whenever there is a great misfortune to deplore, a great crime to brand, or a great act of devotion to admire. When, last year, the news arrived that Poland was once again in action, where is the heart that did not beat faster under the incitement of hope? When, about a month ago, the destruction of the liberties of Cracow became known, whose are the lips over which the word *"Shame!"* has not passed?[2] True, so far this trembling of hope or indignation has been rather sterile, and everyone has soon fallen back into a lethargy that now seems to be the normal state among those peoples who have already acquired their freedom. But does this suggest a lack of either goodwill or energy? No, I believe that it is rather the result of a lack of knowledge, of coordination, of a common center of inspiration. All instinctively said, *"This cause is our own,"* but everybody also said, *"What can I do for it? I am far off, ill-informed, and isolated."*

Take the first Englishman you meet. Speak to him these simple, clear, and incontestable words:

We are all children of the same God, issued of a common stock, and governed by the same providential law. We are all members of humanity, and through it we sustain and improve ourselves. We are thus all brothers, held to a common duty of love and cooperation. And we cannot allow any part of this duty to be violated, without ourselves feeling the pain of such a violation. No single class within a nation can suffer without all other classes being affected in one way or another; likewise inside the great human family no people can suffer due to oppression, superstition, or corruption without their suffering affecting all other peoples, either directly or indirectly. Another people's suffering can, first of all, affect us by setting a dangerous precedent. In addition, when other peoples suffer, the activity, the intelligence, and the sentiment of millions of our brothers can no longer

---

[2] The free Republic of Cracow, established by the Congress of Vienna in 1815, was crushed and its territory annexed by Austria in 1846.

contribute to our own progress. But above anything else, such suffering breaks the divine unity—and therefore saps the foundation—of our common faith; it opens the gates of doubt on what had been eternal notions of justice and right. It degrades our very existence, by attacking it in what we all share in common, namely human dignity and human conscience. Every man is here on Earth to make Good triumph over Evil, the Beautiful over the Ugly, God's truth over the Devil's lies and appetites. Every single one of us is responsible for his brother's safety: it is not only when we kill him, but also when we permit others to kill him, although we would have been able to defend him, that we have to fear the question with which God pursued the first violator of the solid bond of humanity. A desire, a wish, is not enough. Every thought of good which you do not also seek to realize, to translate into acts, is a sin. As a human being, you are endowed with a body and a soul, with intelligence and will, thought and action. God, whom you must represent as far as your feeble nature allows, only thinks in acting: he creates; he manifests himself.

Do you think that anybody would disagree with you, that anybody would fall low enough to reply to you: *"I doubt the truth of what you say?"*

What is missing, then, for this unanimous though tacit agreement to express itself clearly, in broad daylight? for this truly Holy Alliance of Good to establish itself in the face of that League of Evil that has just effaced Cracow? for the peoples who are struggling to learn their self-esteem from the esteem of others to be rehabilitated in love, and to feel that humanity keeps count of their efforts and supports them?

Perhaps nothing is wanting but the courageous first move of a few men of faith, convinced that regardless of its origin, no seed of good is ever sterile in God's earth. I hear say that such men do indeed exist, that this first move is being worked out at this very moment, here where I am writing [in London]. If this is indeed the case—and in the mere hope that it might be true, I feel I ought to suspend any expression of *my* individual thought as to what ought to be done—may those men be blessed! Let them, calm and firm, proclaim that there exists a radical evil, an organized atheism at this moment in Europe, which negates liberty and human conscience through despotism. Let them proclaim that the cause is one; that the struggle ought to be one; and that inertness is a crime and a cowardice where evil acts and defies. Let them plead at the bar of their own nation the cause of all others. Let them explain to their own nation the grief of the present, as well as the sources of the holy and inevitable future. Let them make their own nation feel the intricate bonds that knot together this wider European future with their own. Let them, by a series of legal and peaceable demonstrations, salute martyrdom wherever it appears and denounce tyranny wherever it raises its head! And they will have rendered an immense service to England and to humanity. We are, I repeat it, on the eve of an epoch of renovation. And for every people desirous to enjoy its future benefits, the time has come to profess one's faith and act accordingly.

On Public Opinion and England's International Leadership (1847)

AN ASSOCIATION has recently been formed in London, called the "People's International League," which we think deserves the attention of the public.[1] . . . The association is just taking its first steps, and it is evident that we must see it at work for some time before we can judge it. So for now I merely want to talk about its *objective*: "To enlighten the British public as to the political conditions in foreign countries, as well as international relations between those countries; to disseminate the principles of national freedom and progress; to engage in public advocacy in favor of the right of every people to self-government and the maintenance of their own nationality; to promote a better understanding among the peoples of different countries."[2]

There has always been, since the earliest historical times, a tendency to an ever closer and wider association between the different groups that compose the human race. This should be evident to all those who can read in history something more than mere accounts of battles and biographical information about princes and kings. The providential thought that guides the collective march of societies and tends to draw them closer together has always triumphed, whether in times of war or of peace. And when we see that human civilization suddenly

---

[1] Original title: "The People's International League." Mazzini argues that there is no need for England to engage in an interventionist crusade to support the European revolutionaries. However, England should be willing to threaten counterintervention whenever despotic states such as Austria are planning to suppress a popular insurrection abroad. Given the conservatism of English elites, public opinion should step in and affect the country's foreign policy, by making its preferences clearly known to elected representatives. This essay thus nicely illustrates Mazzini's pluralistic and bottom-up view of international relations, based on the assumption that domestic and transnational societal actors have the ability to actively shape foreign policy.

[2] The People's International League was an association founded by several of Mazzini's English friends, and it included some liberal and progressive MPs. Mazzini hoped to transform this league into a larger European association with representatives from other European countries, but his hope proved too ambitious, and the association was soon overtaken by the revolutionary events of 1848.

breaks down, after having been concentrated for some time around some pivotal country or city, such as Greece and Rome, for instance, we can be sure that it will rise again during the subsequent phase of world history, perhaps with less intensity, but more widely spread. Civilization will then cast its light across a broader surface of our earth, uniting victors and defeated, executioners and victims. In the past, this tendency affected successive generations without them being aware of it, and sometimes against their will, but over the last fifty years it has acquired a regular, progressive, explicit development, and it has often been consciously pursued.

Already during the second half of the eighteenth century, philosophy gave the signal. In 1785, Lessing announced the great and profound idea that the human race is a collective being, endowed with a common life, that advances in its education from one epoch to another, while accomplishing a providential plan.[3] This point of view was then quickly adopted by all historical and literary studies. Men began to value the action and importance of the parts from the higher point of view of the whole. They increasingly recognized the explicit or hidden influence of one people on another. A European literature rose above all the national literatures, and in recent years almost all the great poets and writers have identified with the former, much more than with exclusively national tendencies. There have been numerous translations and surveys of foreign literatures. Thus less fettered by separate interests, literature has indeed contributed to the emergence of joint intellectual achievements and the formation of a *common European sentiment*.

Political economy has accomplished the same in the world of material progress, though with far greater difficulties to contend with. In the eighteenth century, the idea that Europe and indeed our entire planet is a vast common market, where nobody should suffer or be hampered in developing his faculties, as long as there is no inconvenience to others, became central to a whole school of thought in Italy, France, England, and practically everywhere. Members of that school keenly advocated the need to tear down all barriers to the exchange of agricultural and manufactured products from different countries, and to foster international free trade by promoting effective means of transportation, whether by sea, river, or land. All this, they claimed, would progressively draw together different nations. Several important developments have recently confirmed this tendency, first expressed in the world of literature and political economy. As soon as some important event took place

[3] Gotthold Ephraim Lessing (1729–81), German writer and philosopher, an important representative of the European Enlightenment. Mazzini must be referring to some posthumous translation of Lessing's writings, since in 1785 the German philosopher was no longer alive.

among one people, its echoes have been immediately heard elsewhere. Every revolution accomplished somewhere in Europe has been either looked on as a threat, or hailed as a source of hope, all over the continent. The flag of common *principles* has thus been gradually raised above the flag of local *interests*, which had previously remained unchallenged. By the common consent of her populations, Europe is now clearly marching toward a new era of union, of more intimate association. Under the influence of a common thought, the peoples will at last look on one another as members of one great family, bound together by duty and cooperating to support the development and progress of others; they will conceive of themselves as laborers in the great workshop of nature, pursuing different tasks according to their special abilities or their vocation, but all contributing to the same enterprise, whose fruits are to strengthen and improve the life of all. This common trend has now become so evident that it has forced the absolutist governments to overcome all their mutual hatred and jealousies and actually form an *alliance* to oppose these developments.

Europe is now so closely united that it is not possible for a new idea to emerge in one country, without thousands of translators seeking to make it popular everywhere else; it is so closely united at the level of commercial interests that no rise or fall of exchange rates can take place in London or Paris without the shock being felt in Vienna, Genoa, Amsterdam, and Hamburg; so closely united in popular sympathies that the Poles cannot attempt to rise, without the cry of *"Long live Poland!"* resounding at once in London, Paris, Madrid, and in the cities of Romagna.[4] But in the face of all these developments, the official policy of governments has hardly changed. Indeed, it has remained the same it was a hundred years ago, due to some contradiction that we cannot understand. If the governments have sometimes appeared for an instant to quit the old path, this was only some forced concession, the acknowledgement of some fait accompli produced by the aforementioned tendency. Soon thereafter, they have usually fallen back into their old habits. It would seem that for diplomats, the world has stood still since the Treaty of Westphalia. Now, as then, their policy is exclusively founded on *interests*; there is no room for *principles* in their endeavors. There is nothing above those *interests* that could draw them together; each state implicitly perceives the interests of all others as hostile. Only, since now the possibility of war, expansionism, and conquest has become more and more remote, those governments content themselves with diffidently watching one another, or harming each other through commercial tariffs.

[4] The Romagna is a region in central Italy.

Now, as at the time of the Treaty of Westphalia, the great problem for statesmen is that of the *balance of power*; how to prevent one or the other rival power from acquiring too much preponderance; how to force it to inaction. Thus our statesmen do not properly *act* internationally, they merely *resist*. Governments—and here we speak of the best—do not even suspect that it may be their duty to support, direct, and progressively realize the general tendencies of Europe. The thought that these tendencies are inspired by God himself, and that governments exist only to be their interpreters and servants, has remained entirely foreign to them.

There are but two policies in Europe today: that of the absolute governments, which react against the advancing popular movement; and that of the constitutional governments, which do not act at all. The latter is a *retrograde* policy of isolation, inertia, and neutrality; it is a policy of egoism and evil. The foreign policy of England evidently reflects this pattern in its preference for isolation. In 1823, when the dispute between progress and tyranny, between the spirit of national liberties and the usurpation of brute force, had already become evident almost everywhere in Europe, George Canning summed up 'England's policy in these words: "Our stance is essentially neutral; neutral not only between contending nations, but *between conflicting principles.*"[5] In his system, others should either fear England as a mighty adversary, or hope to have her as a powerful friend. But her own foreign policy would always be based on a sublime indifference between the two principles of despotism and democracy. Never openly becoming someone's friend or enemy, never having to choose between the two principles, *that* would be the secret of her power. In the meantime, Europe has changed a lot: the struggle against despotism has become much more widespread; new elements such as, for instance, the Slavic have appeared; great revolutions have taken place; great battles have been constantly fought and several are still ongoing. Yet England—thank God not her inhabitants but certainly her government—has remained impassive. Her policy has continued to reflect Canning's formula; she continues to be *neutral* not only between contending nations, but also between conflicting principles.

But these conflicting principles reflect justice and injustice, good and evil. On the one side men fight for right, on the other they slaughter to oppress. Wherever the voice of an entire nation is protesting, that of a single ruler compels it to be silent. How can you remain indifferent be-

---

[5] George Canning (1770–1827), British statesman, served as foreign secretary (1822–27) and, briefly, as prime minister (1827). As a moderate Tory, Canning was suspicious of both despotism and full-fledged democracy. He was a supporter of generalized nonintervention and strongly opposed foreign military interference by the reactionary powers of the "Holy Alliance," i.e., Austria, Russia, and Prussia.

tween these two voices, these two flags, without committing a crime and without feeling remorse? Just think of it for a moment! The individual who coolly allows some person to be murdered at the corner of a street, while he would have been able to prevent it, will be marked with a brand of infamy forever. So how can we admire the conduct of a nation that remains indifferent and looks on, while everywhere beyond its frontiers men are dying for an idea, killed by tyrants with an unjust ambition, as if it were a show of gladiators? Isn't there a common law to which nations and individuals alike are subject? Are we not all, nations and individuals, bound to do good and to check evil as God's creatures; shouldn't we seek to promote His plan and achieve the triumph of truth over error, of liberty over slavery? Don't the duties of nations grow with their strength? Isn't indifference ultimately but a form of atheism? Isn't the law of Christ, properly understood, a law of self-denial? Doesn't it preach that He who aspires to be the first in the kingdom of Heaven must make himself the last, the servant of his brethren, on earth? When God places a people on earth and tells them, "Be a nation!" he does not say, "Isolate thyself; enjoy thy life as the miser enjoys his treasure, and don't seek to spread My word but rather keep it as a secret." He says instead: "Walk with an upright head among the brethren whom I have given thee, as becomes one who bears My word in his heart; take up thy rank among the nations according to My directions; accomplish thy mission on earth worthily and courageously, for by it thou shalt be judged. Proclaim your Faith openly before the world and the world's masters; do not abandon thy brethren, but assist them according to their wants and thy power, for you are all made after My image."

Neutrality between conflicting principles is immoral in theory; it is, besides, impossible in practice. Life always has a twofold dimension: every people and every individual live *within* themselves and *outside* of themselves; thanks to their own strength and thanks to what surrounds them; hence for themselves and for what surrounds them. Every being influences others and is in turn influenced by others. A people who should isolate themselves from all others would be suicidal. They would suppress half of their own lives. They would foreswear their own external activity, while remaining subject to that of others; they would relinquish their international influence and become passive. England could never accept to descend so low. Hence, she has never been able to unambiguously follow the doctrine enunciated by Canning. Before his time and thereafter, she has frequently *intervened* in the affairs of the world. But she has indeed renounced her natural principle, thus depriving herself of that consciousness of her rights and duties that could have rendered her interventions principled and moral. So England has intervened anomalously, by fits and starts, irregularly and inconsistently, under the momentary impulse of perceived necessity. Sometimes she intervened in favor of nationality, as in Spain, and sometimes against it, as in Denmark. At one time she intervened in favor of emancipation, by recognizing the republics of South America, and several other times against it, as for instance in the treaties of Vienna.[6] Aside from those few instances of active foreign policy, she has refused to exercise any influence and has allowed events to unfold as they might. This has not gained England the friendship of those powers to whom she has essentially abandoned the fate of Europe, as the conduct of the French government clearly shows. She has not cared to enforce existing treaties, which although bad in themselves, could at least have secured some order; just look at what happened in Cracow.[7] So England has progressively undermined any esteem and sympathy that other nations may have felt for her.

Would we then like to see England at the head of a crusade, unleashing war on Europe, and burdening her people with the responsibility of hurling on mankind the force of revolutionary winds? No, far from it. Our intentions, we trust, are too well known to our readers for our words to be interpreted in that manner. But we would certainly like England's behavior to change.

In 1831, a victorious domestic insurrection stirred all of central Italy, without shedding a drop of blood. It was put down by an Austrian army, notwithstanding the principle of nonintervention proclaimed by France and England a few months before.[8] But although the foreign invasion was able to destroy the immediate results of the movement, it could not extirpate its causes. Those deeper causes remained there to be seen and felt, acknowledged as legitimate by friends and enemies. The people, comprising every class, were in a state of permanent protest, although they remained surrounded by hostile bayonets. Compelled by

[6] This passage shows how Mazzini's notion of "intervention" is rather broad, notably including diplomatic pressure and influence. In none of the cases that Mazzini mentions did Britain actually intervene militarily, although it sometimes sanctioned interventions by other great powers, such as France's intervention on the monarchy's side in the Spanish civil war of 1820–23.

[7] The free city-state of Cracow was established at the Congress of Vienna in 1815. Its independence was thus formally guaranteed by an international agreement among the great powers. But when a popular uprising in Cracow in February 1846, aimed to incite a broader Polish fight for national independence, was quickly put down by an Austrian military intervention, and Austria subsequently annexed the city of Cracow, Britain did nothing to seriously oppose it.

[8] In the wake of the successful July revolution of 1830 in France, the secretive Carboneria movement launched several uprisings in central Italy in early 1831. But the insurrection never became a genuine popular movement, and it was thus quickly put down by the Papal army with the support of an Austrian troop contingent. France and England were opposed to an Austrian military intervention at the time but did little to prevent it.

the agitation of men's minds, a diplomatic conference was opened in Rome between the ambassadors of the high powers and the Papal secretary of state. Lord Seymour, then, if my memory serves us, ambassador at Florence, was present.[9] . . .

Now, suppose Lord Seymour, as the interpreter of an avowed moral policy, had been empowered firmly to address the Austrian minister in the following way:

Sir, England cannot be indifferent to the fate of Europe. As a Christian power, she believes in the unity and brotherhood of the human race. She cannot look on indifferently as millions of men in Italy are excluded from the benefit of God's laws and abandoned to the knife of the strongest, just because they demand what they think just and good, which incidentally are all things that England has long since realized at home. England cannot remain calm at the periodical slaughter of men a few miles from her frontiers, when the observance of one or two laws, founded on justice, might forever eradicate the problem. We are thus willing to prevent further usurpations, as we did in 1808 to halt Napoleon's attempt to stifle the nationality of Spain; as we have since done to put an end to the slave trade. England too, Sir, is called on to play a part in Europe. But she reads that part in a humanitarian spirit, according to the principle of liberty that she represents. It concerns us that this principle be not continually crushed before our brethren. In addition, it concerns us that our trade be not constantly checked by crises that result from oppression; that the foreign markets on which our industry relies be not closed by disorders originating from the repressed tendencies of Europe's populations; that our relations with the different countries of Europe be not compromised at any time by some flagrant war between governments and peoples. England, Sir, sincerely desires peace. For this reason, she wishes that the causes of war be eliminated. And for the same reason, she cannot allow that whenever the natural wishes of some population have been fulfilled, and peace has thus been established on a logical and secure basis, you should come, Sir, you a foreign power, to throw the sword of Brennus onto the scale and decree permanent war.[10] Therefore we are determined, if necessary, to throw onto the scale, not the sword of Brennus, the sword of blind force, but rather

[9] Edward Adolphus Seymour (1805–85), British Whig aristocrat and politician, served in various cabinet positions and diplomatic missions in the mid-nineteenth century.

[10] Brennus is the name of a legendary Gallic leader, assumed to have occupied Rome in 387 BC. When the tribute that the Romans had agreed to pay was being weighed, a Roman allegedly complained, whereupon Brennus is believed to have thrown his sword on the scale, crying, "*Vae victis!*" (woe to the vanquished).

the sword of Camillus, the liberating sword, which every human community has a right to draw against arbitrary oppression.[11]

If England had credibly threatened to act this way, do you think Austria would not have changed her behavior? Do you think the victims would not have been saved? Do you think Italy would now be on the eve of a general conflagration? We might mention a virtually infinite number of specific examples, but the one discussed above should be sufficient. We are firmly persuaded that bold language, worthy of England, and in conformity with the principle that guides her, would have sufficed and would indeed still suffice to secure the peace of the world on the basis of progressive development. But we equally believe that by refusing to hold such language, the English government is increasing the risk of a European struggle, into which it would be inevitably drawn.

Now, since the government, evidently astray, has lost all power of initiative and allows itself to be led by opinion, it remains for public opinion itself to suggest this language to its representatives. The goal of the "League" is to form public opinion on international questions and thus affect English foreign policy, and we cannot but praise its objective. In consequence of the government's neutral and indifferent attitude, public opinion has hitherto neglected the study of foreign questions, saying: "What does it matter to us?" But the recent violation of the Treaty of Vienna, the threats of the northern Powers to Switzerland, aimed at preventing any improvement of her domestic institutions, and the angry bearing of Austria in Italy, seem at length to have awakened the public from its lethargy. Hence the time seems well-chosen to furnish it with materials on which to form its judgments.

Europe has much changed during the last twenty years. New desires and new needs have manifested themselves. New elements have arisen, which if not reasonably satisfied, are capable of convulsing all of Europe on their own. And the English people know scarcely anything about them. The English people are still very imperfectly acquainted with Italy, notwithstanding the immense sympathy she elicits. You are still very imperfectly acquainted with Poland; with the moral and intellectual progress she has made since the first partition in 1772; with the popular tendencies that have progressively reached even her nobles; with her poets, some of which, like Mickiewicz, Garczyński, and others, are equal to the mightiest of modern poets and sing of Poland's griefs, her aspirations, and her entire soul. The English people are still more unacquainted with present-day Greece, which, perhaps more than any other country, holds in her bosom the solution to the oriental question. You know

---

[11] Marcus Furius Camillus (ca. 446–365 BC), Roman soldier and statesman. He defeated the Gauls and is believed to have taken back the unjust tribute originally paid to Brennus.

nothing of Switzerland, that small but phenomenal country, which since 1308, has held up high the republican flag amidst the monarchies of Europe; nothing of its *national* movement, which exasperates the absolutist courts; nothing of the organization of the Pact of 1815, which was devised to condemn that country to impotence, and, by rendering internal convulsions inevitable, to keep the path open for the influence of foreign cabinets. The English are completely in the dark about everything relating to the Slavic movement; the movement of those populations of Bohemians, Moravians, Slovenes, Croats, and Serbs, which clench the heart of Austria, as with a net, and are connected to both the Polish movement and the destinies of Greece. All this is unknown land to the English, even in its very names. The whole Slavic race, the only one that has not yet spoken its word to Europe, has gradually arisen over the last twenty years, but the growing sound of its advance has not yet been able to pierce England's inattentive ear. . . .

It is time that England opens her eyes to these things; it is time that she joins her life to the life that ferments in the hearts of millions of her European brethren. It is time for England's voice to be raised, as in the noble days of the Reformation, so that victimized nations may feel that they have a sister who is ready to protest with them and for them, in the name of Truth and Justice. Let me repeat that this is the object of the *League*, and I sympathize profoundly with it. The League's first actions will show whether this sympathy can be expanded into active cooperation.

CHAPTER EIGHTEEN

Concerning the Fall of the Roman Republic (1849)

ROME HAS FALLEN![1] It is a great crime and a great error.[2] The crime belongs to France; the error to civilized Europe, and above all to your England. I say *to your England*, for in the three questions that are now at issue in Rome and that cannot be stifled by brute force, England appears to me—as it appeared to us all—to be especially concerned. All three of these questions had already been raised in Rome long before the French entered the city: first, the question of principle, of international right, of European morality; second, the political question, pertaining to the so-called balance of power in Europe and the preservation or expansion of influence; and finally the religious question. The question of principle is, thank God, sufficiently clear. A population of more than 2 million men, having peacefully, solemnly, and legally chosen a form of government through a regularly elected constitutional assembly, is deprived of it by foreign violence. It is then forced again to submit to the power that had been abolished, and this without the population having furnished the slightest pretext for such violence, or made the slightest attempt against the peace of neighboring countries.

The calumnies which for months have been systematically circulated against our republic are of little importance; what matters is that it was necessary to first defame those whom the powers had determined to destroy. But I affirm that the republic, voted for almost unanimously by

---

[1] Mazzini wrote this article in English soon after the fall of the Roman Republic of 1849. It was published in the London *International Magazine* and addressed to a British liberal and progressive audience. Language and sentence structure have been partially updated.

[2] Rome had been a free republic for four months between February and May 1849, with Mazzini as its leading political figure, though executive authority was formally held by a three-person presidency, or triumvirate. The decisive revolt against the theocratic rule of Pope Pius IX had begun in November 1848; subsequently a Constituent Assembly was elected by universal suffrage, and the resulting republican constitution was one of the first fully democratic constitutions of Europe. However, the republic was to be short-lived. French President Louis Napoleon, who would soon declare himself emperor Napoleon III and needed the pope's benevolence, took the lead in a counterrevolutionary intervention: his troops landed at Civitavecchia on the coast northwest of Rome, joined by 4,000 men from Spain. Meanwhile Austrian forces advanced from the North and the king of Naples threatened intervention from the South. The revolutionaries put up a staunch resistance, but on July 3 the French Army entered Rome; the Republic had fallen and the pope's temporal power was restored.

the assembly, had the general and spontaneous approbation of the country. Of this, the explicit declaration of support by almost all the municipalities of the Roman State, voluntarily renewed at the time of the French invasion and without any initiative on the part of the Roman government, is a decisive proof. I affirm that with the exception of the city of Ancona, where the triumvirate was obliged to energetically repress certain criminal acts of political vengeance, the republican cause was never sullied by the slightest excess; there was never any censorship imposed on the press before the siege. Not a single condemnation to death or exile bore witness to a severity we could have rightfully exercised, but which the perfect unanimity that reigned amongst all the elements of the State made unnecessary. I affirm that, except in the case of three or four priests, who had been guilty of firing on our combatants and were thus killed by the people during the last days of the siege, not a single act of personal violence was committed by any fraction of the population against another. Hence, if ever there was a town presenting the spectacle of a group of brothers pursuing a common end, bound together by the same faith, it was Rome under republican rule. The city was inhabited by foreigners from all parts of the world, by the consular agents, by many of your countrymen: let any one of them arise and deny under oath, if he can, the truth of what I say.[3]

Terror now reigns in Rome. The prisons are filled with men who have been arrested and detained without trial. Fifty priests, whose only crime consists in having lent their services in our hospitals, are confined in the Castle of St. Angelo. Among the citizens, those best known for their moderation are exiled. The republican army is almost entirely dissolved, the city disarmed, and the "factions" sent away to the last man. Yet France does not dare to consult in a legal manner the will of the populations; instead it has reestablished the papal authority by military decree. I believe that since the dismemberment of Poland, no more atrocious injustice has been committed; no greater violation of the eternal right that God has given to the people—namely, that of appreciating and defining for themselves their own life, and governing themselves in accordance with their own appreciation of it [the right to self-determination]—has occurred. And I cannot believe that it is good either for you or for Europe that such things can happen in the eyes of the world without even a single nation arising out of its immobility to protest in the name of uni-

---

[3] In addition to those foreigners who had aleady been living in Rome, numerous foreign volunteers moved there to support the republic, representing a new phenomenon of international mobilization for a national cause. Particularly well known is the case of Margaret Fuller, a leading figure in the American transcendentalist movement, who took charge of a hospital in Rome and married Giovanni Angelo d'Ossoli, an Italian nobleman involved in the revolution.

versal justice! It means to enthrone brute force where, by the power of reason, God alone should reign; it means to substitute the sword and dagger for law; to decree a ferocious war without limit of time or means between oppressors who are rendered suspicious by their own fears, and leave the oppressed abandoned to the instincts of reaction and isolation. Let Europe ponder these things. For if the light of human morality is obscured but a little further, in that darkness there will arise a strife that will make those who come after us shudder with dread.

The balance of power in Europe is destroyed. It used to consist in the support given to the smaller States by the great Powers, but now the former are abandoned. France in Italy, Russia in Hungary, Prussia in Germany, a little later perhaps in Switzerland: these are now the masters of the Continent. England is thus made a nullity; the "celsa sedet Eolus in arce,"[4] which Canning delighted to quote, to express the moderating function that he wished to reserve for his country, is now a meaningless phrase. Let not your preachers of the theory of material interests, your speculators on extended markets, deceive themselves; there is history to teach them that political influence and commercial influence are closely bound together. Political sympathies hold the key of the markets: the lowering of the tariff by the Roman Republic will appear to you, if you study it, to have been a declaration of sympathy toward England to which your government did not think it necessary to respond.

And yet, above the question of right, above the question of political interest, both of which were of a nature to excite early the attention of England, there is, as I have said, another question being agitated at Rome of a very different kind of importance, and which ought to have aroused all those who believe in the vital principle of religious reformation—it is that of liberty of conscience. The religious question that broods at the root of all political questions showed itself there, great and visible in all its European importance. The pope at Gaeta was the theory of absolute infallible authority exiled from Rome forever; and exiled from Rome was to be exiled from the world.[5] The abolition of the temporal power evidently drew with it, in the minds of all those who understood the secret of the papal authority, the emancipation of men's minds from the spiritual authority. The principles of liberty and of free consent, elevated by the constituent assembly into a living, active right, were about to destroy the absolutist dogma that now from Rome aims more than ever to enchain the universe. The high aristocracy of the Roman Catholic clergy well knows the impossibility of retaining the

[4] The Latin phrase can be translated as "the God of the winds happily observes from his fortress."

[5] For the duration of the revolutionary Roman Republic, the pope had fled into exile in the city of Gaeta, in the kingdom of Naples.

soul in darkness, in the midst of light inundating the intelligences of men; for this reason they carried off their pope to Gaeta; for this reason they now refuse all compromise. They know that any compromise would be fatal to them; that they must reenter as conquerors, or not at all. And in the same way that the aristocracy of the clergy insists on the inseparability of the temporal and spiritual powers, the French government, in its present reactionary march, feels that the keystone of despotism lies in Rome—that the ruin of the spiritual authority of the Middle Ages would have entailed the ruin of its own projects—and that the only method of securing to it a few more years of existence is to rebuild for it a temporal domination.

England has understood nothing of all this. She has not understood all that was sublime and prophetic in this cry of emancipation, in this protestation in favor of human liberty, issuing from the very heart of ancient Rome, in the face of the Vatican. England has not felt that the struggle in Rome was about cutting the Gordian knot of moral servitude, against which she herself has long and vainly opposed her Bible societies, her Christian and Evangelical alliances; and that if only she had extended a sisterly hand to the movement, a mighty pathway for the human mind could have been opened there. She has not understood that one bold word, "respect for the liberty of thought," opposed to the hypocritical language of the French government, would have been sufficient to inaugurate the era of a new religious policy, and to conquer for herself a decisive ascendancy on the Continent.

Is England beginning to understand these things? You answer me: yes. But I doubt it. Political and religious indifference appears to me to have taken root too deeply with you to be vanquished by anything short of those internal crises that now, alas, will become more and more inevitable. Nevertheless, if it is true that the unequal struggle that went on for two months in Rome has borne fruit; if indeed you begin to understand how much brutality there is in the league of four powers against the awakening of the Eternal City; if you understand all that is grand and fruitful for humanity in this cry of country and liberty, rising from among the ruins of the Capitol; and how much it would be noble, generous, and profitable for England to respond to this cry, as to that of a sister toward whom a debt of gratitude is owed—then you can still do us a great good. You may console (this you have always done) the exiles among our former combatants, whom the French government tears from their homes to cast them out—poor mistaken souls, who dreamed of the fraternity of France—in utter physical destitution, and in despair of mind! You can save for us these brothers and their spirits, by preserving them from the attacks of doubt and of unmeasured, self-destructive reaction. You can, by your press, by the voice of your meetings, fix on the forehead of the French Republic the mark of Cain; on the front of Rome the glory of a martyrdom that contains the promise of victory. You can give to Europe the consciousness that Italy is being born anew, and to Italy a redoubled faith in herself. You may do more. The Roman question is far from being resolved.

France finds herself placed between the necessity of giving way to a new insurrection, and that of prolonging indefinitely the occupation by her troops, thus changing intervention into conquest. Assemble, associate, organize a vast agitation for the political and religious independence of the peoples. Tell your government that honor, duty, and the future of England demand that your flag shall not hang idly in atheistic immobility, amidst the continued violation of the principle it represents; that France does not have the right to dispose of the Roman States as she pleases; that the will of the Roman people ought to be expressed, and that it cannot be freely expressed while four hostile armies are encamped on its territories. Call on France to fulfill her promises. As the elected representatives of the people, we could not normally admit that the people should be asked to express for a second time what they have already peacefully, completely, and in the most unfettered manner declared. Under normal circumstances, it would be tantamount to suicide, it would mean abandoning our most sacred right. But, since violence has now annihilated the consequences of that right of ours, it is for you now to recall France to its engagements, and to say to her: "All that you are about to do is null and illegal, if the will of the populations is not consulted." And if your government remains silent, if France pursues her course of violence, then you should aid us, you men of Justice and Liberty, in the struggle. With or without the aid of the peoples, we will recommence this struggle. We cannot, we will not, sacrifice our future and the destinies toward which we are called by God, to the caprices of egoism and of blind force. But the assistance of the peoples may spare us many bloody sacrifices and much reactionary violence, which we men of order and peace have always striven to avoid but in the powerlessness of exile may not be able to prevent.

August 6, 1849.

CHAPTER NINETEEN

On Nonintervention (1851)

THE PRINCIPLE OF Nonintervention in the affairs of other nations is a product of the negative and purely critical spirit of the last century.[1] It was originally a useful and righteous protest against the lust of conquest and the appetite for war, which had until then characterized the activity of Europe. As such, it was a step forward; a real step in the intellectual progress of the human race. First put forward by thinkers of the European liberal movement, it would have been capable, had it been actually followed, of serving that movement in a most effective manner. Had it been observed in the case of the French Revolution, France would have been left to her own free and spontaneous development. But the instinct of the Absolutist party was to reject a principle that threatened to destroy the prevailing system; so what followed was the war of the Royal Allies, and France had to call forth a Napoleon to repel intervention by intervention on a grander scale.

Since that time the fate of the principle has been peculiar. Seized by the very men against whom it had been intended to act, and who had positively no belief in it whatever [i.e., the conservative rulers], it was erected as a protective canopy over that diplomatic parceling out of the continent of Europe that was iniquitously concocted at Vienna after the fall of Napoleon. Thus the principle of Nonintervention was turned against the cause in whose service it had at first been promulgated. The plan succeeded. Some continued to believe in the original and true meaning of the principle; and indeed, we still see many in whose minds the principle has worked itself out to just and liberal conclusions. But on the whole, a huge confusion fell on the intelligence of the nations: it came to be understood that the principle of Nonintervention meant that the arrangement of 1815 should not be altered except by the diplomats who had made it; that every government recognized by that arrange-

---

[1] Mazzini wrote this essay for a British liberal audience. In the mid nineteenth century, prominent liberal intellectuals such as Richard Cobden and John Bright were advocating British nonintervention in continental European affairs. Against this view, Mazzini insists that from a principled moral point of view, the rule of nonintervention can be valid only in a world of free and self-determining nations. Nevertheless, he acknowledges that from a more prudential, or consequentialist, viewpoint, the rule ought to be seen as prima facie valid also in the imperfect world of existing states, provided of course that everyone respects it.

ment should be allowed to do as it liked with the populations included within its bounds; and that in case of any rebellion among those populations, having a tendency to disturb the status quo, the various governments might combine to put that rebellion down.

This was such an atrocious perversion of the original meaning of the principle, and it has led to such flagrant enormities on the Continent, that thinking men there have begun to hate the very phrase Nonintervention, and to wish that it were for a time at least dismissed from the language of mankind. Only in England is the phrase still repeated with any degree of respect. Here, indeed, the principle of Noninterference, according as it does so peculiarly with the habits of thought engendered by our insular position and our peculiar national occupations, has degenerated into a kind of selfish indifferentism. "Let every nation attend to its own affairs; let other nations work out their freedom as we have worked out ours; whether they succeed or not is not our concern"— such is the sole theory of foreign policy propounded or indeed acted on by many of the public men of England.

Now, in the first place, it has to be observed of this principle of Noninterference, the very terms in which it is put forth necessarily presuppose something, take something for granted. When it is said that the true principle of the mutual relations of nations is the principle of Nonintervention, a state of things is presupposed in which all the due conditions of Nationality have been attended to. It is between certain things called *Nations* that the principle of Nonintervention is to hold; the principle of Nonintervention is not to take effect except on the supposition that the parties concerned are distinct Nations.

But what is a Nation? According to any possible definition of this word, a nation is a larger or smaller aggregate of human beings bound together into an organic whole by agreement in a certain number of real particulars, such as ethnicity, language, physiognomy, historical tradition, intellectual peculiarities, or active tendencies. Thus *the Russians* are a nation—they are a specified mass of human beings who share a certain number of real particulars, the aggregate of which is expressed by the name *Russians*. So also *the French* are a nation; *the English* are a nation; *the Spaniards* are a nation—these names implying in each case a certain number of real distinguishing characteristics impressed by nature herself on the fragments of the human race to which the names refer. It seems to be the design of Providence that the general purposes of the world shall be pursued through the medium of these distinct national organisms, each acting the part for which its peculiarities best adapt it. Hence the profound sacredness attached to the idea of nationality: faithfulness to it is the highest kind of heroism, and treachery to it is the deepest kind of infamy yet recognized in history. Hence even those conquests that have produced, or been supposed to produce, beneficial results, have always ended in the merging of the conquerors with the conquered, so as not to destroy the feeling of national independence and unity, but only reinvigorate it by somewhat changing the organism.

It is between nations in this sense, surely, that the doctrine of Noninterference ought to hold. The meaning surely is that, seeing God has divided the human race into masses so evidently distinct; each with a separate tone of thought, and a separate part to fulfill, this arrangement should not be needlessly tampered with by attempts of one nation to dictate to another its line of policy, or arrest its course of internal development. It was surely not meant that, if this natural arrangement were changed and the inhabitants of Europe were flung together haphazardly, half a nation under one government and half under another, with some governments including five or six fragments of five or six different peoples, the principle of Nonintervention would still be as reasonable as before. If half of England were attached to France and the other half to Denmark, would not the governments of France and Denmark find themselves entangled by the strong tendency of the severed halves of England to reunite themselves; and would it be fair to set up any abstract doctrine of Nonintervention as a reason why the two masses of Englishmen whom Nature had destined to form one, should turn their backs to each other, take no concern in each other's affairs, and disavow their dearest instincts? Now, is this not a fair description of certain parts of that diplomatic dismemberment of Europe, misleadingly called a Political System, in perpetuation of which the doctrine of Nonintervention is cunningly invoked? Without discussing other instances where, especially in Eastern Europe, those enduring realities of ethnicity, language, and cherished tradition, on which alone a national system can be reared, were ruthlessly disregarded by the arrangements of 1815, let us just think of what was done to Italy. Here, of a country naturally one in everything that constitutes a nation, a fraction amounting to one-fourth of the whole was handed over to a foreign state [Austria] to be governed according to the most absolute principles of despotism. The remainder was left cut up into small states between which all national relationship was barred, and which were all at the virtual mercy of the first foreign power. Is the doctrine of Nonintervention to be set up as a reason why this unnatural arrangement should be considered inviolable, or why it should be regarded a crime for the Lombards, Romans, Tuscans, and Neapolitans still to feel as parts of an indestructible Italian people? A nation is a more permanent thing than a political system, and it ought to be guaranteed by higher maxims of inviolability. Destroy the current political system in Russia, Spain, or England, and Russia, Spain, and England will still remain as real as before—facts engraved, so to speak, on the solid substance of the globe. But destroy the political system that has its center in Vienna [the Habsburg monarchy], and there remains nothing at all answering to the name of Austria. The charters by which Italy and Hungary exist as separate nationalities are more ancient and more sacred than that which has handed them over to one and the same master.

But even if all this remained unchanged; if the idea of Nationality continued to be treated as an unsubstantial crotchet; if it were argued that the notion of a really national system is a mere pedantry; that there was never a time when the division of Europe into states could have been made to coincide with its division into nations; and that consequently it was necessary to assume some actual arrangement of states, as convenient as possible, and protect *that* by a decree of permanent inviolability—in short, even if the principle of Nonintervention between governments or de facto states were substituted for that of Nonintervention between nations or de jure states—still all this would not affect the need for some vigorous discussion of cases such as that of present-day Italy. For, surely, when the rule of Noninterference is set up as the sole rule of political relationship between states, it is implied that this rule shall be absolute. If the rule means anything on the lips of those who rely on it as a ground for doing nothing on behalf of Italy, it must mean that in every state the government must deal directly and alone with its own people, and that if any dispute arises between the government and the people, they must settle it entirely between themselves. If the government of a state is despotic and if the people, roused by unjust treatment or seized with the passion for freedom and progress, resist that government, carry on a war of the press against it, and at last, in spite of police and military force, defeat it; then, according to this rule, the decision is final, the revolution is legitimate, and it must be accepted as an indisputable fact that Providence means that state to order its internal relations in a new manner. But should the government of a neighboring despotic state, either invited by the vanquished party or fearing the contagion of liberal ideas in its own territory, militarily invade the convulsed state and so interrupt or repeal the revolution, then the principle of Nonintervention is at an end, and all moral obligation on other states to observe it is from that moment annulled. As much as the principle of Noninterference was previously revered, to the same degree interference is now entirely lawful. In other words: the same theory which proclaims Noninterference as the first law of international politics must include, as a secondary law, the right of interference to make good all prior infractions of the law of Noninterference.

There is no escaping this conclusion. Nor is it difficult to apply this conclusion to the present state of European affairs. What does the principle of Nonintervention actually mean today? It means precisely this: Intervention on the wrong side; Intervention by all who choose, and are strong enough, to put down free movements of peoples against corrupt governments. It means cooperation of despots against peoples, but no cooperation of peoples against despots. It means that if after years of injury and protest, the brave Hungarian nation is provoked to a universal revolt against its corrupt government and dares to draw the sword in self-defense, beats the armies of its corrupt government, and comes close to a well-earned renovation of its ancient liberties, then it would be lawful for a Russian Czar to step in, but not at all lawful for the free English people to push that interfering Czar back. It means that if in an Italian state such as Piedmont, Tuscany, or Naples, any symptom of free life should arise, then Austria shall have a right to send barbarian troops to extinguish it, even in defiance of the government of that state, while no other nation of the world shall have a right to say *Nay* to Austria. It means that if, following the flight of a pope from Rome and his refusal to return or to exercise his functions through regular deputies, the Roman people shall calmly, unanimously, and wisely proceed to govern themselves, showing that they can do without the pope as their secular sovereign, then it shall be lawful for a sister republic like France to send an army, with a lie on its banners, to compel the Romans to take back their pope on his own terms, and unlawful for Protestant Britain to do anything else than look on and smile.[2] It means that a few hundreds of thousands of soldiers, paid and drilled by despotism, shall march from spot to spot all over Europe, crossing rivers and frontiers according to orders sent from a few great capitals, doing foul work wherever they go and trampling out all germs of high and promising vitality. It means that, God alone knows, one day these hirelings of despotism might be prepared to march even on our own soil of England. That, and much more, is what Nonintervention practically means at present.

But it begins to be felt that even understood in its fairest sense, the doctrine of Nonintervention between states and nations is poor and incomplete. People begin to feel that not only is every nation entitled to a free and independent life, but also that there are bonds of international duty binding all the nations of this earth together. Hence, the conviction is gaining ground that if on any spot of the world, even within the limits of an independent nation, some glaring wrong should be done, casting a blight over a populous area of many square miles and

[2] Mazzini is referring to the flight of Pope Pius IX from Rome in late 1848, following a popular insurrection, which led to the proclamation of the revolutionary Roman Republic. Republican France took the lead in a military intervention against the Roman Republic (Alexis de Tocqueville was the French minister of foreign affairs at the time), with the goal of reinstating the pope.

sending up a cause of offence toward heaven—if, for example, there should be, as there has been in our time, a massacre of Christians within the dominions of the Turks—then other nations are not absolved from all concern in the matter simply because of the large distance between them and the scene of the wrong, or because traditional diplomatic courtesy would counsel against raising one's voice. In one way or another, nations should exert an influence on the general affairs of the world, proportionate not merely to their numbers, but also to their intrinsic moral qualities and their capacity for acting nobly. This need is perceived more widely, and the likelihood of meeting it increases, as the improvement of our means of transport and communication between one land and another reduces our earth to a more manageable compass, making its inhabitants more conscious of being but one family.

The whole problem is indeed very difficult. Governments are the natural organs and representatives of states in their dealings with other states, and war is in itself a deplorable means for settling international disputes. However, I hope that the world still has something to discover in this regard. I hope that out of all those current plans and proposals, which many believe to be premature and Utopian—Peace Congresses, Western Committees on Progress, European Courts of Arbitration, and Universal Industrial Exhibitions—a new type of international relations will gradually emerge, the exact character of which we cannot foresee, but which shall be equally distinct from a wretched neutrality on the one hand, and from a boisterous military activity on the other.

This result is not to be arrived at by shutting our eyes and our hearts to what is actually happening around us. Instead, we should allow each case of contemporary international wrong to produce its full impression on us and to stimulate us to some immediate and appropriate course of action. The theory of international politics can be perfected in no other way than by dealing sincerely and thoroughly with individual cases as they successively arise.

CHAPTER TWENTY

America as a Leading Nation in the Cause of Liberty (1865)

Dear Conway,

You ask for my opinion regarding the question of the right to vote for colored men.[1] Can you have the slightest doubt about it?

You have abolished slavery. Abolition is the crowning moment of your glorious struggle, the religious consecration of your battles, which otherwise would have been nothing but a lamentable carnage. You have decreed that the sun of the Republic will shine for all; that whoever breathes the air of the Republic is free; and that, just as God is one, so wherever liberty is not a mere haphazard fact but a *faith* and gospel, the stamp of mankind is one. How could you now mutilate this great principle? How could you degrade it and reduce it to the proportions of that half-baked liberty granted by the Monarchies? How could you tolerate that some men amongst you be only half of themselves? How could you proclaim the dogma of half-responsibility, and create on the republican land of America a class of political serfs that reminds one of the Middle Ages?

Can there be Liberty without the vote? Isn't political liberty the sanction and guarantee of civil liberty? Isn't the right to vote the seal of human nature that affirms itself via the moral world, as the right to work and property is the seal of human nature in the physical world? Or will you deny this and thereby turn your democracy into an incipient aristocracy? Will you decree that color conveys moral inferiority? Now, ignorance is indeed a mark of inferiority; but you did not choose to place intellect as the foundation for electoral rights. Had you done so, you would have met quite a few objections of a different kind, but you could not be accused of betraying your proclaimed principle itself. You could not be accused, I mean, of applying a different standard to two sections of God's children; you could not be accused of saying: "These colored men are called to be the armed apostles of our national union, and they shall give their lives for that purpose; but their life will not be represented in the councils of the nation."

[1] Mazzini had made the acquaintance of Moncure Daniel Conway, an American clergyman and abolitionist (1832–1907), in London in 1863. The two men met several times and had a frequent exchange of letters.

Furthermore, is not the vote the first step toward popular education? Does not the very consciousness of a function to fulfill prepare man to progress? And is not the elevation of a reasonable being in his own self-esteem the most meaningful first step toward education, for both the child and the ignorant man? So what are you afraid of? Blunders? But have you *whites* perhaps never made any mistakes? And, anyway, is it not through blunders that we eventually reach the truth? Give the colored men the vote and education with it; you will shorten for them the period of mistakes. But do not put on the same level the great republican principle, which you have declared to be holy and intend to extend to all of Humanity, and the small amount of evil that could spring from the few transient blunders of a minority. One thing is practically certain: if you give the vote to the colored men, they will undoubtedly vote for those who have called them into political existence. However, if they remain unjustly deprived of that right, they will become a tool of extralegal agitations in the hands of anyone who will promise them the vote.

Probably you have been told these things repeatedly and much more forcefully by your American compatriots. But there is one argument that, as far as I know, has not yet been touched on by your countrymen, and that nevertheless seems to me to be of vital importance for you and for us all. Your task has now changed, and you have a sacred duty before you; but you will not be able to fulfill it until you have first bravely confronted and resolved the difficulty in front of which you now appear to hesitate.

There are two different stages in the life of every great Nation: the first is devoted to one's self-constitution, to the establishment of domestic order, and in some way to the preparation of all those elements and faculties by which a Nation can subsequently carry out its task in the world and fulfill the mission that was assigned to it by God for the good of all mankind. A Nation is a living mission: her life is not her own narrow property, but rather a force and a function in the universal Providential scheme.

The second stage begins once the Nation has affirmed and assured its own existence; once it has gathered and displayed to everyone the force and the qualifications it possesses for the fulfillment of its mission. Then the Nation rises and stirs, performing noble deeds in harmony with the general *aim* of humnaity. You have triumphantly gone through the first stage: now you are on the threshold of the second one, and you find yourselves facing the alternative of either betraying your national duty or of proceeding toward the goal.

Your combined forces have produced an incredible amount of energy that is wholly unknown to our old rotten European monarchies. Your men and women have been constantly devoted to the national cause, and the courage of your makeshift soldiers proved to be truly indomitable. But, above all, you have now erased that one black spot, Slavery, which was sullying your glorious republican flag. By all these glorious deeds, you have struck deep in the heart of Europe the conviction that there is in you an exceptional power, an almost incalculable strength at the service of human progress. All the numerous and ever-increasing republican elements of Europe have discovered in you their true representative. You have become a *leading* Nation. Now you must act as such. Your place is already marked in the great battle that is being fought all over the world between Right and wrong, Justice and arbitrary rule, Equality and privilege, Duty and selfishness, the Republic and monarchy, Truth and lies, God and the Idols. You must now take up that place and occupy it worthily.

As workers of Humanity, you must feel that to stand aloof would be a sin; that indifference at this very moment when the cry of God's children is calling you would be atheism. You must, first, drive off the American continent the enemy who took advantage of your internal troubles and dangers to insinuate himself along your borders and establish there an outpost of Caesarism.[2] You must then help your republican brothers, mainly morally, and materially if needed, whenever the sacred battle is being fought and you have the ability to effectively inspire and support those who toil and bleed for truth and for justice. There lies your mission, your glory and safety, your future. The fathers of your Republic would speak the same language today; keep in mind that those Great men were speaking to the American *child*, whereas now you have become a *giant*.

But to fulfill your duty, to achieve this mission, you must not have any threatening agitation at home. This suffrage question, until resolved, will be a source of perennial agitation for you. The question of suffrage is sacred, and it should be nourished and advanced by those among you who agitate for the sake of logic and religion. But that same question is also a weapon in your enemy's hands, a Damocles' sword in the hands of 4 million political serfs. Hence the question of suffrage will unavoidably absorb you and weaken you; it will keep you powerless and inert abroad, until it is resolved.

Think of it, dear Conway, and speak of it. You may, of course, make any use you want of what I write; but such thoughts as these will be more readily listened to if they are expressed by an American. A foreigner is always suspected of pleading his own cause which, God knows, I am not.

Ever faithfully your,
Joseph Mazzini
(London, October 30, 1865).

[2] Mazzini is referring to France, which under Napoleon III had invaded Mexico in 1861 and installed Maximilian of Habsburg as king of Mexico.

CHAPTER TWENTY-ONE

To Our Friends in the United States (1865)

IF IT IS TRUE that duties are proportionate to power, today new duties are arising for the United States. After the Civil War and the abolition of slavery, the power of the United States has become immense, not only on the American continent but also in Europe. Now you can—and therefore you must—be a guiding and instigating force, for the good of your own country and that of Humanity. To fulfill your duty it is sufficient that you stand for the principle of your own national life, both within your geographic boundaries and beyond. The principle of your life is the republican principle; the principle toward which progressive Europe is leaning and which, whether latent or openly professed, underlies every European struggle today.

All over Europe, and beyond Europe, there are ferments of a great struggle between States constituted by kings in the most arbitrary way, and Nationalities defined by the needs and aspirations of the people— between republican faith and monarchical interests. You must come forth and take your part in this battle. It is God's battle.

Every Nation lives a double life, internal and external, which is the manifestation of the same principle in two different spheres. There is a period, historically the first in a people's life, during which a Nation must necessarily think only of constituting itself. For you, this period has today been completed. Your Nation's vitality and force have lately been clarified beyond any doubt. Hence, a new period is now beginning for you. You are summoned by the admiration, the sympathies, and expectations of all of progressive Europe to affirm yourselves before kings and peoples, and to carry out a service for the general progress of Humanity. The monarchical powers are federated to promote their own narrow interests. It is now time that republicans in turn abandon their old system of isolation, which has resulted in an unworthy sentiment of inferiority, and form an alliance everywhere. Don't we already hold a common faith? And isn't every faith essentially aimed at the diffusion of one's ideas?

Furthermore, the alliance of which we speak is not only a duty and a glorious moral task, but a necessary defensive measure for the United States. Suffice it to look at Mexico. The audacious step that Louis Napoleon has taken there is no more than the beginning of an aggressive politics that dynastic Europe will not abandon. This politics has already successfully lured Spain; and it is now seeking, however vainly, to lure England as well.[1] You are currently too powerful and therefore feared, but be assured that the European despots will not miss any occasion to weaken you, damage you, and dismember you if possible. Shall you leave it to despotism to choose when and where to harm you? Even in such an event, you could doubtless win on your own, but only with grave sacrifices of American blood that should instead be saved, and of American wealth that should be put to better use.

You could elude the present danger by means of a timely and brotherly alliance with the European republican Party. That would allow you to strike evil at its roots and carry out a sacred mission toward Europe. You would promote the triumph of Right, Truth, and Justice and lay the foundation for a new moral, political, and commercial Era for your country. The European map must be redrawn. Old States will disappear; young and new nations will come to life; and these will recognize with special ties of gratitude the help they received from you in their time of need. If you approve of these views, our envoy will explain to you our aspirations, our hopes, and our desires.

London, December 1865.
On behalf of the European republican Committee,
Giuseppe Mazzini

[1] In July 1861, following Mexico's suspension of its payment of interests on foreign debt, France under Napoleon III launched an invasion of Mexico that was at first supported by Britain and Spain. With the United States Army immobilized by the American Civil War, French troops were able to enter Mexico City in June 1863. Maximilian of Habsburg was subsequently installed as king of Mexico. He ruled from 1864 to 1866, when Napoleon III announced the withdrawal of French forces, due to sustained popular resistance and growing threats of American intervention.

CHAPTER TWENTY-TWO

Principles of International Politics (1871)

I.

As I have already said on several occasions: one must judge the social and political acts that constitute the life of nations, as well as the different doctrines that presumably direct them, on the basis of the Moral Law.[1] The spectacle that we have before our eyes today of a great nation fallen to the depths for having deviated from that Law should glaringly confirm our principle.[2] What applies to all nations is especially true of rising nations. The morality of their social orders and of the standards that guide their political conduct is not just a matter of duty; it also affects their future to a significant degree. Just as commercial life and general economic development rest on the availability of credit, so the overall life of a people and its national growth rest on the faith that other peoples place in them. Now, to be worthy of such faith, a new people invariably needs to follow a precise and agreed-upon program, in domestic matters but especially in international affairs.

From economic markets to political alliances, everything becomes quite easily available to any nation that lives a normal life founded on a moral principle. What matters here is that the foundations of that principle be well-known. Also, the principle's actual consequences

[1] Original title: "Politica Internazionale." Mazzini's international political thought, expressed with particular force in this essay, establishes him as one of the leading pioneers of modern liberal internationalism, or democratic Wilsonianism. First, the pursuit of a principled foreign policy, centered on ideas of nonaggression, national self-determination, and international cooperation, is a matter of moral duty. It is also in the long-term self-interest of even the most powerful nations. Second, the newly established Italian nation ought to play a civilizing role in international relations, by supporting the liberation of subject peoples across the European continent. Furthermore, Europe's smaller and newly independent nations should establish a defensive alliance among themselves, which would result in growing mutual trust and bring about the possibility of lasting international peace. Finally, like several other prominent liberals and radicals of his time, Mazzini thought that Europe ought to colonize Asia and Africa to "civilize" local populations and make them ready for genuine self-determination.

[2] Mazzini is referring to France, which had just suffered a humiliating defeat at the hands of Prussia and lost Alsace-Lorraine.

should become both logically and practically visible in the nation's deeds. Where such a principle is absent and there is no standard of behavior apart from the arbitrary will of individuals and rulers, foreign peoples will look on the nation with mistrust, suspicion, and jealousy. Any such nation's success due to its own crime or someone else's cowardice may well impress other peoples, or at least scare them into short-term consent and seeming reverence; but their attitude will only last up to the first signs of the usurper's weakness or decline. Two historical examples may illustrate this further: the first Napoleon rejected the idea of Nationality, the soul of a new Era, by substituting his own power for the force of *principle*.[3] But this meant that as soon as his streak of military victories was interrupted, all of his Genius, strength, and prestige quickly disappeared in the face of Europe's sudden bounce of renewed hostility. Similarly, under the last Napoleon's rule, France had proudly sanctioned the degrading submission of all European Governments, and in consequence she could not find a single ally in her first hours of crisis only a few years later.[4] The same fate might now await England, if it persists in excluding from its foreign policy any pursuit of the *principle* of Liberty, which long ago made it powerful internationally and still inspires its domestic life.

We believe that every individual or collective being has a *goal*. This is what all our Great men from Dante onward have taught; and the *goal* that most accurately reflects God's design reigns supreme. The mere existence of that *goal* generates a *duty* to achieve it, or at least to attempt doing so. Life entails a mission. The steady, committed fulfillment of that mission constitutes life's ultimate value and ensures its progress.

Humanity itself has its own *goal*. That goal consists in the progressive discovery of the Moral Law and its expression through actual *deeds*. The *means*—the method for achieving this goal—consist in Association; that is to say, progressive association of human faculties and strengths, achieved through a steadily expanding and more intense communion of each human being with every other. Thus our human *reality* will be infused with genuine *love*. When all of God's children are free and equal, pursuing common thoughts and deeds under the same faith, and every

---

[3] Napoleon I (1769–1821) came to dominate continental Europe during the first decade of the nineteenth century. But Napoleon's fortunes began to turn after his fateful invasion of Russia in 1812, and he was finally defeated by a coalition that eventually included almost every major European power.

[4] Napoleon III, also known as Louis-Napoléon Bonaparte (1808–73), became emperor of the French in 1852 and was deposed after France's humiliating defeat against Prussia in 1870.

human life is illuminated by an awareness of the Moral Law, just like every drop of morning dew is illuminated by the rising Sun, then our *goal* will be achieved. Then Humanity, transformed, will be able to move on toward a new and higher goal.

Nations are the individuals of Humanity; and all of them must work toward accomplishing their common *goal*. But each of them must do so according to their own geographical position, their own particular abilities, and the means that are naturally at their disposal. In each case the combination of these particular conditions points toward a *special goal* that every people ought to pursue, while also striving to achieve Humanity's *common goal*. Where a people is *aware* of both their special goal and the particular contribution they can make toward the common goal—Humanity's ultimate ideal—by pursuing this special goal, there we have a Nation. Where there is no such awareness, we just have a crowd, or at best an ill-defined people that will sooner or later be absorbed by another.

The National Pact [agreement on a written constitution] is the beginning and actual guarantee of a people's fraternal progress. The declaration of *principles* that must preface any such pact ought to recognize the *common* goal of Humanity. But the same Pact should also clearly identify the nation's *special* goal; that is, the part of the general project to be accomplished by that specific people. Each time a people disavow the common goal, or prevent the fruits of progress from benefiting Humanity as a whole, by diverting them exclusively toward their special goal, they are reduced to a lower rank. In past epochs, once a nation had achieved its special goal, it would die over the course of several centuries. Today this is prevented by every nation's awareness of humanity's common goal and collective life, which were previously unknown, and the law of Progress that governs this collective life. However, any Nation that guiltily disowns its duty loses all virtue and moral *initiative* and cannot restore itself except by making amends.

By openly acknowledging their *special* goal, the millions of men and women who belong to a particular group freely express their associational bond, thus recognizing that they constitute a nation. The nation's special goal, publicly declared, will inform its domestic organization. No doubt, similarity of special goals among different peoples allows for better understanding and more intimate international relations. But only the recognition of a shared *common* goal makes long-term international *alliances* possible.

War becomes sacred, and can thus be justified, only under two circumstances: when vital progress toward the common *goal* is impossible by any other means; and when other states oppose a people's freedom to achieve its own mission.[5] Every other war is a fratricidal crime; and whenever such blatant breaches of the moral Law are committed, all the nations that recognize and accept the common goal should bond together to oppose the crime. Like the members of a family, the nations should support each other against aggression. They are called on to fight such Evil wherever it manifests itself and to promote the Good wherever possible. Those nations who remain passive in the face of unjust wars inspired by dynastic or national egoism will in turn find nothing but passive disinterest if one day they are themselves attacked.

These are what I take to be the guiding principles of all international politics. I have outlined these principles early on, because over the following pages I want to rely on them to judge past and present European events. Like all guidelines derived from a genuinely moral conception, these principles are quite simple and straightforward. But their proof lies in History, which, when examined properly, shows that each time they were violated there were disastrous consequences, both for the violators themselves and for other peoples that did not prevent evil when they could have done so.

The science of international politics is actually simpler and less difficult than one might be led to think, as long as one relies on a few principles all derived from religion and the idea of Duty. It is only when all common faith is destroyed, and the collective sense of religion is weak—as has been the case in Europe for almost three centuries now—that this same science can become complex and obscure. When there is no common faith, the political life of Nations falls prey to a short-sighted materialism, which elevates the *self* into its guiding principle and relies on *force* or *faits accomplis* as its proof. It then becomes necessary to deal with opposing claims to historically acquired half-rights, which are likely to result in endless suffering and disagreement.

Over the past three centuries, this shortsighted materialism has given rise to the intricate and extremely unreliable science of Diplomacy. Today the main task of diplomacy consists in achieving multiple and frequently interrelated backroom deals; and typically the concessions that these deals imply are either just corrupt lies, or otherwise they imply the subjugation of one state to another. The practice of diplomacy is usually full of lofty slogans, but those are only designed to veil one's real intentions. In short, Diplomacy is fatal to the education of peoples, and the ends it pursues are always sterile, if not outright evil. A truly

[5] The first part of the sentence seems to suggest a right of violent insurrection as a last resort; the second part appears to justify military counterintervention, aimed at offsetting a previous foreign intervention. Mazzini develops his thinking on the ethics of military intervention more fully in his essay "On Nonintervention" in chapter 19 of this book.

republican order would transcend both the ends of Diplomacy and the practice itself, by decreeing that international politics become a transparent matter of public intercourse among peoples.

For almost three centuries now, there has been no common moral principle and thus no clear ethical standard guiding international relations. So long as the Christian conception of morality was alive and well, to some extent it guided and exercised a unifying influence on different events as they resulted from the circumstances and from human passions. The preaching of the Gospel had slowly transformed the Northern men [Germanic tribes] that had so dreadfully invaded Italy and other regions into territorial settlers. That same preaching subsequently promoted the emancipation of the serfs; and as soon as this goal had been achieved, the Christian Crusades were launched to challenge the fatalism of the Orient in the name of Europe. Finally, from time to time, different church councils and Papal letters uttered words of peace, moral unity, and common faith into the world. Needless to say, those times were half-barbarous: feudalism dismembered any people who tried to come together and unite; and a *dualism* persisted within Christianity itself between the spiritual and corporeal worlds. Yet, notwithstanding these apparently insurmountable and perennial causes of discord and war, there was a general tendency for everyone to accept a few moral principles that prevented the worst from happening. At a minimum, those moral principles could be relied on to shorten the duration of wars, to fasten the decline of feudal orders, and to bring the peoples somewhat closer together.

But beginning in the sixteenth century, the slow dissolution of Christianity opened a void in Europe that to this day has not been filled. We thus lack a common moral faith, an open or tacit agreement that could make the peoples understand and trust one another. Different political arrangements—most of them sterile and inefficient—have succeeded each other on the brink of this void, the result either of isolated inspiration or plain dynastic greed. Some of the most influential writers in the field of international law appealed to antiquity, as if the moral standards developed for polytheist peoples could ever guide relations among Christians. Then came the doctrine of the European *balance of power*, promoted by England. With the signing of the Westphalian peace, this doctrine sanctioned the equality of two irreconcilably opposed beliefs; and thus hostilities were suspended between France, Austria, and Spain. The ensuing peace was supposed to last forever, but it came to an end already with Louis XIV. Thereafter, new attempts to reestablish a European balance followed at Utrecht and elsewhere; but they too were soon challenged by the feisty sword of Frederick II and entirely came to naught with the rise of Prussian militarism and the unjust division of Poland. Thus, this hoped-for *equilibrium* resulted in roughly seventy years of war on the European continent.[6] The pursuit of *balance* translated into steadily growing military arsenals, which were paradoxically aimed at preventing war. It also sanctioned the principle that *any conquest achieved by one Power must be counterbalanced* by the conquests of others. The implications of this principle became evident at the peace of Campoformio, which led to the sale of Venice to Austria in compensation for French gains on the Rhine.[7] But these agreements were children of materialism and therefore condemned to perish in impotence, anarchy, and crime. God's approval was missing.

Today Europe's nations have all but abandoned any hope of finding a solution to international conflicts. Hence, they follow England's lead and bow down before the theory of *nonintervention*. But this theory is not based on any *principle*. Instead, it implies a negation of all those principles that have marked Humanity's main intellectual achievements up to our present time: unity of God and the Moral Law, unity of the human family, unity of purpose; brotherhood and association among peoples, and finally acknowledgement of a duty to combat Evil and promote the triumph of what is Good. The theory of nonintervention is nothing but Atheism transplanted into international life, or the deification of Egoism if you prefer. Its essence was expressed by a French monarchic statesman with the following words: "Chacun chez soi, chacun pour soi."[8] But these words are not just extremely immoral; they are also plainly absurd. If accepted by everyone, this maxim would deprive us of one of the most potent levers of Progress, which as history shows has almost always been achieved through acts of intervention and war. So

---

[6] The Peace of Westphalia (1648) ended the European religious wars, sanctioning what Mazzini calls the "equality between two irreconcilably opposed beliefs," that is, Catholicism and Protestantism. As Mazzini points out, the European balance was repeatedly challenged, not least by the expansionism of Louis XIV, king of France from 1643 to 1715, and Frederick II, who ruled Prussia from 1740 to 1786. European international relations were extremely conflictual during the latter half of the eighteenth century, from the War of the Austrian Succession (1740–48) to the Congress of Vienna (1815). Hence, Mazzini refers to this period as "seventy years of war."

[7] The peace treaty of Campoformio (1797) was signed between Austria and Revolutionary France at the end of Napoleon's first victorious campaign in Italy. Austria was forced to cede the Netherlands and some territories on the left bank of the Rhine to France, and it lost the region around Milan. But it gained large territories in northeastern Italy (most crucially, the Veneto), which sanctioned the end of the centuries-old Venetian Republic.

[8] The phrase can be translated as "everyone should mind their own business, without interfering elsewhere." It was most likely pronounced by Prince Talleyrand (1754–1838), France's chief negotiator at the Congress of Vienna.

long as nonintervention is practiced by some and not by others, as is presently the case, evil purposes are likely to triumph. The evildoers know that anyway, nobody will stop them for the sake of Justice. Of course, no single nation could stop them on its own: any single nation that took it on itself to uphold nonintervention as a general rule would condemn itself to frequent wars with all those who refuse to accept it. At the same time, any nation that were to adopt the rule of nonintervention as an absolute guideline for its own foreign policy would renounce half of its own life; it would lose the esteem and love of all peoples, and anyway, it could not eliminate occasional wars of necessity. In England an influential school of thought led by Cobden and Bright used to cry out for "Peace at any cost"—but this only encouraged Russia to be daring and largely determined the Crimean War.[9]

The blood of all those Martyrs, whether peoples or individuals, who have sacredly intervened and died outside of their native land for the sake of Justice and Truth represents a permanent challenge to the cold, abject, and cowardly doctrine of nonintervention. I believe that this doctrine is indeed a blasphemy against the notion of Duty; it suggests an undeniable lack of conviction in our present time and the need to find a new faith.

As for Italy's contemporary international life, one need not waste many words: there is no such thing. The men of the Monarchy have no awareness of an Italian mission in the world; they have no long-term vision or political design. Their only conception of policy is to drag oneself along from day to day in an uncertain and weary existence, relying on short-term gambits and always following those who seem powerful at the moment. The rare statesmanlike phrases that our leaders in charge of foreign affairs haughtily utter, as if they were the expression of a genuine doctrine, are in most cases just stolen from a Russian or British dispatch and would be laughable if they didn't make one blush. Wars and peace agreements have always been imposed on us by others; morality and the future of Italy as a nation have played no role in our alliance decisions. Indeed, while we were rising up in the pursuit of Liberty and National unity—or at least that's what we claimed—Italy invoked the help of a tyrannical ruler. Italy invoked the help of France—

[9] Richard Cobden (1804–65) and John Bright (1811–89), two influential establishment liberals and proponents of British nonintervention in continental European affairs. Note how Mazzini's views on intervention and war are significantly more radical when he writes for his fellow Italian revolutionaries, as he does in this essay, compared to the more discerning and moderate stance he takes when writing for foreign, and especially British, liberal audiences. See e.g. "The European Question: Foreign Intervention and National Self-Determination," chapter 16 of this book, 195; and "On Public Opinion and England's International Leadership," chapter 17 of this book, 204–5.

that same France that had actually prevented our national unification through its unrighteously acquired and maintained possession of Rome; that same France that requested the dismemberment of our lands, which was granted without delay.[10] Then we entered an alliance with Prussia against Austria; and soon thereafter we were about to ally ourselves with imperial France against Prussia and thus against the unification of Germany. Only France's precipitous defeats and our insistence on certain facts (others have recently *discovered* a powerful agitation of the French Left) prevented this from happening. Tomorrow we will again be allies of Austria. The hack writers of the monarchical faction, who are afraid of finding themselves without a master, are already preparing the ground. Further examples of our corrupt Diplomacy abound: for instance, it aligned itself with the supporters of the Turk, and together with them told the Greeks: "You should not actually claim your land." Then our Diplomacy promised England, at the latter's request, that it would not move an inch in the recent war without alerting it. Finally, our Diplomacy has of course insistently wooed Prussia, although the latter took a vital part in extinguishing Poland as an independent nation. In short, history will remember the first twelve years in the international *life* of this newly risen Italy as an age of denial.

II.

Today Italy lacks any real foreign policy. Our rulers lack any faith in moral norms and in the Nation's duty that the Government should fulfill. This lack of conviction and the related neglect of Italy's mission in the world condemn us to live centered on the *present*. Without any deep understanding of our own tradition and no conception of the future, we are overwhelmed by daily events to such an extent that we have come to fear them. Now that the French nation has fallen, articles are published in the mouthpieces of the Italian government that seek to prove that the only viable foreign policy for us is to actually have none. All this suggests that there is no real difference between today's unified Italian Nation and the old Duchies of Modena, Tuscany, or Parma. Like those former Duchies, Italy remains utterly weak and passive; she has

[10] France had sent an expeditionary force to quash the revolutionary Roman Republic and to reinstate the pope in 1849; thereafter it maintained a military garrison in Rome for almost two decades. In a secret alliance treaty signed in 1858, France promised the king of Piedmont-Sardinia to support the political unification of northern Italy; and in exchange, Piedmont agreed to cede the town of Nizza (where Garibaldi was born) and the Savoy region to France, which Mazzini sees as a regrettable "dismemberment" of Italian lands.

no objective and no name among the peoples. As a consequence she plays no meaningful role in the congress of Nations and lacks any civilizing initiative. But a People that rises without contributing a new element of progress to the common cause, and that adds no stone to the edifice slowly erected by Humanity, has no reason for living. Indeed it lacks any life. It will almost inevitably slip back into being dominated, either directly or indirectly, by the first foreign power that wants to master it. In international society, those who play no meaningful role and don't contribute anything to the common good may have their right to existence questioned.

Yet if there is a people that based on its geographical position, traditions, and natural abilities is expected by other peoples to play a great civilizing role in Europe, it is certainly us. Expectations were huge at the time of the first Italian movements, and they still remain high although they have been somewhat lowered in the wake of repeated disappointments. If there was ever a time when a people, provided that it wanted to do so, could take on an important mission and build a great and successful future for itself, this is certainly it. Today nobody holds the initiative amidst the rising tide of national movements. All are therefore waiting for someone to pick up the torch of life that has visibly fallen from the hands of others, in order to raise it for the solace and protection of all doubt-ridden peoples. The peoples are threatened today by the advancing shadow of selfishness.

Italy has a twofold mission, which is eloquently suggested by her History, the particular circumstances of her recent resurgence, and the broader conditions of present-day Europe. If Italy were to accomplish this mission, she would place herself at the forefront of a new Era.

The first part of Italy's mission consists in the abolition of the Papacy. This would establish once and for all the universal principle of inviolability of the human *conscience*. Another likely benefit would be the replacement of the dogma of human *fall* and *redemption* with a more timely belief in Progress. But this is a religious mission, of which I do not intend to speak here at length. In any case, a significant amount of peaceful propaganda will be required before a people of religious believers, such as the Italians undoubtedly are, shall approve the necessary decrees to complete this mission. The second mission is of a more political nature: it consists in promoting the principle of Nationality as the supreme foundation of international order and as a guarantee of future peace. This latter mission is intimately connected with the former: it does in fact aim at a new European settlement, which in all great historical Epochs has always been the prelude to a religious transformation. The development of the National principle needs to be primarily achieved through moral influence; but it also needs to be backed up by the force of arms when necessary and when the circumstances are propitious.

Nationality is the vital force of the epoch that will soon be upon us. Almost all the wars fought in Europe between the last years of the first Napoleonic Empire and our present time originated from that principle. Quite often those wars were provoked by peoples that aimed to achieve their own *nationality* or wanted to protect it from the assaults of others. On other occasions, war was promoted by monarchs who wanted to preventively gain control over and undermine a *nationalist* uprising that they foresaw as inevitable.

Today, several peoples in Europe are called on by providential tendencies to strengthen their internal bonds so that they can live their normal life, and freely and spontaneously fulfill their role on the continent. However, those peoples are for the most part split up and divided. The servants of others, they have been subjugated by states with a different *goal*. They have been violently separated from other branches of the same family; and this makes them weak and uncertain in their movements and in the expression of their legitimate aspirations. The Europe that has emerged from dynastic conquests and treaties is clearly not the Europe that had been outlined by God's hand; indeed according to His providential design, the great rivers and mountain ranges should have marked the division of labor among our continent's inhabitants. So long as the map of Europe is not reordered and brought into line with this God-given design, the *peace* that we are all seeking will remain a fantasy of unsound minds. In short, we cannot enjoy the rewards of peace without first achieving Justice.

Different *Nations* represent the diversity of human abilities. They are thus called on to reach their common *goal* by *associating*; not by becoming confounded with or submerged into others. Each nation forever retains the right to fashion its own life, for only those who are self-determining and affirm their own *individuality* can fruitfully associate. The pantheists of politics [the conservative statesmen and diplomats] reject this right and fear that the principle of *nationality* contains the seeds of rivalries and permanent warfare. But they forget that until now, most nations have never been free and have never been based on the popular will. Their political life has mostly been subject to the monopoly and ambitions of ruling families. These ruling families, for their part, deny the providential design suggested by geographical features and revealed by history; they frustrate the *means* necessary for a people to achieve its objective; and without fully realizing it, they validate the notion of *universal monarchy*, which has tempted so many powerful rulers and has caused so many futile bloodsheds in Europe. Free *nationhood*, or universal national self-determination, is the sole guarantee against the despotic rule of a single people over several others, just as *individual liberty* is the sole guarantee against the despotic subjection of human beings.

Our Epoch is destined to witness a rearrangement of the Map of Europe, which will be achieved through a series of inevitable battles. But if one Nation made itself the pivot of this movement by virtue of its intellectual wisdom and the strength of its will, it could shorten those battles and come to hold the *initiative* in matters of human progress for many centuries to come. The idea of free *nationalities*, which today more than any other thought stirs the minds of Europe, should constitute the basis of Italy's true international life. Italy must take inspiration from this thought when choosing its *alliances*. Quite naturally, Italy's position ought to be one of leadership among today's rising nations, rather than one of servitude to the older nations that are beginning to decline.

Italy is a new fact of international politics, a new people, a *life* that only yesterday did not exist. She does not yet have any binding ties other than with the Moral Law itself, which is sovereign over all nations, be they young or old. She is not a party to the dynastic treaties that date from before her birth; hence those treaties do not bind her, especially when they don't agree with standards of Justice and eternal Right. Italy should say so loudly and act freely according to this assumption. Tradition is *sacred*, and we should generally respect it. However, some distinctions are necessary: think of religion, where there is not just the Tradition of a single church or a single epoch, but rather the tradition of Humanity as a whole that embraces and explains them all, thus ruling above the rest. As to our own [republican] political tradition, it does not encompass all the past, but rather only that part of the past that clarifies the Moral Law and points out the way toward Progress; it does not stray toward Evil, but rather aims toward the Good and would perpetuate it if accepted. Now, a People that come into being as a Nation do not only have a duty to verbally renounce the guilty deeds of their fathers; they also have a splendid opportunity to do so through their actions. Every new life is pure; and God does not give life merely for it to be soiled in the accumulated mire of antecedent corrupt lives.

If Italy wants to be great, prosperous, and truly powerful, she needs to make her own the notion of an allocation of tasks in Europe according to the natural tendencies and the mission of peoples. She must resolutely plant on her frontiers the flag of Liberty and Nationality, and this *goal* must inform every act of her international life.

Italy is today facing her third mission on earth. First, the Rome of the caesars pursued the goal of *political* Unity, which it took over from the previous Republic; and it accomplished this goal as much as was possible at the time, supported by the arms of its Legions. Second, the Rome of the popes tried to achieve *moral* Unity, and it partially succeeded thanks to the proselytism of its priests and its believers. However, neither the Rome of the caesars nor the Rome of the popes recognized the collective movement of Nations decreed by providence. Indeed, this would have been impossible. Those past political entities did not see anything in the world but their own power and their *individual* human subjects. They had no cooperating, intermediate agents between themselves and the pursued *goal*; and thus they found no instrument to attain their goal other than absolute, despotic *authority* over the bodies or souls of their subjects. But today's Rome of the People—the Rome of the Italian Nation—believes in Progress, the collective life of Humanity, and the division of labor among Nations. Our *goal* consists in uniting all other Nations in the brotherly pursuit of a common undertaking, both as their leader and their supporter in times of hardship.

Let me briefly come back to the twofold mission to which, as I mentioned, Italy is preordained [the abolition of the papacy and the promotion of national self-determination]. This mission has been implicit in the very first requirements of our own national resurgence. Italy's resurgence would indeed not have been possible without going to war, on the one hand against the Papacy, that custodian of old unlimited *authority,* and on the other hand against the Austrian Empire, that most forceful negation of the principle of *nationality* throughout Europe. It now won't be possible to complete our resurgence except by moving ahead along this path until its very end; hence what may be just a moral duty for others is actually a vital requirement for us.

In many regards, the best alliances are those that are made with whoever is both powerful and close enough to come to our aid when necessary. Yet our allies should not be too powerful, lest they exploit the pretext of services rendered in the past—or the lure of common endeavors—to impose their will on us and to overstep in their selfish expansionism all the limits agreed on in the pacts of alliance. This rule should be followed even by long-established peoples, who are living a normal life and have no special mission to pursue; but Italy, more than others, has recently undergone the very painful experience of what damage can follow from violating this rule.[11] As a new people, we deserve to become a secure member of the community of nations only if we add a new and useful element of life to the already existing elements. We will thus be able to form lasting alliances only if their purpose is in agreement with our deeper political faith. Our natural allies are to be found among the peoples who rightfully aim either to solidify their national unity or to attain it with some probability of success. The long-established and tradition-

[11] Italy's alliance with France became increasingly fraught with tensions after 1860, given in particular France's support for the pope and the French government's related opposition to making Rome the capital of a newly united Italy. It is only after France's defeat by Prussia in 1870 that Rome and the surrounding lands could be annexed to the new Italian state.

ally powerful nations will for a long time look down with instincts of envy and suspicion on a rising nation like ours, whose progress threatens them with new countervailing influence and economic competition. Only among new peoples will we find sincere friendship, founded on the importance of our own friendship for them. This friendship could be further solidified in several ways: we should offer other emerging nations the diplomatic support that the established powers deny them, and they will be forever grateful; we ought to further deepen our already established commercial relationships with them; and we should directly invest in the new markets that will develop with the growth of life in those renewed lands. Our mutual friendship could benefit greatly from the enjoyment of diverse mutual advantages without any danger attached.

If Italy wants to be able to influence future international developments, her first priority in foreign policy should be to make herself the soul and center of a League of Europe's smaller States, closely united in a collective defense pact against the possible usurpations of one or the other great Power. This alliance could include Spain, Portugal, Scandinavia, Belgium, Holland, Switzerland, Greece, and the Romanian-Danubian principalities. If all these countries joined, the League would add up to a material force of more than 64 million men united by a pact of independence and freedom. At a later stage it should not be difficult to obtain the adherence of England to this League, which would thus become able to effectively resist any attempt at usurpation by a single great Power. It bears reminding that international acts of aggression are usually planned and executed by great Powers individually, with others diffidently watching.

The establishment of such a League would greatly enhance Italy's moral influence, which could thus be exercised toward a future reorganization of Europe along the following lines: *unified Nations secure in their independence and possibly with free confederations among them* as a guarantee against violent international collisions. With this goal in mind, we should constantly remind our Italian representatives to pursue several specific objectives, namely: find a definitive settlement for the Iberian Peninsula by means of a union between Portugal and Spain; transform the Swiss Confederation into a broader Alpine confederation with the addition of Savoy and the German Tyrol; and achieve a Scandinavian Union, as well as a republican Confederation of Holland and Belgium. But the true objective of Italy's international life and the most direct path to its future greatness lies elsewhere—in a brotherly alliance with the Slavic family. Today the travails of the Slavic family constitute the most vital European problem. The Slavic family, vast and potentially very powerful, could add a new positive energy to the community of

Nations. But if left to go astray by our imprudent mistrust, it could also be the cause of long wars and grave dangers. . . .

III.

The first and most important consequence of the Slavic uprising will be the breakdown of the Austrian Empire and the Turkish Empire in Europe. These events have now become all but inevitable; and their onset should be hastened as much as possible, for the sake of general civilizational progress and for Italy's future benefit. Unless our rulers come to share this assessment, they cannot even pretend to be pursuing anything resembling a genuine international politics. Sure, they may for some time continue to live off tactical gambits, like the Monarchical ministers—obtaining an apparent advantage today and paying for it tomorrow with dishonor and possibly with the subjection of their entire country to foreign rule. Moving from one alliance to the next, without guarantees or clear norms of behavior, they will find their nation completely abandoned when international support is most clearly needed. Unless our rulers radically change their course of behavior, they will inevitably continue to tremble before France, before the Prussian victories, and even before the foolish threats of the pope. As long as the Italian people accept all this, we will reduce a nation of 26 million that has twice already led the world to be an absolute nothing in Europe. I am of course aware that unfortunately, our rulers may well continue to misgovern, but at least they should keep silent. Without a moral standard, with no understanding of the future, no consciousness of a specific *goal* and no *method* to achieve that goal, a genuine international life is impossible. . . .

If Italy were to aid the uprising of the Illyrian Slavs and of those who form the greater part of European Turkey, she would be rewarded with the affection of the entire Slavic family. We would inspire those peoples politically and acquire the right to privileged economic relations with them. Our nation could thus, if she only wanted, take the lead in promoting a new political arrangement. The likely advantages for Europe and for Italy are undeniable and indeed of vital importance. To the North, a new Slavic federation would be positioned between Russia and Germany. If Hungary were to liberate herself from the Austrian Empire and join that federation, Germany would no longer have to fear Russia's predominance in the region and France and Italy would no longer have to fear any Teutonic domination, since Italy in particular, thanks to her alliance with the Slavs, who are no friends of either Austria or Germany, could threaten a two-front war against any Teutonic invader if necessary.

To the South and the East, Constantinople would come to enjoy Western liberties forever. Young nations, determined to defend their independence, would constitute a barrier against the advance of Czarism. Russia would thus be confined to its natural borders. As a consequence, a very large and exceptionally fertile land would become accessible to the influence of European civilization and to European production. Two of the three great roads to the Asian world would be opened up to and made safe for European commerce. And thanks to the Italian initiative in the Balkans, our own commerce would gain preferential access to that region.

We have mentioned the Asian world. If we look to the future and beyond our current frontiers, the main elements of our European uprising today converge toward Asia. Europe was once populated by Asian migrants who brought us the first seeds of civilization and the first national tendencies. Today, providence leads Europe to carry back to Asia the civilization that grew from those seeds on its own privileged lands. We are the sons of the Vedic peoples. After a long pilgrimage full of hardship, we are led back by an unknown hand toward our civilizational cradle.[12] We feel almost compelled to exercise our moral mission there, by transforming the religious idea. Similarly, by pursuing our industrial and agricultural activities in those lands, we will contribute to changing the material world. Europe is pushing at Asia's borders and invades its different regions: the English have conquered India; Russia is slowly advancing in the North; China is periodically forced to make concessions; the Americans are moving beyond the Rocky Mountains; European colonies and trade are generally spreading across the Asian continent. Italy was once the most powerful colonizer of the world,[13] and she should not lose out on this wonderful new movement.

Our foreign policy must insist on opening up for Italy all the roads that lead to the Asian world. We must pursue this goal with the same tenacity that Russia since Peter the Great has displayed in her attempts to conquer Constantinople. If we solved this problem, we could also contribute to the great civilizing mission suggested by our times. The means by which to achieve our goal are the following: first, establish an alliance with the Southern Slavs and with the entire Hellenic element; second, systematically increase the Italian influence at Suez and Alexandria; third, invade and colonize the Tunisian lands when the oppor-

[12] There have long been speculations, which Mazzini clearly follows here, that the ancient Vedic civilization, centered in the northern part of the Indian subcontinent, was the cradle of what later became the Indo-European civilization.

[13] Mazzini is referring to the Roman Empire, which he sees as the historical antecedent of modern Italy.

tunity presents itself. An inevitable trend is calling for Europe to civilize the African regions. Just as Morocco is for the Spanish and Algeria is for France, so Tunisia should become our own. This should be obvious if one considers that Tunisia, the key to the central Mediterranean, is connected to the Sardinian-Sicilian island system and lies only twenty-five miles away from Sicily. Tunis, Tripoli, and the Cyrenaica belong to that part of Africa up to the Atlas Mountains that truly fits into the European system. This entire region is of the utmost importance for its contiguity with Egypt, and through Egypt with Syria and with Asia. Already in the past, the flag of Rome was unfurled on top of the Atlas Mountains, after Carthage had been vanquished, and the Mediterranean became known as *Mare nostrum*. We were the masters of that entire region until the fifth century. Today the French covet it and they will soon have it if we don't get there first.

Are these plans to which we refer and which we will eventually carry out utopian? The men of the Monarchy will sneeringly say so, for they are *practical* men. However, History is more *practical* than them: it will tell you that we have been pursuing the Unification of Italy for thirty-nine years, often sneered at by *practical* men. Today it is almost achieved, at least in material terms. History will also tell you that while being sneered at, we have been predicting the Unification of Germany for at least as long, and it is now being accomplished. Similarly, we were looked down on when we claimed that France had lost any power of *initiative*, and today the facts prove us right. In 1848, *practical people* thought that the Five Days of [popular resistance in] Milan would be impossible, but they actually happened. In 1849 those same people insisted that we would not be able to defend Rome against the French for even two days, but we ended up successfully defending it for two months. The Venetians were told that they should take down their republican flag because without dynastic help they would be incapable of resisting Austria for even a couple of weeks. Indeed, Venice turned to the Monarchy for help, did not receive any support from it, and nevertheless it held out for as long as eighteen months.[14] So far, all those *practical* people have just been able to follow in our own footsteps whenever they realized that we were successfully advancing. They then usurped our plans and exhausted them, wearing our own

[14] The "Five days of Milan" refer to a five-day-long popular insurrection in March 1848 by the citizens of Milan, which the Austrian occupation forces could repress only with some difficulty. In 1849 the revolutionary Roman Republic, led by Mazzini himself, held out for several months against a vastly superior French expeditionary force. Similarly, the revolutionary Venetian Republic, proclaimed in 1848, resisted for several months against the Austrian imperial army.

clothes and soiling them with a cravenness that nobody had foreseen but ourselves.[15] . . .

As we have said many times, great ideas make for great peoples. But an idea becomes great only insofar as it reaches beyond one's own national boundaries. And a people can only become great by achieving a distinguished and sacred mission in the world, just like the value of an individual human being is measured by what he accomplishes for his own country.

Every Nation's domestic order reflects the sum of the means and the efforts that have been marshaled in the pursuit of its international goals. Just as commercial intercourse and exchange generally determine the value of goods and actually stimulate their production, so a nation's foreign relations determine the value and dynamism of its domestic life. National life is a *means*, while international life is the actual *goal*. The first is the work of men; the latter is outlined and indeed prescribed by God. Every Nation's prosperity, its glory, and more generally its future are determined by how much and how well it approaches the *goal* that has been assigned to it.

[15] Mazzini is referring to the Piedmontese monarchy, which unified Italy on its own terms between 1859 and 1870, essentially annexing other Italian regions. Frequently those annexations were legitimized through token plebiscites that exploited patriotic popular sentiments across the peninsula.

Index

DATE DUE

FEB 1 0 2016